PENGUIN CLASSICS

THE PRAYERS AND MEDITATIONS OF ST ANSELM

ADVISORY EDITOR: BETTY RADICE

ANSELM, bishop and theologian, was born at Aosta *c.* 1033, the son of a Lombard nobleman. After a restless youth, he entered in 1059 the monastery of Bec in Normandy, whose prior was then Lanfranc, who was to precede him in the see of Canterbury. During the next thirty years Anselm wrote several of the philosophical and theological works that have been so influential and which earned him the title of 'the father of scholasticism'. He was elected abbot of Bec in 1078, and in 1093 King William II consented to nominate him to the archbishopric of Canterbury. Henceforth, Anselm's public life was almost wholly conditioned by dissensions with William II and Henry I over relations between the church and the state as represented by the king. In 1097, due to William II's determined efforts to get rid of the archbishop, Anselm went to Rome for three years; during that time he wrote *Cur Deus Homo*, one of the best known works on the Atonement, and attended the Council of Bari. He returned to England when Henry I came to the throne, but Henry soon claimed rights in respect of abbots and bishops that a council in Rome had been unable to recognize: Anselm was again in exile abroad from 1103 to 1107. He died in 1109 in Canterbury.

BENEDICTA WARD is a member of the Community of the Sisters of the Love of God, an Anglican religious community whose mother house is in Oxford. She holds a degree in history from Manchester University and a D. Phil. from Oxford. She has written articles on medieval topics and translated several texts. Her most recent publication is *Miracles and the Medieval Mind* (1982) and she is at present preparing a translation of the *Institutes* of Cassian. She is the tutor in history at the Centre for Medieval and Renaissance Studies in Oxford.

THE PRAYERS AND
MEDITATIONS OF
ST ANSELM

❀

*Translated and with an introduction
by Sister Benedicta Ward, S.L.G.
With a foreword by
R. W. Southern*

PENGUIN BOOKS

Penguin Books Ltd, 80 Strand, London, WC2R 0RL, England
Viking Penguin Inc., 40 West 23rd Street, New York, New York 10010, U.S.A.
Penguin Books Australia Ltd, Ringwood, Victoria, Australia
Penguin Books Canada Limited, 2801 John Street, Markham, Ontario, Canada L3R 1B4
Penguin Books (N.Z.) Ltd, 182–190 Wairau Road, Auckland 10, New Zealand

—

This translation first published 1973
Reprinted 1979, 1984, 1986

20

—

Printed and bound in Great Britain by Antony Rowe Ltd.,
Chippenham, Wiltshire

Set in Monotype Ehrhardt

ISBN 978-0-14-044278-6

CONTENTS

Contents

Contents

FOREWORD

In his *Prayers and Meditations* Anselm created a new kind of poetry – the poetry of intimate, personal devotion. These poems were not written in lines and stanzas, but in the rhymed prose which was a fashionable literary mode in the late eleventh century, and with the intricate antitheses which were a special feature of Anselm's thought and art. The carefully constructed form and choice of words convey the heightened emotion of poetry, and it is one of the great merits of this translation that both the emotion and poetic form have been carefully preserved.

The form and the emotion cannot be separated. What Anselm attempted was, first of all, to stir up his own sense of horror, compunction, humiliation, and self-abasement at the recollection of his sins, and then to communicate these feelings to the reader, by arranging his words to give them their fullest possible effect. They were (he said) to be read 'not cursorily or quickly, but slowly and with profound and deliberate meditation'; and we find in fact that it is impossible to read them in any other way. Eye and mind alike are arrested by the intricacies of construction and thought, and Anselm's literary art serves to enforce the principles of meditation on which he insisted.

The practice of meditative prayer was already very ancient when Anselm began to write his prayers, but he introduced some important innovations both as regards the public for which he wrote and in his manner of writing. Until his time meditation had been essentially a monastic exercise, and Anselm certainly wrote largely for monks; but he also wrote to meet the increasingly articulate needs of lay people, especially of women in great positions who had the time, inclination, and wealth to adopt the religious practices of the monastic life. Such women were among the earliest recipients of his prayers, and one of them, Countess

Mathilda of Tuscany, was one of the main agents of their dissemination.

In his manner of writing also Anselm made a distinct break with the past. When he started to write, extracts from the Psalms formed the main texts for private devotion. In addition, there were already in existence several collections of short prayers for private use, but they had not yet established themselves as a distinct form of religious literature. Anselm's prayers made the distinction at once complete and irreversible. They were longer, more subtle, more personal, and theologically more daring, than any earlier prayers in use in the West; and they were clearly unsuitable for public use.

Most of Anselm's prayers are addressed to individual saints. In casting them in this form he was following an established devotional practice, but here too he did something which was new. He threw himself before the saint with so personal an appeal and so vivid an evocation of the saint's personality, that his prayers have a visual quality like a picture by El Greco. The saint stands out as a central dominating figure in a brilliant and varied canvas.

The Prayer to St Peter is a good example of Anselm's method. He addresses St Peter in every possible guise: as a worn-out sinner addressing the chief of the apostles, as a scabby sheep addressing the shepherd of the flock, as a wounded desperate soul addressing the door-keeper of heaven. Then, by a subtle change of view, the reader's attention is directed to the fact that St Peter himself had needed and received mercy and forgiveness. Thereafter the prayer turns into a petition to God and St Peter, sometimes jointly, sometimes singly, and ends in a final intricate pattern of imploration. It is altogether much too elaborate and artificial for our taste, but it leaves an intense sense of the contrast between the squalid sinful soul and the glory to which the soul aspires.

The main art of Anselm in his prayers is directed towards bringing out this contrast. He piles up images and epithets to emphasize the misery, squalor, and desperation of the sinful soul, overwhelmed in the mire and stench of its own making, just managing to articulate entreaties to the shining friends and collaborators of God. The misery of the individual soul would seem simply vast and shapeless were it not given a certain degree of form by the precise rhythms of Anselm's prose, the refinement of his language, and the extraordinary boldness of his imagery. It is by these devices that Anselm arouses the sinner's interest in his condition, and keeps this interest alive even while he is being bludgeoned into numbness by the long enumeration of his evils. For instance, in his very long Prayer to St Paul, Anselm explores every aspect of Paul's career to find an avenue of approach along which the sinner can travel with confidence. But all in vain. Everywhere he comes up against an impenetrable wall of sin. Then he stumbles on some words of St Paul in his Epistles to the Thessalonians and Galatians which suggest the contrasting images of a nurse and a woman in labour. With this flimsy aid Anselm finds a new approach to St Paul, now depicted as a tender nurse and mother. There is indeed a faint absurdity in this double image, but it serves to provide a climax for the prayer by suggesting a further image of Jesus dying in spiritual childbirth so that his children in the faith may live. The two images are then combined, and tossed to and fro – 'both Paul and Jesus are mothers, both are fathers too' – until the prayer ends in a general sense of consolation.

This small example brings out the baroque side of Anselm's prayers – the sometimes wild extravagance of the word-play and association of ideas. In the curious ambiguity of mother and father images it also contains a hint of the psychological complications of Anselm's life; he was a man who had lost his mother and quarrelled with his father, and he was always seeking to replace them in his spiritual life. The prayers are not just exercises in generalized devotion and idealized imagery; they are also reflections of a tormented and tumultuous spirit, which only slowly found peace in prayer and meditation.

Of all Anselm's prayers there can be no doubt that the most important and original are those to St Mary. They happen also to be the best documented. Anselm sent them from Bec, probably in 1072, to a friend at Caen called Gundolf with a letter explaining how they came to be written. He says that an unnamed friend had asked him to write a prayer about St Mary, and he had done so; but the friend was not satisfied, and he wrote a second. The friend was still dissatisfied, and he wrote a third. A careful examination of the manuscripts has shown that even the third of these prayers did not at once satisfy Anselm, for he continued to make alterations and additions for some time after its original composition. The composition of these three prayers, therefore, gave him a quite unusual amount of trouble, and he tells us that the main source of this trouble was the dissatisfaction of an unnamed friend. Yet as so often happens where an author tells us how he wrote something, his account is rather misleading. I think that the unnamed friend is probably a fictitious character introduced to satisfy the literary convention that an author should write only under pressure from outside; it was Anselm's own desire for completeness of expression which drove him on. It is clear, for instance, that the third prayer did not supersede the two earlier ones as his letter suggests, for he preserved all three and always kept them together. Nor did any of them cover the same ground as the other two: they dealt with different aspects of the subject; and, if we look at them carefully, we can see that they form a logical sequence and describe a process of spiritual growth. The first prayer is a meditation addressed to St Mary 'when the mind is heavy with lethargy'; the second, 'when the mind is filled with fear'; the third, when the sinner 'seeks the love of St Mary and Christ'.

This progression from inertia to a vivid apprehension of the being and love of God is the programme which Anselm follows in his prayers. It is also the programme of his theology, especially in the greatest of his early theological works, the *Proslogion*, which he wrote in a single gust of inspiration in 1078. The first step of spiritual progress is the stirring up of the soul from its state of torpor. This leads to fear and horror, and to an awakening of the desire to know and love God. The resulting movement is a two-fold process of intellectual illumination and spiritual purification. Roughly speaking, when the emphasis is on intellectual illumination the result is theology; when it is on spiritual purification the result is the kind of prayer which is exemplified in the collection which is printed below.

The third Prayer to St Mary is the fullest statement of this programme in devotional terms, and in its extraordinary freedom of verbal and imaginative elaboration it is Anselm's greatest achievement in this mode. Since no translation, however good, can entirely capture the spirit of the original, the reader may wish to have a few lines of Anselm's own words as he reaches this highest point in his verbal and devotional flight. I have arranged the lines to make comparison with the translation (lines 175–189) easy, and the reader will notice the rhymes and assonances which are especially important:

Omnis natura a deo est creata, et deus ex Maria est natus.
Deus omnia creavit, et Maria deum generavit.
Deus qui omnia fecit, ipse se ex Maria fecit,
et sic omnia quae fecerat refecit.
Qui potuit omnia de nihilo facere,
noluit ea violata, nisi prius fieret Mariae filius, reficere.
{Deus igitur est pater rerum creatarum,
{et Maria mater rerum recreatarum.
{Deus est pater constitutionis omnium,
{et Maria est mater restitutionis omnium.
{Deus enim genuit illum per quem omnia sunt facta,
{et Maria peperit illum per quem cuncta sunt salvata.
{Deus genuit illum sine quo penitus nihil est,
{et Maria peperit illum sine quo nihil omnino bene est.

Most of Anselm's *Prayers and Meditations* were written in the decade between 1070 and 1080, when he also wrote his first two theological works, *Monologion* and *Proslogion*. These and the letters to his friends at Canterbury were his earliest writings, and they show a striking similarity of theme and method: they are all about the mental and spiritual awakening which is the origin of love. They all have the same fanciful, yet precise, word-play, which expresses Anselm's feeling for the subtle links between words and reality.

In his later years there was a change both in his style and in his habits of thought. His writing became more solid, less fanciful, less fragile. We can see the results of this change in the latest of his meditations, the *Meditation on Human Redemption*, which is the devotional counterpart to his last great theological work, the *Cur Deus Homo*. This work, and the meditation associated with it, were written about twenty years later than the main body of his *Prayers and Meditations*. The *Meditation* was probably composed in 1098 in the peaceful surroundings of the small monastery at Liberi in southern Italy where the *Cur Deus Homo* was completed. It is a theological medita-tion, and the reader will easily detect the change of tone from the personal and effusive self-examination of the earlier prayers.

When he wrote this last meditation Anselm was an elderly archbishop of sixty-five, a man more worn by experience and troublesome duties than the monk who had begun to write nearly thirty years earlier. He died eleven years later in 1109. After his death he had many imitators. His prayers set a fashion for long theological meditations and elaborate prayers. Some of the best of these imitations became attached to the genuine body of Anselm's *Prayers and Meditations*, and circulated under his name. Until forty years ago (when a Benedictine scholar, Dom André Wilmart, finally cleared up the whole matter) nobody could distinguish the genuine from the spurious elements in the collection. But now that the difference between the genuine and the spurious has been made clear, we can see how far Anselm outshone his later imitators in the brightness of his imagery, the beauty of his prose, and the originality of his thoughts. These qualities by themselves would be sufficient to make his prayers worth reading; and it is unlikely that anyone will read them without sometimes being drawn into the paths along which Anselm invited the reader to follow him.

R. W. SOUTHERN

PREFACE

Anselm was born in 1033 in Aosta, then in the kingdom of Burgundy. He came north after the death of his mother, and three years later he entered the abbey of Notre Dame at Bec in Normandy, where Lanfranc was prior. When Lanfranc went to Caen, Anselm replaced him as prior at the age of thirty, and fifteen years later, in 1078, he became abbot, at the death of the founder of the abbey, Herluin. In 1093 William Rufus appointed him Archbishop of Canterbury, and he held this office until his death on 21 April 1109. It was while he lived at Bec that he did some of his most creative writing, including the *Prayers and Meditations* and the *Proslogion*.

They are the earliest of his writings to have survived. They were written, according to Eadmer, 'at the desire and request of his friends', as the overflow of his own devotion: 'anyone can see without my speaking about them with what anxious care, with what fear, with what hope and love he addressed himself to God and his saints and taught others to do the same.'[1] His own prayer made him a spiritual guide to others from the beginning of his life as a monk, and it was in this capacity that he was most esteemed by his contemporaries. The *Prayers and Meditations* stand in some ways between the conversations and discussions, which formed so large a part of his teaching, and the great treatises, by belonging to his daily life and conduct, but forming also a part of his literary output. Until the end of his life he was ready to have the prayers copied as a definite collection, under his own name, sending them to those who asked for them, his last known recipient being the Countess Mathilda of Tuscany.

Since the time of Anselm's death, however, it has been virtually impossible to know which prayers were really his, or

1. VA, 1, viii.

to form a true picture of him as a devotional writer. The collection was enlarged almost at once by the addition of prayers by Ralph of Battle, and in the ensuing centuries it continued to take to itself a host of anonymous writings. By the seventeenth century when the Jesuit, Théophile Raynaud, edited the *Prayers and Meditations*, there were 111 pieces of devotional literature going under this name. The edition prepared in 1675 by the Maurist, Gabriel Gerberon, included them all, and these in turn were printed by Migne among the works of Anselm in volume 158 of the *Patrologiae Latinae*. In the last fifty years, however, Dom Wilmart has distinguished nineteen of the prayers and three of the meditations as the genuine work of Anselm,[2] and these have been printed in a critical edition by Dom F. Schmitt.[3]

It is now therefore possible to form some idea of Anselm as a devotional writer, and to estimate his place in the development of Christian spirituality. He wrote no formal treatise on prayer, but in the *Prayers and Meditations* and in the *Proslogion* he shows a pattern of prayer and an approach to praying which had an influence so profound on Christian devotion that it has been called 'the Anselmian revolution'.[4] This way of prayer is also expressed and explained in the Preface to the *Prayers and Meditations* and in some of the letters which were written to recipients of the prayers. In order to see the extent of this 'revolution', and its relation to the tradition of Christian spirituality, it seems necessary to examine not only the prayers themselves but also the background of devotion out of which they grew, in liturgy and in private prayer. The *Prayers and*

2. Wilmart, *Auteurs spirituels et textes dévots du moyen âge Latin*, Paris, 1932, pp. 162–201.

Wilmart, Introduction to Odo Castel's French translation, *Les Meditations et Prières de S. Anselme*, Paris, 1923, Pax XI.

3. Schmitt, *Meditations and Prayers*, vol. 3, *Letters*, vols. 3–5, *Proslogion*, vol. 2.

4. R. W. Southern, *St Anselm and His Biographer*, Cambridge University Press, 1963, pp. 42–71.

Meditations are of interest, too, for the light they throw on Anselm himself, both as a monk and as a scholar, especially where they contain the germ of ideas which appear more fully in his later works.

The *Prayers and Meditations* that went under the name of Anselm have been widely used for centuries. There were translations into Middle English, some of which survive, and more recently there have been translations into French and Italian. In 1856 Dr Pusey wrote a learned and perspective introduction to a translation into English by 'a younger friend' of some of the material in PL158, which included four of the genuine prayers of Anselm and two of his meditations. Since Dom Schmitt's edition of the Latin text has appeared, Sister Penelope, C.S.M.V., has translated the three meditations and some of the prayers, though not those addressed to the saints.

Translator's Note

This translation has been prepared in the conviction that these prayers are of lasting value in themselves, as well as for the light they throw upon Anselm and on the development of Christian spirituality. I have been aware of subtleties in the Latin which cannot be conveyed in English, and for this reason have sometimes resorted to paraphrase rather than translation. Some of the prose, especially in Meditation 2, is artificial and mannered to a degree; I have not tried to make this more palatable, nor have I tried to reinterpret the many passages of self-abasement which to modern taste must seem overdone.

Most of Anselm's references to the Bible are approximations rather than direct quotations. The references given in the notes are to the Revised Standard Version, including the numbering of the Psalms.

The prayers and parts of the *Proslogion* have been set out in broken lines, in an attempt to convey the rhythm of Anselm's complex rhymed prose, which is closer to our conception of poetry. The broken lines may also help to a more meditative reading of the prayers, if such be undertaken. In the arrangement of the lines I have been helped by reference to three early Anselmian MSS., where the prayers are carefully punctuated for reading aloud. These are MS. Rawlinson 392, a late eleventh-century copy of most of the prayers, the three meditations, and the *Proslogion*; MS. Bodley 271, the work of the great Canterbury school of illuminators, produced early in the twelfth century; and the Oxford 'Littlemore Anselm', contained in MS. Auct.D 26, and discussed at length by Otto Pächt in his article on the illustrations to Anselm's *Prayers and Meditations*.[5] It is fair to suppose that the way Anselm cast his sentences and the effects at which he aimed can be seen from these early MSS. The prayers were written both for the ear and for the understanding, and this gives to the punctuation a special significance. Where possible in the translation, I have rendered the final medial point by a full stop, and the mid-sentence pauses or breaks by a comma, semi-colon, or new line, and sometimes by a conjunction. But the rhythm of English is not that of Latin, and at best this use of the MSS. punctuation has been a matter of intuition, of listening to the sentences and trying to catch their rhythm. This is especially true in the *Proslogion*, where I have used broken lines and continuous prose for different parts, with no justification but a feeling for the sound.

This work was undertaken at the suggestion of Professor R. W. Southern and I am deeply grateful for the opportunity of profiting by his wider scholarship, as well as for his patient advice and criticism. I would also like to record my gratitude to my community for making the work possible, and especially to those sisters who have edited, corrected, and typed the MS. My thanks must also go to the librarians of the Bodleian Library for their assistance with books and manuscripts. And finally I

5. Pächt O., Illustrations of St Anselm's Prayers and Meditations, *Journal of the Warburg and Courtauld Institutes*, XIX, 1956, pp. 68–83.

offer the book, with all its defects, to the Rev. A. M. Allchin, without whose friendship and encouragement it would never have been completed.

Benedicta Ward, S.L.G.

Fairacres, Oxford
July 1970

ABBREVIATIONS

PL: Migne, J. P., *Patrologiae Latinae cursus completus*; the references are to volume and column.

Rev. Bén.: *Revue Bénédictine.*

Schmitt: Schmitt, F. S., *Sancti Anselmi Cantuariensis Archiepiscopi Opera Omnia*, i–vi, Nelson, 1938–61. This text has been used throughout for the translation of the *Prayers and Meditations*, the *Proslogion*, and the letters. The prayers and letters are numbered according to Dom Schmitt's edition.

VA: *Vita Anselmi* by Eadmer; the references to the *Vita Anselmi* are to book and chapter, and may be found in R. W. Southern's edition, in Oxford Medieval Texts (reprinted 1972).

Precum Libelli: ed. Wilmart, A., *Precum Libelli Quattuor Aevi Karolini*, Ephemerides Liturgicae, Rome, 1940.

INTRODUCTION

I. BACKGROUND TO THE 'PRAYERS
AND MEDITATIONS'

I. The Liturgy

The Divine Office

The *Prayers and Meditations* themselves give little indication of the sources that formed them; unlike John of Fécamp, Anselm does not quote directly from other writers, and the very form of the prayers prevents direct reference to their teaching; they are the words of a man praying to God, not discussing ideas about Him. In such spontaneous effusions, words and phrases already known are recalled to the memory as they are prayed in the heart, becoming the present prayer of the one who uses them. However, it seems reasonable to consider the liturgy as one of the formative influences on Anselm's prayer. As a monk he was bound to the daily recitation of the Benedictine Office, with the additions of Norman monasticism, and as a priest he would celebrate the Eucharist at least on Sundays and major festivals, if not more frequently. This continual round of corporate worship is the setting of Anselm's life in the years when he was writing the *Prayers and Meditations*, and it seems proper to relate them to this context, though in doing this it is well to recall the reservations expressed by Edmund Bishop when he was investigating the liturgical sources of the *Book of Cerne*: 'The best security for right judgement will be found to lie in the conviction that, after the best efforts, the results in any particular case are to be looked on as only tentative.'[1]

Chapters 8 to 20 in the *Rule of St Benedict* contain the arrangement of the psalter for recitation at the Divine Office, by day and night; the basic plan is that the 'psalter with its hundred and fifty psalms be chanted every week and begun afresh every Sunday at Matins',[2] the psalms being distributed between the lesser hours of Prime, Terce, Sext, None, and Compline; the major hours of Lauds and Vespers; and the Night Office. By the eleventh century a whole series of extra psalms, prayers and offices had been added to this basic structure, so that monks of a fervent monastery like Bec would be occupied for a very large part of the day in corporate attention to the God of the Bible as set before them in the liturgy, and particularly in the psalter. The great monastic house with its ordered life of prayer was what men respected most in Christian living in these centuries, and this meant for the monks a change in emphasis in the horarium, and indeed in their understanding of the monastic life. For them, the liturgy was no longer, as it was for St Benedict, only a part, although the best part, of a whole daily life directed towards God. It was worship, their rendering to God of that which is due to Him, but it was also an asceticism, an exercise of charity towards the living and dead, a social obligation, a way of life. Some idea of what this meant for monks in the eleventh century can be seen in the directory of the customs of Anglo-Norman monastic houses drawn up by Archbishop Lanfranc while Anselm was still at Bec.[3] The *Trina Oratio*, the Gradual Psalms, the Penitential Psalms, Psalms for the Dead, and Psalms for Benefactors were said after various Offices, as well as the daily recitation of the Office of the Dead and of All Saints.

This continuous round of psalmody gave the monk a rich and deep knowledge of the psalter, which would be absorbed almost unconsciously. And it is clear when Anselm uses the psalter that this is the kind of understanding he has of it. When he uses the language of the psalms he is not quoting: he is speaking with the language of the scriptures, as in the Prayer to Christ:

'The joy of my heart fails me'; my laughter is 'turned to mourning';
    'my heart and my flesh fail me';
'but God is the strength of my heart and my portion for ever.'
    'My soul refuses comfort,' unless from you, my dear.

Here three psalms are woven together with Anselm's own thoughts, and are prayed spontaneously by him. This is the traditional monastic use of the psalter, where the words of the

Hebrew psalms become the prayer of Christ and his Christians: 'For many members united by love and peace, under one head, our Saviour himself, form one man . . . and the words of the psalms are either the words of Christ, and of the Church, or of Christ alone, or of the Church alone in which we are made partakers.'[4]

Chapter 9 of the *Rule of St Benedict* mentions the other basic element in the Office: 'The books to be read at Matins shall be the inspired scriptures of the Old and New Testaments, and also the commentaries on them which have been made by well-known and orthodox Catholic Fathers.' This meant that Anselm would hear lections from the Bible read 'continuo' through the year, but it is not possible to distinguish this from his personal reading of the scriptures in its effect on the prayers. The same is true of his reading of the Fathers, though it is clear that he was not influenced by the symbolic interpretations of scripture common to the four Fathers most used in the homilies of the Office – Augustine, Jerome, Leo, and Gregory. As with the psalter his was a simpler and more personal use of the scriptures.

By the eleventh century the Office had been embellished with responses, antiphons, and hymns. There are echoes of these in the prayers of Anselm, notably in the Prayer to St Peter, which begins with a direct reference to the hymn for the feast of St Peter and St Paul, and the first antiphon of vespers. But it will be more convenient to notice these few allusions when the prayers are discussed individually.

The Kalendar and the Mass

Between the *Rule of St Benedict* and the life of Bec in the time of Anselm lay five centuries of development in both Office and Mass. The non-clerical community of Monte Cassino had been replaced by communities of ordained priests, concerned for the celebration of the mysteries, with more and more solemnity and frequency. The content and shape of the Mass, and the pattern of the liturgical year were more or less stable by the eleventh century. The ninth and tenth centuries in Western Europe had seen a steady process in the stabilization of government, and in this the re-ordering of the Christian life had pride of place. Charlemagne completed the ecclesiastical legislation of his father and continued the reform of the Church begun by Boniface and Chrodegang. In this he re-emphasized their policy of using the liturgy as a means to bring about order and uniformity. By the mid eleventh century a basic pattern of liturgical worship had been established throughout Gaul, though there were regional variations and additions. Each monastery had its own form of the Kalendar, with local additions to a basic structure. The saints Anselm addresses in his prayers had their place in the liturgical year, in Mass and Office, with the exception of St Nicholas, who became popular in the West after the translation of his relics in the eleventh century, which occasion may have inspired Anselm's prayer.

The only prayer of Anselm which is directly connected with the Mass is the Prayer before Receiving the Body and Blood of Christ. It is the prayer of a priest before receiving Communion, and, like earlier prayers of this kind, is a prayer for purity before receiving the Sacrament. Private prayers for the priest before Communion had become customary in Gaul during the eighth century, and there are many examples of these.[5] What makes Anselm's prayer different is that it is personal and ardent, and at the same time scriptural and theological. The Eucharist is described in words from St Paul, and seen as the pledge of redemption, the sign of reconciliation, and the point of incorporation of Christians into the Body of Christ. This is a wider view than that of the earlier prayers, and it is also free from the pressures of scholastic definition and controversy that were to come later. This is the one prayer of Anselm which might have been used in a liturgy – it is short enough and of the same type as other private prayers in the Mass, but there is no evidence that this happened.

The other prayer of Anselm connected with liturgy is the Prayer to the Cross. The devotion to the cross of the Lord was well known in the West long before the twelfth century. The account of Constantine's vision of the cross and its subsequent discovery in Jerusalem by St Helena were the subject of hymns and legends and poems, such as Cynewulf's 'Elene'. The discovery of the cross and its later recovery from the Turks were commemorated in the feasts of the Invention of the Cross on 3 May, and the Exaltation of the Cross on 14 September.

The actual service of the Veneration of the Cross which was incorporated into the Gallican liturgies for Good Friday was derived from the ceremonies for Holy Week conducted in Jerusalem in the fourth century and described in the diary of Etheria, a devout pilgrim to the Holy Places.[6] The inspiration for this and similar liturgical celebrations of the passion of the Lord came from St Cyril, Bishop of Jerusalem, who gave to the primitive concept of the Paschal mystery this added dimension of historical celebration. Part of the service consists in the kissing of the cross, while the Reproaches are sung, and, after these, the hymn *Pange lingua*, by Fortunatus, Bishop of Poitiers, who wrote it for the procession bringing a relic of the True Cross to Queen Radegunda in 760 A.D.

The veneration of relics of the True Cross spread in the West from pilgrims returning from Jerusalem, and it was a short step from venerating a cross that contained a relic of the True Cross to venerating any cross or crucifix. The actual veneration of the wood itself had a mystique of its own, of which the eighth-century *Dream of the Rood* is perhaps the most famous example. In this poem, as in the hymns of Fortunatus and in the whole of the early history of devotion to the cross, it is Christ who reigns from the tree, the Christus Victor, who is adored:

> Brightly that beacon was gilded with gold,
> Jewels adorned it, fair at the foot –
> Wondrous that tree, token of triumph.[7]

In this poem, however, there is also the idea of the suffering of Christ, of His blood upon the tree, where is 'the Lord in agony outstretched'. These two themes, of the victory of the cross and its cost, form the liturgy of the cross, whether it is in the Mass, the Office, or the Good Friday Veneration, and it is these two themes that form Anselm's prayer. In popular devotion the aspect of cost and suffering could and did become a sentimental pity for the crucified; and, on the other hand, the power of the wood could equally well become a form of magic, as medieval miracle stories abundantly testify, including one incident at least in Eadmer's life of Anselm.[8] But this prayer is in the liturgical tradition and very far from idolatry or sentiment. In the first line it is the cross as a symbol of the cross of Christ, which was itself a symbol of redemption, which is venerated. The whole prayer continues this idea of the cross as the sign of life and redemption, freely chosen and not inflicted; it was a line of thought which Anselm was to work out more thoroughly in *Cur Deus Homo*, in reply to objections to the 'shame of the cross'. There are echoes in the prayer of the *Pange Lingua*'s praise of the 'sweetest wood'; there is reference to the passage from Galatians used as an introit for the feast of the Holy Cross, and that from Philippians used on Maundy Thursday as the introit; and the 'joy' which comes to the world through the cross recalls the Byzantine Liturgical Trisagion, *Crucem Tuam*, used also in the Western Veneration of the Cross. There were many other prayers to the cross,[9] both before and after Anselm, but this, like so many of his prayers, holds a balance between the formal and austere tradition of the liturgy and the ardent personal fervour which came into devotion in the twelfth century; it is not a liturgical prayer, but a personal prayer which has its roots in the liturgy.

The Prayer to God and the Prayer to Christ belong to the tradition of private prayer and seem to be without direct liturgical associations; the Prayer for Friends and the Prayer for Enemies are also of this kind. In the prayers to the saints, however, it is possible to see some connection with the official liturgy of the saints, in Mass or Office. The three prayers to St Mary are full of the titles and honours familiar in the Eastern liturgies connected with her – most of all, the ancient title of *Theotocos*, the God-bearer, is Anselm's first and main title for her. The four main feasts of Our Lady had been introduced to the West by the Syrian pope, Sergius (687–701), and retain some traces of their Greek origin. The early texts about the Mother of God, in the liturgy and in sermons, are concerned most of all with the mystery of the Annunciation, and use two texts from St Luke – the angel's greeting and the acclamation by Elizabeth – as the basis of their meditation. The free assent of Mary to God's action, and the resulting grace and blessedness of her as the Mother of God, are likewise the basis of the third prayer of Anselm – a prayer which, H. Barré says, 'crowns and sums up all the Western tradition of the Fathers about the Virgin Mother of the Saviour'. [10] The *Lacta mater* of St Augustine which was taken up and used in homilies and sermons in her Office, especially in Spain, appears near the end of this third prayer. The idea of praying to Mary and asking her help and intercession was already established in the liturgy, and Anselm has no hesitation in using it. The basis and background of his devotion to Mary seems to be liturgical as well as scriptural, but it is the fervour and love that fills the prayer, and his personal relationship to Mary herself that make it one of the greatest of Marian devotions.

The saints first venerated in the liturgy of the Church were those who after Mary most nearly touched the mystery of Christ – the Apostles and St John the Baptist. By the eleventh century their liturgy in Mass and Office was fully established. The feast of the Nativity of St John the Baptist and that of the Visitation present the same aspect of the life of St John the Baptist as the first part of Anselm's prayer: he is the hidden witness who recognized Christ from the womb. The latter part of the prayer, with its recurrent meditation on the Lamb of God, may have been influenced by the use in the Mass of the *Agnus dei* before Communion – but here again it is impossible to distinguish between the influence of the Bible and that of the liturgy, which after all is composed almost exclusively of biblical material.

One more direct reference to the liturgy is in the Prayer to St Peter, where Anselm uses the idea of Peter as door-keeper of heaven, as prince of the apostles, and as shepherd, in the same way as the liturgy. The 'faithful shepherd', the 'prince of the Apostles', is used in the Magnificat antiphon for the first Vespers of St Peter and also in the Office hymn at Lauds, *Jam, bone Pastor, Petre.*

The Prayer to St Paul and the Prayer to St John the Evangelist are in no way related to their liturgies, but rather to their own writings, and the basis of the Prayer to St Stephen is the seventh chapter of Acts, a choice which may or may not be connected with its use as the epistle for the feast. The point Anselm makes about the joy of Stephen in his martyrdom, when the stones bring forth the 'sound of his goodness', recalls the second antiphon for Lauds of St Stephen, 'The stones of the brook were sweet unto Stephen'.

The other biblical saint addressed by Anselm is St Mary Magdalene. The great outburst of devotion to her was to come in the next century and be connected with her relics and with Vézelay, but from the time of Bede her commemoration was known to the West.[11] In the liturgy she was commemorated by Mass and Office on 22 July, under the three aspects of penitent, witness of the resurrection, and apostle to the apostles. Anselm uses the first two ideas in his prayer, addressing her as the witness to forgiving love and to the power of the risen Christ; this Paschal understanding of St Mary Magdalene is also familiar from the Easter sequence, *Victimae Paschali Laudes*, where she is addressed and questioned about her experience at the empty tomb. The conflation of the three Marys of the Bible was common ground, though Anselm may have derived it directly from the homily by St Gregory used for her feast.

The two non-biblical saints addressed in the prayers are St Benedict and St Nicholas. The Prayer to St Benedict uses material from the *Rule of St Benedict*, not from the liturgy which is based on the *Dialogues of St Gregory*. The Prayer to St Nicholas may have been written on the occasion of the translation of this saint's relics from Myra to Bari and is one of the earliest of the evidences of his cult in the West. There is, of course, no possibility of liturgical influence here, though there is the reference to the repeated use of the name of the saint – 'Nicholas – great Nicholas', by those who pray to him for help, which may be connected with the Litany of the Saints.

One other element in the liturgy of the saints that can be seen as a connection with private prayers such as Anselm's is the collects. These prayers take the form of the Roman *orationes*, in which God is addressed directly, under various titles, some reference is made to his mighty acts in and through the saint, and a petition is made to God through the prayers and merits of the saints, the whole prayer being offered through Christ in the power of the Spirit. This pattern is basically that of these longer and more complex prayers. In Anselm's prayers, there is always the address under various titles, a mention of the special merits of the saint and God's work in him or her, petitions for help, and usually a trinitarian ending, all of which are much elaborated. The definite difference is that Anselm addresses his prayers to the saint rather than to God. This is not the method of the collects, but rather of the semi-liturgical devotion of the 'Litany of the Saints', which came into use in Rome in the sixth century, and was a popular medieval devotion.

2. The 'Preces Privatae'

The tradition of private devotion in the two centuries before Anselm was strongly liturgical. What called forth the admiration of laymen in the ninth and tenth centuries was the monastic organization of prayer in an ordered life of dedication to God; it seemed the proper response of mankind to the command to 'pray without ceasing'. The same spirit that led to the multiplication of prayers and Offices within the monasteries led to its imitation outside. There was a demand by laymen for schemes of prayer approximating to the monastic pattern. Such prayer books were used at court and by great ladies, such as Mathilda of Tuscany and the Princess Adelaide, in fact by those economically and socially in the best position to profit by them. They consisted primarily of arrangements of the psalms, running parallel to the monastic Office, and with the same idea of sanctifying the whole day. There is no doubt that the psalter was the prayer book *par excellence* of the age, and Alcuin recommended it to Charlemagne in glowing terms: 'If you come to the psalms with a serious mind, and look with the spirit of understanding, you will find there the word of the Lord incarnate, suffering, risen, and ascended . . . you will find every virtue in the psalms, if you deserve to find the mercy of God in revealing to you their secrets.'[1] These books of extracts from the psalms for private use contained also prayers, among which were short prayers to connect the Hours with the stages of the passion of Christ, a development known as early as the third century in Hippolytus.[2] There were long prayers of contrition, similar to the Irish penitentials, and groups of psalms such as the penitential psalms. The book which Anselm sent to the royal lady Adelaide contained such extracts, *florilegia*, from the psalms, for her private use.

The psalms in the *libelli* were copied by scribes directly from choir psalters, and with them were copied the 'psalter collects'[3] – short prayers, in the form of a Roman collect, which directed the psalm to a Christian meaning. Since the fifth century one way in which the Old Testament words were given a New Testament meaning had been by the use of these prayers addressed to God through Christ, which were read at the end of a psalm, and in which a few words from the psalm were taken and developed into a prayer; no attempt seems to have been made in them to interpret the whole of a psalm. It is possible to see how this would have looked to Anselm from the eleventh-century book of prayers preserved in the Bodleian MS. D'Orville 45.[4] Here a short prayer, usually one sentence only, follows each psalm in the way described; thus psalm 23, 'The Lord is my Shepherd', is followed by this collect: 'Lord, be our shepherd, and we shall lack nothing. We desire no other leader than you, no pasture other than your glory. Lead us in the paths of righteousness, and we shall not go astray. In the valley of the shadow may we not be overcome.' These collects were included with their psalms in the *libelli*, and to these were added other parts of the Office, hymns, canticles, the *Te Deum*, and the collects for feasts of the saints. By the ninth century a litany of the saints was also included, often as a preface to a prayer of contrition.

A certain development took place in private devotion to the saints and this can be illustrated from the Carolingian prayer books. The four Carolingian *libelli* printed by Dom Wilmart contain collects for the Common of Saints, and hymns for their Offices. The *Libelli Turonensis* contains also a litany of the saints, in the traditional form, asking mercy from God, Father, Son and Holy Ghost; then petitions are made to the saints in an hierarchic rather than historical order: St Mary, the apostles, martyrs, confessors and religious founders, and virgins; this is followed by a long confession of sins.[5] In the prayer ascribed to St Ephraim in the *Libelli Trecensis* petitions are made to the same groups of saints, but at greater length than 'have mercy upon us'; each saint has a separate prayer, of identical pattern but different content.[6] Another form of this is found in the prayer ascribed to St Gregory, which, like Jewish paradigm prayers, asks the help of saints of the Old Testament with reference to God's mighty acts in their lives: for instance, 'Elias, who raised the dead, pray for me,'[7] or, more fully, as in the *Libelli Parisini*, 'Lord Jesus Christ, I adore you who called Adam at midday and said to him, "Adam, where are you?," and I beseech your mercy that I may deserve to walk in the light of noon and not in the shadows of death.' [8] It is this pattern of prayer to the saints, in the liturgical collects, and in the expanded litany, that lies behind the longer prayers that developed at the beginning of the eleventh century. A group of prayers to the saints is found in many MSS., often in close juxtaposition to the litany of the saints, and they form a distinct group, related to the sequence followed in the litany: prayers to God, Father, Son and Spirit, followed by prayers to Mary, the apostles, martyrs, confessors, and sometimes virgins. Usually the saints selected from these categories are St John the Baptist, St Peter and St Paul, St John the Evangelist, St Stephen, St Benedict, and either St Martin or St Nicholas.[9] This is the same group of saints that Anselm selects for his much longer and more complex prayers, which nonetheless contain some of the same elements as the *libelli*: there are references to the merits and life of the saints as the ground of intercession, and there are long passages of self-abasement, which can be associated with the forms of self-examination put after the litany of the saints in the more formal Carolingian setting.

The Prayer to God is the shortest of the prayers and the one most like the Carolingian prayers, with brief petitions, based on the last part of the 'Our Father'. It is followed by the Prayer to Christ, the prayer which belongs most completely to the new style of personal devotion, and is furthest from the liturgy. It is a prayer directed to Jesus Christ, not to God through Jesus Christ. Christian prayer in the New Testament had been made to God through the mediation of Christ, though prayer direct to Jesus as the Lord was also known, as in the prayer of St Stephen at his death, 'Lord Jesus, receive my spirit'. The mediation of Christ is the core of Christian prayer, but there was also a tradition of praying to Christ in the first three centuries, especially in the prayers of the martyrs, who followed the example of the proto-martyr in calling directly on Jesus, like Genesius of Rome, 'Christ is on my lips, Christ is in my heart, no torments now can take him from me.'[10] The Arian controversy of the fourth century led to an increasing stress in official worship on the equality of the Son with the Father, and in some quarters this led to an over-emphasis on the Son. The Council of Carthage therefore in 397 decreed that prayers directed to Christ were not admissible in the liturgy: 'No one is to name the Father in place of the Son in the prayers, or the Son in place of the Father. At the altar prayer is always to be directed to the Father.' Thus, in spite of Arius, the tradition of prayer directed to Christ found no place in the official liturgy of the Church, but it continued in private and popular devotion from Hippolytus through Ambrose and Gregory, to flower again in the Middle Ages.

This private tradition of prayer to Christ revived and developed in the eleventh century, with a new stress on the person of Jesus in his earthly life and especially in his passion, as related to the person praying. Anselm's Prayer to Christ is one of the great compositions in this tradition. To emphasize the 'to Christ' directive he uses the title, 'Lord Jesus Christ', and it is not so much Christ as the second person of the Trinity that he addresses, as Jesus, incarnate Lord, 'My Redeemer, my Mercy, my Salvation'. This personal relationship with Christ evolved rapidly after Anselm, but it is there in other eleventh-century prayers, such as those of Peter Damian – in his prayer to the Cross, for instance, the idea of personal commitment in regard to the passion of Christ and the immediateness of the scene are very striking: 'My Redeemer, I see you with the eyes of my soul, fixed to the Cross with nails, I hear you speak with a clear voice to the thief . . . may I bear here the marks of the nails and be conformed to the sufferings of the Crucified, so that I may deserve to come to Him to the resurrection in glory.'[11]

The Prayer to Christ contains a meditation on the sorrows of St Mary at the Cross, the forerunner of many such. The Carolingian prayer books contain prayers to St Mary, notably the *Singularis merita*, which occurs again and again.[12] The praise of Mary as Virgin and Mother, the contrast made between her holiness and man's vileness, and urgent petitions for her help, characterize these prayers. By the eleventh century this simple prayer form was being expanded, and one instance of this by Maurillus of Rouen shows the way in which this was happening: 'Before whom then shall we desolate wretches more properly groan and weep for all the evil of our unhappy state than before the true and undoubted mother of mercy? . . . See, Lady, the prodigal son, with worn and naked feet, sighs, shouts, and calls to his mother, from a huge and stinking darkness – I know not how often he begs her to love and reconcile and excuse him to his Father.'[13] This expanded version of the *Singularis merita* was printed by Migne incorrectly under the name of Anselm.

The intercession of Mary was sometimes asked together with that of St John the Evangelist, as the two at the foot of the Cross. There is one version of this in the *Book of Cerne*,[14] and a later extension of this is the *O intemerata*, one of the most popular of Carolingian prayers.[15] It is directed to Mary and John rather than to God or Christ. The reference to the *luminaria divinitatis ante Deum lucentia* is interesting, since the theme of light recurs in other prayers to St John the Evangelist, presumably with a recollection of the Fourth Gospel and its image of Christ as the light of the world that shines in the darkness. In Anselm's prayers the picture of St John is, in one, the friend who reclined on the bosom of the Lord at the Last Supper, and, in the other, the rich friend who will give to the poor who ask. Both these ideas are present in embryo in this Carolingian prayer to St John the Evangelist: 'Open the gate of life to me when I knock, and let not the prince of darkness prevail against me; let him not lift up the foot of pride against me. Let not the hand that was held out to save you reject me. Help me according to your word and lead me to the banquet of love, where all your friends dine with you . . .'[16]

The idea of taking incidents in the life of a saint and applying them to the particular needs of the present situation is the basic one in these early Carolingian prayers. The prayers to St John the Baptist see him pre-eminently as the Baptizer, the one who cleanses, and the witness who points to him who should come. He was popular as the first ascetic, and later with the introduction of the feast of his beheading from the East he was given the status of a martyr. Anselm addresses him first as the witness from the womb of his mother, and then as the one who witnesses to the Lamb of God who takes away the sin of the world. He makes no mention of him as either virgin or ascetic, though the idea of cleansing is present in Anselm's prayer as in the older Carolingian one: 'St John the Baptist, precursor and martyr of Christ, most holy virgin, I pray you obtain for me by your prayers from the Lord the grace of abstinence in both food and drink, in thought, word, and deed . . .'[17] The prayer given in the *Book of Cerne* is closer to Anselm in its thought on baptism and on the Lamb of God: 'St John the Baptist, who deserved to baptize the Saviour of the world with your own hands in the waters of Jordan; be an intercessor for me to the mercy of God our redeemer, that he may deliver me from the darkness of sin and lead me into the light of grace, who takes away the sin of the world and has promised to grant us the kingdom of heaven.'[18]

In the Prayer to St Peter, Anselm uses the traditional ideas of him as the key-bearer of the kingdom of heaven and the shepherd; but the equally popular concept of him as the rock, the foundation upon which Christ would build his Church, is absent. In art and in liturgy as well as in private devotion these are the main images under which St Peter is seen, and there are many prayers in the Carolingian books that bear this out. Prayers to St Paul, the other Roman martyr, are not so frequent; when they do occur, it is the event of his conversion or some aspect of his teaching that is used. He is *Vas electionis*, a quotation from Acts, which is also used in the Mass of St Paul in the introit. Anselm's prayer to him is concerned with him as a 'mother', as bearing sons in the faith, based on the fourth chapter of the epistle to the Galatians; it seems to have no parallel in liturgy or private devotion.

The earlier private prayers to St Stephen picture him as the proto-martyr, the one who, after Christ, most loved his enemies. This is the theme of the first part of Anselm's prayer, and may be compared with this Carolingian prayer: 'St Stephen, first and glorious martyr saint, you are first in that choir of martyrs who have come before God out of great tribulation, and suffered persecution for righteousness' sake. Pray for me, a miserable sinner, to the Lord, for you prayed for your enemies and for those who stoned you. Help me, for you are one with the holy Lord Jesus, the great martyr and your friend.'[19] The last part of Anselm's prayer, centred on the text, 'he fell asleep in the Lord', is very like the meditations on heaven and the bliss of the saints which reached their apogee in Peter Abelard's *O quanta qualia*. It can be compared with the twenty-fifth chapter of the *Proslogion*, where Anselm considers 'which goods belong to those who enjoy this good and how great they are'. Heaven, for the writers of the Middle Ages, was the fullness of God, and is therefore described by analogy with the fulfilment of the five senses[20] – as Julian of Norwich later put it: 'Eternally hid in God, we shall see him truly and feel him fully, hear him spiritually, smell him delightfully, and taste him sweetly; we shall see God face to face, simply and fully.'[21]

The Prayer for Friends and the Prayer for Enemies of Anselm have their forerunners in the Carolingian prayer books, and clearly these are more appropriate subjects for private prayer than for liturgical intercession. The *Liber Coloniensis* has a prayer 'for our enemies',[22] to be used as a preparation for confession, and in the *Manual of Prayers of St John Gualbert* there is an interesting parallel to Anselm's prayers, for both friends and enemies: 'Lord Jesus Christ, Son of the Living God, if anyone wishes me ill or has done me harm or is my enemy, if anyone opposes me or persecutes me – Lord, forgive them. I can love my friends in you and my enemies for your sake. Lord, direct my paths in your sight. Hear my prayer, Christ Jesus, who with the Father . . .'[23]

Thus the liturgy and the *preces privatae* can be seen to have formed part of the background to the *Prayers and Meditations*. They were not so much a conscious source as a mental climate forming and shaping Anselm's life and prayer. There is the element of the liturgical use of the Bible and especially of the psalter; there is the way of praying to the saints and the choice of the group he uses; there are the long passages in every prayer about sin, which find their more formal counterpart in the Carolingian forms for confession; there are the more directly liturgic-ally-inspired prayers, such as those before communion and to the Cross. It would not be possible to suggest either liturgical texts or texts of private prayers with certainty as a conscious source for Anselm's prayers, but it is possible to see them as the ground on which his genius worked.

3. 'Meditari aut Legere'

The prayers of Anselm are linked with the Carolingian liturgy and with the *preces privatae*, which were themselves so close to the liturgical pattern, but they are in no sense liturgical prayers; their content and the method they employ belong to another aspect of Christian devotion. The prayers are, in fact, in some sense also meditations – just as, of course, the meditations are also prayers – and belong to that assimilation and rumination of divine truth through the reading of the scriptures which is *lectio divina*. The fragmentation of the concept of prayer inevit-able upon its more schematic analysis has made the use of such terms as 'reading', 'meditation', and 'prayer' misleading. For Anselm and his predecessors these were different aspects of the same thing, not separate exercises in their own right. Reading was an action of the whole person, by which the meaning of a text was absorbed, until it became prayer. It was frequently compared to eating – 'Taste by reading, chew by understanding, swallow by loving and rejoicing,'[1] and the text 'O taste and see how gracious the Lord is' was applied more often to the reading of the scriptures than to the Eucharist before the twelfth century. In the fourth century the *Apostolic Constitutions* had recommended 'prayer that is fed by *lectio divina*, exercised in psalmody, prolonged and assimilated by brief prayers'.[2] It was in the same tradition that Bede wrote of 'the *majestas Domini* which is communicated to us in the *majestas scripturae*'.

The other side of the same coin is seen in the writings of the Fathers: their theology is continually rising up into prayer, or rather there is no distinction between the two. In Cyprian, Irenaeus, and especially Origen, prayer welled up spontaneously as they wrote their commentaries. Their theology, in the ancient sense of the word, was a hymn, a prayer, the point where knowledge and love become praise. The *Sanctus*, the *Te Deum*, were therefore called theologies and conversely theologians were those whose prayer is true. In Origen this prayed theology was prompted by a devotion to Christ which has at times a medieval sound, as in this sentence from a homily on the Feet Washing: 'Jesus, my feet are dirty. Come and be my slave; pour water into your basin and wash my feet.'[3] To take only two other examples of this personal aspect of theology, St Hilary's discussion of the doctrine of the Trinity breaks into this petition: 'Almighty God, bestow upon us the meaning of words, the light of understanding, the nobility of diction, and the faith of the true nature. And grant that what we believe we may also speak.'[4] And there is this familiar passage from the greatest of the confessions: 'To praise you is the desire of man who is but a part of your creation. You stir him to take delight in praising you, for you have made us for yourself and our heart is restless until it finds its rest in you.'[5]

It was through the *Rule of St Benedict* that this way of prayer was mediated to Anselm. As Dom Butler has shown,[6] St Benedict transmitted the teaching of Cassian on prayer which in its turn was based on the theology of Origen. Here the way into prayer was through meditative reading, with the aim of purity of heart and compunction of tears. Abbot Nestorius is recorded as saying, 'Strive to apply yourselves to holy reading so that this continual meditation may finally impregnate your soul and form it in its own image.'[7] And the two Conferences attributed to Abbot Isaac deal with the subject in detail.[8] St Benedict says little about prayer but it is all in this tradition of meditative reading as the way into prayer. In the brief chapter *Of the Oratory of the Monastery* he merely says, 'If anyone wishes to pray secretly, let him just go in and pray',[9] but at once he makes the connection with Cassian by adding, 'with tears and fervour of heart.' There is the same connection in the chapter *On Reverence in Prayer* – 'our prayer therefore ought to be short and pure,' 'we shall be heard . . . for purity of heart and compunction of tears.'[10] In the chapter *On the Observance of Lent* this prayer is linked to reading: 'Let us refrain from all sin, and apply ourselves to prayer with tears, to reading, to compunction of heart, and to abstinence.'[11] Here reading, compunction and prayer are all classed together. Nor is there a contradiction of this way of reading in the chapter *Of the Daily Manual Work* where the books given out for reading during Lent are to be read *'per ordinem ex integro'*.[12] The fact that the book was to be read in its entirety may have been mentioned specifically here in order to underline the penitential nature of this particular piece of reading: it was to be an *ascesis*, much as the Desert Fathers had recited a great number of psalms *'per ordinem'*, but the next chapter makes it clear when it refers to reading that even in this case the continuous reading of the book was not to take precedence over the impulses of grace; the point of the reading, as always, was prayer.

It was this perspective of reading meditatively that Anselm re-affirmed in his *Prayers and Meditations*. By the eleventh century for all practical purposes *lectio divina* was identified with *lectio continua,* the corporate liturgical reading of the scriptures and the Fathers. At Bec the time for reading may have been more than that at Cluny but it was not great, and the more usual way of reading the scriptures was to listen to them being read. The prayers Anselm composed provided material for reading, in the tradition of *lectio divina* as a starting point for prayer.

The way into prayer could be through the reading of the scriptures, through the recitation of the Office, through reflecting on liturgical texts or the psalms in private; it could also be through the use of the material Anselm provided. And in all these the basis was the Bible and its assimilation. The *Prayers and Meditations* are not, like those of John of Fécamp, full of direct quotation, but they are made up from the remembered language of the Bible: Anselm had so assimilated divine truth through reading, that the scriptures had become his spontaneous prayer. The texture of the *Prayers and Meditations* is composed of biblical words and images, and Anselm's personal devotion is given mysterious depth by this. He writes according to that medieval view which sees life as being entirely transfigured by the redemption wrought by Christ; it is a world in which everything becomes a revelation of love so amazing that nothing is insignificant. The Old Testament, therefore, is seen as a revelation of Christ just as much as the New, so that when Anselm gives instances of the raising of the dead he refers to Elijah and Elisha as well as St Paul;[13] and the fiat of Mary reaches 'all just men who died before his birth'.[14] Anselm was to extend this even further by proposing the understanding and analysis of the very nature of the existence of God as a subject for meditation, in the *Monologion* and the *Proslogion*, a step which in his successors led to a division of theology and prayer, in which the term 'theology' came to be limited to a study of the nature of God. But in the *Prayers and Meditations* the old tradition of *lectio divina* is still basic.

4. *John of Fécamp*

In this tradition of meditative reading there is a writer close in time, place, and outlook to Anselm; indeed some of his writings have been attributed to Anselm until very recently. John of Fécamp, or Jeannelin, as he called himself, with the diminutive that recalls Anselm's term for himself, *homuncio*, lived first as a hermit near Ravenna. Then he joined his uncle, the great Benedictine reformer, William of Volpiano, at Fruttuaria. In 1017 John was sent to the Abbey of the Holy Trinity at Fécamp, where eleven years later he became abbot. He ruled Fécamp conscientiously but without enthusiasm until he died in 1078, never ceasing to regret his lost solitude and with his real interest in prayer rather than administration. Anselm became Abbot of Bec in the year of John's death, so that the years of his first writings, which included the Prayers, overlapped with the last years of John. Fécamp is not far from Bec and John must have known at least by repute so notable a young teacher and scholar, but nothing is known of any direct contact between them. The *Confessio Fidei*, which belongs to John's last years, has a more philosophic tone than his other writings, an expansion possibly due to the influence of Anselm; and there is a reference of his which fits Anselm well: 'Unde modernos laudo doctores et eorum scripta libenter lectito qui dum antiquorum dicta revolvunt, ex multorum lectione radicem veritatis remandendo inveniunt, Quanto enim sunt iuniores tanto perspicaciores, et eo magis florent ingenio quo de pluribus fontibus hauserunt.'[1] *

What Anselm knew of his older contemporary is still more uncertain, but from internal evidence it would seem likely that Anselm had read at least the *Confessio Theologica*, and was familiar with John's style and thought. This passage in particular

---

* I praise those modern scholars who have turned over the ancient writings, seeking to discover the real roots of many books, and I willingly read what they have written. Those who are young are nonetheless the more perspicacious, and their skill flowers since it draws from so many sources.

from the second book of the *Confessio Theologica* has close affinities with Anselm's meditations:

At that tremendous judgement 'scarcely shall the just be saved'; and I, the most wretched of men, what will be done to me, what shall be said of me, when I am brought before his judgement seat, who knows all the transgressions I have committed? But I pray you, my King, Father, and my God, by that eternal judgement, by the propitiation of sinners, make my heart contrite and a fount of tears, that I may weep for the wounds of my soul day and night, until the accepted time, until the day of salvation. Otherwise my great iniquities, my innumerable sins, which are now hidden, will on that tremendous day appear in the sight of the waiting angels, archangels, prophets and apostles, saints, and all just men. Have mercy upon me, Lord, have mercy on me; cast me not away in my sins, vices, guilt, and negligences. For you do not desire the death of a sinner, but that he be converted and live. Have mercy upon me; do not keep my evils stored up to be punished in the next life, in the pains of hell, in the tremendous judgement, but punish them in this present life as much as and how you please. Behold, I am in your hand; do unto me as seems good to you.[2]

Anselm's *Prayers and Meditations* are closer to John's writings than they are to the liturgical tradition and the Carolingian *preces*, but in themselves they are as different as the men who wrote them. The chief note of John's work is a profound serenity and peace, '*tranquilla et secura*', and he is filled with longing for 'the one thing necessary', the vision of God. As Dom Wilmart put it, John '*a pris plaisir à traiter les mêmes sujets par les mêmes moyens et dans les mêmes termes*'.[3] He finds the way to that one thing necessary through the words of the scriptures and the Fathers. His own description of his work, 'my words are the words of the Fathers',[4] is true; his writings are a tissue of quotation from the Bible and the Fathers, though they are put together in a way entirely his own, and also contain fine original passages. Like Anselm he knows the Bible intimately, but, characteristically, he is selective: he quotes mostly from St John's Gospel, Revelation, Ephesians, Hebrews, the Psalms, and the Song of

Songs, the books in fact that correspond to his own contemplative way. By contrast, there is no book of the Bible that Anselm does not use freely, and yet he quotes far less from the Bible and not at all from the Fathers. John is a mosaic of quotations from Augustine and Gregory, his words are the words of the Fathers; but Anselm, equally in the tradition of Augustine and Gregory, writes as being himself one of the Fathers.

Both men have an ardent desire for God, and experience it in the piercing of contrition and love which is compunction; both turn their energies to shake off the 'torpor' that holds them back, but in doing this John has none of the intellectual fire of Anselm; again, he restricts his thought to the one thing necessary; Jean Leclercq suggests that this was a deliberate asceticism on his part.[5]

Both men sent their prayers to other people and gave detailed instructions for their use. John wrote to the Empress Agnes in much the same terms as Anselm to Mathilda and Adelaide – the prayers are to be 'read with reverence and meditated with fear' – but John has a warning which Anselm never chose to give: 'This book ought to be read only by those whose minds are not involved in carnal desires . . . but with tears and great devotion . . . the proud mind should not dare to touch the secret and sublime words of divine eloquence, lest by chance it speaks to them wrongly.'[6] John's prayers are for the elect, for the contemplatives, but Anselm's apparently for any who need and want them.

In another way also they differ: John does not produce finished meditations. For him writing is not an act of prayer; he offers material for reading which can thus become prayer. But in many cases Anselm does write and pray at the same time; his prayers are already written as prayers, with the exclamations and spontaneous expressions in the text. This gives them for the modern reader the sense of being too much; they seem overwrought, too finished, as Dom Wilmart said, *'un peu abondant'*,[7] but there is on the other hand great profit in having a prayer exactly as a saint has prayed it, down to the intimate communications of his soul with God.

In the prayers of John of Fécamp and Anselm we have the forerunners of the great meditations of the next century, such as those of William of St Thierry; in Anselm the stream of liturgical piety joins the tradition of *lectio et meditatio*. It remains to be seen what Anselm made out of this inheritance in his teaching about prayer and in the *Prayers and Meditations* themselves.

2. THE PRAYERS AND MEDITATIONS

1. The Anselmian Pattern of Prayer

Anselm wrote no formal treatise on prayer, but his writings contain certain indications about the way in which he understood it. In a Preface to the *Prayers and Meditations* he explains how they are to be used, and gives the same kind of instructions to Gundolf, Adelaide, and Mathilda in the letters that accompanied the prayers he sent them. The first chapter of the *Proslogion* sets out the same pattern of prayer, and in the prayers themselves there are definite indications about the tradition of spirituality which they represent, especially in the Prayer to St Mary Magdalene.

There is a basic pattern that emerges from all these sources: the prayers are meant to be said in solitude, and the aim is to stir the mind out of its inertia to know itself thoroughly and so come to contrition and the love of God. This is to be done by a quiet and thoughtful reading of the text of the prayers, but only as much of them as achieves this aim; they are not to be read for the interest of reading them but as a way into prayer, and for this purpose they are divided into paragraphs. Anselm anticipates the criticism that the prayers are too long when in his letter to Gundolf he assures him that they are not meant to be read straight through, but to provide varied material to be used as needed. He is not concerned that the reader should *like* the prayers; he means his heart to be changed by them.

'In cubiculum meum'

The *Prayers and Meditations* are not meant to be read in the congregation of the faithful but in the secret chamber, not only in the inner room of the heart, but literally apart, in solitude. The *Proslogion* emphasizes this inner and exterior withdrawal:

> Come now, little man,
> turn aside for a while from your daily employment,
> escape for a moment from the tumult of your thoughts.
> Put aside your weighty cares,
> let your burdensome distractions wait,
> free yourself awhile for God,
> and rest awhile in him.
> Enter the inner chamber of your soul,
> shut out everything except God
> and that which can help you in seeking him,
> and when you have shut the door, seek him.
> Now, my whole heart, say to God,
> 'I seek your face,
> Lord, it is your face I seek.'[1]

This taking oneself aside in order to have leisure for God is one of the great themes of medieval monasticism, the '*otium*', '*quies*', '*sabbatum*', which is understood to be the major occupation of the monk. It means to be free from the usual occupations in order to enter more deeply into the work of prayer and this is the teaching of Cassian's *Conferences*. The work of the monk is to withdraw from the common lot of men to seek purity of heart and so to see God. This approach has more in common with the desert hermits than Cluny or the Carolingian liturgy, but for all that Anselm, like indeed the hermits, has not withdrawn from the *koinonia*; he has only entered more deeply into the fullness of the people of God, where he talks with Christ and the saints as a man talks with his friends.

'*Excita Mentem*'

Once this withdrawal has been made, a more difficult task faces the Christian; he has been made in the image of God, but that image has been overlaid and obscured in him and he no longer knows God as he was created to do. Cassian's Abbot Isaac compares the soul to a feather,[2] which has to be freed from the earth in order to rise upwards as it was meant to do. Anselm calls that which impedes the soul 'torpor' – a dullness, a sloth, a weight, and the first task in prayer is to shake off torpor and so be ready to enter into the experiental knowledge of God which is prayer.

Anselm uses the same terminology of mental effort in preparation for prayer and for theological speculation, '*excita mentem*', '*excitandum legentis mentem*', to stir up the mind in order both to pray and to understand. For Anselm reason is a gift of God which, like the emotions, can be used to kindle the spirit. This freeing of the mind for prayer is not just a setting aside of the irrelevant; it is a complete emptying by purgation, a knowledge of sin in the light of God, and an understanding of man's situation with regard to his Creator and Redeemer. This torpor is no easy thing to dispel and Anselm uses every means in his power to this end. The prayers demand a seriousness of purpose before they can begin to be understood; they are subtle and personal writings, requiring an effort of thought and attention in which every resource of language is used to stir the one who prays out of his self-focused state, through self-knowledge, to dependence on God, and so to the threshold of prayer. The liturgical tradition laid emphasis on the discipline of the will as the antechamber to prayer; Anselm uses in addition the intellect, the imagination, and the emotions. In both cases these are only ways into prayer; nonetheless with Anselm it is a new kind of beginning.

'*Compunctio Cordis*'

The centre of Anselm's teaching on prayer is in the word 'compunction'. By reading the prayers one is to be 'moved to the love or fear of God, or to self-examination'.[3] The steady discipline of attention in reading continues until one is moved by love or fear, which generally begins by awareness of sin and personal self-abasement. It is a matter of seeing steadily and truly the real situation of man before his Creator, the sinner before his Redeemer and Judge. Each of the prayers contains a long passage of self-scrutiny, where the horror of sin is brought to light by knowledge of the love of God. This is the first kind of compunction, a piercing of sorrow and dread, which leads, through a realization of its resolution in the love of God, to that other compunction of longing desire for God.

This doctrine of compunction was transmitted to the Middle Ages through Cassian, St Benedict, St Augustine, and, above all, St Gregory. St Augustine's conversion is described in terms of compunction: 'But it was in my inmost heart, where I had grown angry with myself, where I had been stung with remorse . . . it was there that you had begun to make me love you . . .';[4] and later he wrote, 'You touched me and I am inflamed with love of your peace.'[5] Cassian's *Conferences* deal with this approach to prayer and Dom Butler has shown how this was reflected in the *Rule of Saint Benedict*.[6] It was through St Gregory and St Benedict that Anselm received this teaching.

The references in the *Rule of Saint Benedict* to prayer 'with compunction and tears' have already been discussed, but the same pattern is to be seen elsewhere in the *Rule*. In the Prologue the whole life of a monk is described in terms of this two-fold piercing: 'Let us open our eyes to the divine light, let us hear with attentive ears the warning . . . and so our heart shall be enlarged . . . and we shall share by patience in the sufferings of Christ, that we may deserve to be partakers also of his kingdom.' Among the 'Tools of Good Works', St Benedict lists: 'To fear the Day of Judgement. To dread hell. To desire eternal life with all spiritual longing,' and in the chapter on 'Humility' there is the same pattern: 'The monk will presently come to the perfect love of God which casts out all fear,' where he acts, 'no longer for fear of hell but for love of Christ.'

In the *Moralia on the Book of Job* St Gregory takes up this

theme of compunction and describes it more fully, especially
in Books XXII and XXIII. 'A man has compunction of one
kind when he is shaken with fear at his own wickedness, and of
another when he looks up to the joys of heaven and is strength-
ened with a kind of hope and security. One emotion excites
of pain and sorrow, the other tears of joy.'[7] 'When the
light of truth pierces our hearts it makes us at one time full of
sorrow, from its display of severe justice, and delights us at
another by disclosing inward joys.'[8] 'For the fire of tribulation
is first darted into our mind from a consideration of our own
blindness, in order that all rust of sin may be burnt away, and
when the eyes of our heart are purged from sin, the joy of heaven
is disclosed to us . . . for the intervening mist of sin must first
be wiped away from the eye of the mind, and then it is enlight-
ened by the brightness of unbounded light that is poured upon
it.' 'When the virtue of compunction moves our hearts, the
clamour of evil longings is silenced.'[9]

It is just this grace of compunction that Anselm asks for in
the Prayer to St Mary Magdalene, in words and images very
close to those of St Gregory:

> Ask urgently that I may have
> the love that pierces the heart; tears that are humble;
>   desire for the homeland of heaven;
>   impatience with this earthly exile;
> searing repentance; and a dread of torments in eternity.[10]

This passage is set in a prayer of tears and longing and is indeed
the two-edged sword of compunction, piercing with terror and
tenderness, fear and delight.

Like St Gregory Anselm is not concerned with a transitory
feeling of sorrow. After describing the state of prayer which may
follow from compunction St Gregory says, 'The more a man
contemplates heavenly things, the more does he amend his life,'[11]
and this is a connection which Anselm takes for granted. In the
Prayer to God this intimate connection of the life of prayer with

the life of Christian charity is made explicit: he asks for the mercy of God and for this piercing of the heart, but along with it go the living of a good life and the following of the will of God. This sober moral basis for the life of prayer is fundamental to an understanding of the prayers, and was by later imitators easily blurred.

'*In Caelis*'

The tears that God gives begin as sorrow for sin, and that is the first stage of compunction. There may be despair or terror at the horror of sin and the judgement it deserves, as in the first of the meditations, but this is not the end. 'Whither shall I flee?'[12] the sinner asks when faced with his doom, but the tears of this compunction turn into tears of love and longing and delight: 'But it is he, it is Jesus; the same is my judge between whose hands I tremble.' Like St Gregory, Anselm is a doctor of *suspira*, the longing for heaven, for union in love with God. The end of all the prayers is the same, union with God, the Blessed Trinity, in the bliss of heaven. For it is not on earth that Anselm expects to know God in his fullness; there is a foretaste given sometimes in prayer, but, like John of Fécamp, he does not expect it to last long; it is a rare gift of God's mercy, not the habitual state of any man. We see here indeed in a glass darkly, and, as St Gregory says, 'The mind falls back at once to itself, having seen some traces of truth before it, it is recalled to a sense of its own lowliness.'[13] It is in heaven that the full vision will be known. The Prayer to St Stephen and the twenty-fifth chapter of the *Proslogion* are marvellous examples of this devotion to heaven and the longing which the soul has for it.

2. *The Content of the Prayers*

It is a traditional and simple way of prayer that Anselm sets out, though 'costing not less than everything', but there is nothing austere or simple about the language he uses to convey it. The prayers are written in a rhymed prose which is mannered and elegant to a fault; they are polished literary products, every word in its right place, 'the whole consort dancing together'. There is antithesis, the use of parallel grammatical constructions, the rhetorical question, the careful build-up of each phrase and sentence to a climax, combined with balance and form. What makes them highly mannered works of medieval literature and of no other age is the almost childish play with words, the love of a jingle, so that *'horror terribilis'* inevitably becomes *'terror horribilis'*, and *'electa dilectrix'* is sure to be also *'dilecta electrix'*.

But most of the time in Anselm's prayers these are not mere exhibitions of literary skill. He is not using words for their own sake; they are for him, as for the whole monastic school of *'grammatica'*, an expression of inner coherence, and their order and balance are vital to his meaning. Moreover, these are no literary compositions in their own right, they are prayers, and they have a definite aim. If their language is subtle and complex, demanding an effort, this is a part of the *'excita mentem'* which is the first stage of the way. The effort required 'stirs up the mind' from its 'torpor', not for the sake of the words, but for the freeing of the soul from itself for God.

This is not to say that the prayers are uniformly of the highest literary quality. There are passages, especially in Meditation 2, which are overwrought and artificial. But at their best they combine clarity of thought and intensity of feeling in language finely wrought and expressive.

The imagery of the prayers is as vivid as the style; images are used that recur in devotional literature throughout the Middle Ages. They include the similes of sin as dryness; and of grace as a dew, a rain, a stream, to 'make fresh my dry places'. Others include the likeness of devils to wolves, the soul without God to an orphan, as well as the familiar Christian images of the Christian life as a warfare, the Fall as the overlaying of the image of God in man, self-knowledge as seeing oneself in a mirror. The absence of images of the Christian life as a journey or an ascent is interesting: perhaps there is something here of the monk and scholar, who preferred to see life from within the cloister.

One side of Anselm's imagery, however, needs more comment: he has, and this might almost be called his distinctive quality, an interest in spiritual psychology. When he addresses the saints he is interested only in two things, what God has done in them and how they have experienced his work. It is not their miracles, their appearance, their glory even, but themselves as people that Anselm cares about. Thus St John the Baptist is the friend of the Bridegroom; St Peter is the shepherd who, after his repentance, cares for Christ's flock; St Mary Magdalene is pre-eminently the lover, the one forgiven and therefore loving much; St John the Apostle is the intimate friend of the Lord. To take instances from only one prayer: in Prayer 14 the reason given for the Lord's delay in appearing to St Mary Magdalene at the tomb is 'for only in such broken words can she tell out a grief as great as hers'. When the Lord does speak to her, 'she responded to the gentle tone in which he was wont to call, "Mary"'; and when Mary's tears eventually turn to joy they do not end in a shout of rejoicing, rather they continue to 'flow from a heart exulting'. This is a new way of imaginative insight into the sensations of scriptural persons which later found expression in *Jesu Dulcis Memoria*, and the *Stabat Mater*.

This interest in persons was also expressed in the prayers on the theme, new in intensity in the eleventh century, of tenderness and compassion for the Saviour and his Mother. It was no desire for an outpouring of emotion, nor was it an early instance of 'humanism', that caused this, but a radical change in theological understanding of the doctrine of the Atonement. A new dimension of love and understanding was replacing the remote, objective, salvation act, and in this the *Cur Deus Homo* was to play its part. Already in the prayers Anselm has made this revolution in understanding, and sees man as face to face with God, a sharer in the redemption of Christ. 'Would that I with happy Joseph might have been there' at the taking down of the body of Christ from the Cross; this is a far cry from the *Vexilla Regis* and the *Christus Victor*; it is the beginnings of the *devotio moderna* and the imitation of Christ.

The notes that follow on each of the prayers and the meditations are not intended to be exhaustive; they are simply indications of what is there. The basic structure of the prayers and the elements they contain are the same throughout, but they are assembled in a variety of ways. Most of them are set in the form of a dialogue: the person praying addresses the saint, relates him to Christ, and to himself, and the prayer is woven around these three. Scriptural incidents and phrases are taken up and made the pivot of the developing meditation. Each prayer begins with praise and adoration; then follows self-abasement and contrition, leading on to compunction of heart, and desire for God; there is some form of petition, and the end is renewed thanksgiving and adoration. But within this framework each prayer has its own tone and colour. Because of their importance the *Proslogion* and the *Meditation on Human Redemption* have been given separate consideration.

3. The Prayers

1. Prayer to God

This is the shortest of the prayers, with brief petitions, and it is in the style of the Carolingian prayers. It may be a pattern prayer for the rest, or, alternatively, a prologue to praying the rest. It is based on the last part of the Lord's Prayer, in a series of petitions for forgiveness and for help in making progress in the Christian life. It is in this prayer that Anselm is most explicit in linking prayer to the whole Christian life of charity. The request for 'a true and effective mind' is typical of Anselm and the school of monastic scholarship which he represents.

2. Prayer to Christ

This is the prayer that belongs most completely to the 'new style' of devotion of the eleventh and twelfth centuries. It is first found in the collection sent to Countess Mathilda in 1104.

The goad Anselm uses to stir up the spirit to desire God is a passionate lament for not having seen Christ after the flesh. In a dialectic of the absence and presence of God he uses the image of an orphan deprived of his father to express this grief. It is not, as in the other prayers, the estrangement caused by sin that Anselm is thinking of here; it is quite definitely the fact that he did not know the Lord in his earthly life that grieves him. He dwells in imagination on the details of the passion of Jesus; it is the nails, the spear, the wounds, the suffering of the man who 'suffered under Pontius Pilate' that move him, and beside the figure of 'the Lord of angels humbled to converse with men' he sees the figure of Mary as the Mother of Sorrows. From the text of John 19, 25, he draws a detailed picture of her grief, especially of her tears; it was a picture that was to become very familiar in medieval art and piety.

But it is not only the sufferings of Christ that he wants to share; the meditation is truly theological, for it goes from the Cross to the Resurrection, the Ascension, and the second coming. In the passage about the *myrophores* at the tomb it is possible to see a reflection of the way of dramatizing Easter which had its roots in the liturgical drama of Easter night, but was taking more definite form as a liturgical play at this time.[1]

The prayer ends with an expression of longing, put in the words of the psalms. The ending is of a piece with the tone of the prayer – instead of asking for union with God, 'blessed forever', as in other prayers, here Anselm is concerned with the coming of Christ: 'Until I hear, Soul, behold your bridegroom.'

3. Prayer before Receiving the Body and Blood of Christ

This prayer was included in the collection sent to the Countess Mathilda. For notes on this prayer, see Introduction p. 30.

4. Prayer to the Holy Cross

Another of the prayers included in the collection of 1104. For a discussion of this in relation to other *Adoratio Crucis* prayers, see Introduction pp. 31–2.

5. Prayer to St Mary (1)

This is the first of three prayers to St Mary that Anselm sent to Gundolf in 1072. It was written at the request of an importunate monk of Bec and did not satisfy the author. The titles of this and the other two prayers mark a familiar progress, from the 'torpor', 'the mind weighed down with heaviness', of the first, to the piercing fear, 'when the mind is anxious with fear', of the second, to that other compunction of longing, 'for her and Christ's love', in the third prayer.

Here Mary is given her true place in the economy of salvation as 'the most holy after God, because she bore the son of the most high': it is as the God-bearer, *Theotocos*, that she is honoured. She is acclaimed as above women, angels, saints, but only for this reason, 'that she brought forth the Saviour of the lost human race'.

Before the light of her sanctity the sinner sees his falling short and is ashamed. Sin is called a wound, a bite, an ulcer, a poison, a bad smell, but most of all it is a 'torpor', a huge dullness that must be broken through. In his need the sinner asks for Mary's intercession, and uses a reason that recurs in other prayers and has something unexpected to say about the intercession of the saints: 'If you refuse to help me, will not your mercy be less than it ought to be?' It is for the honour of God, and that his will of love should be fulfilled, that sinners and saints alike should ask for mercy. The prayer ends with the familiar 'that God may be glorified forever'.

6. Prayer to St Mary (2)

This second prayer did not satisfy Anselm either. It is longer than the first and is concerned with the intercession of Mary as Mother of men.

After a series of titles for Mary, as Virgin and Mother, the sinner is introduced and this time the setting is a law court. The throng of heaven looks on at the judgement of the accused, and the Judge is Christ himself. The sinner knows his guilt and the justice of the Judge, so he turns to the Mother of Christ to be his advocate, as being the one closest to the mercy of his heart. This image has a meaningful place in the whole context of Anselm's understanding of the Atonement and the relationship of justice and mercy which he worked out later in *Cur Deus Homo*; it was a good thing to say, but it proved a dangerous way of saying it. Out of its context such a scene could easily be seen as ascribing justice to Christ and mercy to Mary, as two opposing forces. Nothing was further from Anselm's intention; he asks here for Mary's intercession just because of her unique share in that aspect of the love of God which we call mercy:

> The son of Man in his goodness came
> of his own free will to save that which was lost;
> how can the mother of God not care
> when the lost cry to her?

Mary has by grace all that her Son has by nature, and all she has, she has only from him; this is the place given her in the awed theology of the early Church. But after Anselm this unity was lost in the West, and became a source of division – mercy belonged to Mary, justice to her son. She was seen popularly as a capricious goddess who would treat her devotees with unscrupulous favouritism and a doubtful kindness, as witness the unfortunate 'yonge Hugh of Lyncoln' in the Canterbury Tales, who for his love of the Lady found himself in the unenviable position of continuing to sing her praises with 'my throte kut into my nekke boon'. In popular miracle stories of

Our Lady, the devils called her '*illa mulier*', 'that woman', and protested that she overthrew justice, 'doing just what she likes with God and we cannot complain'.

7. Prayer to St Mary (3)

This third, 'great' prayer to St Mary contains Anselm's reflections on the place of Mary in redemption; he worked over the prayer with great care and considered it still to contain all he had to say about her to the end of his life.

Here Mary is honoured as 'Mother of my Lord and God'. Because she bore Christ through her all good comes to men, and she is the Mother of all the redeemed. The main section of this very long prayer deals with the relationship of God and Mary in creation and recreation, analysing the way in which the initiative of God has chosen to be contingent upon the assent of man. This is done in a passage of great beauty which inevitably loses much in translation: 'God gave his own Son . . . that all nature in you might be in him.'

The salutation of the Angel and of Elizabeth, the proclamation of Emmanuel, God with us, leads to a deeper joy: 'The Saviour and Judge of the world is our brother'; mercy and justice are one in 'the blessed fruit of thy womb'. Not only is all mankind saved by the '*fiat mihi*' of Mary, but the whole creation can again become transparent with glory. Through her childbearing the four elements, 'heaven, stars, earth, waters, day and night', which were corrupted by the misuse of fallen man, 'rejoice in their loss, for they have been given life again'. And not only are they restored to the original glory of their creation, but God is among them, 'visibly sanctifying them by use'.

This restoration of life is not even limited to the visible creation; through the son of Mary, 'those in hell rejoice that they are delivered', 'all just men who died before his birth exult that their captivity is broken', and 'the angels wish each other joy in the rebuilding of their half-ruined city'. It is a cosmic view of redemption in which, as in an icon, Christ is the central figure, and Mary shows him us and us him, while all around redemption is poured out in earth, heaven, and hell.

What Anselm honours in each of the saints is what God has done in them, and that is the basis on which he asks their prayers. In the case of Mary, in whom God has done everything and who has no other claim than to be 'full of grace', Anselm pours forth prayer and praise without reticence. In the end he sees the interpenetration of God and Mary in the work of salvation as a whole: 'I love you both . . . and I serve you both . . .

> And in this let my life be consummated
> that for all eternity all my being may sing
> 'Blessed be the Lord forever. Amen.'

8. Prayer to St John the Baptist

This prayer was probably among those sent to Adelaide in 1070. It is addressed to John as the baptizer and witness to Christ as the Lamb of God. It begins with praise of the infant John 'You knew God before you knew the world', and in contrast to his holiness Anselm sees himself as 'a guilty, creeping thing'. He explores the truth about the fall of man in vivid and perceptive terms:

> What was I, O God, as you had made me –
> and how have I made myself again!

God has created man in his own image, and man in heedless ingratitude has persisted in choosing evil and obscuring the image of God by the image of sin. This theme of the *imago dei* is familiar in the Eastern Fathers, especially in Gregory of Nyssa, and it occurs again in the Prayer to St Peter.

Anselm sees himself as worse than the devil, with less excuse for sinning, and this self-knowledge sickens him:

> If I look within myself, I cannot bear myself;
> if I do not look within myself, I do not know myself.

In this dilemma he acknowledges his guilt and the justice of any punishment decreed for him, but he turns for help to the witness of 'him who takes away the sin of the world', John the Baptist. There follow several brief meditations on this phrase, and the prayer ends on a note of confidence in the promises of God in Christ.

9. Prayer to St Peter

Peter is here addressed as the prince of the apostles, the shepherd of the sheep, and door-keeper of the kingdom of heaven. This is vividly depicted in the illuminated letter at the beginning of this prayer in the Littlemore Anselm: the first half of the picture shows Peter receiving a key from Christ while some sheep graze at his feet; in the 'S' itself Peter leans over and beckons to some Christians who look up trustingly as he points them towards the gates of heaven.

In the first half of the prayer the image of the sinner as a sickly sheep is worked out in great detail, but Anselm himself seems to have felt that the imagery had run away with him, so he explains its meaning more plainly. Then he recounts his misery again, putting it more clearly, before both Christ and Peter. He reminds Peter both of his denial of Christ and of the commission given him by the Lord to 'feed my sheep', and asks,

> is this misery of mine so huge
> that it cannot be met by the wideness of your mercy?

He prays for the bread of mercy rather than the stone of justice, and ends with a prayer to the 'door-keeper' to lead him from the kingdom of sin into the kingdom of heaven.

10. Prayer to St Paul

This prayer also was probably one of those sent to the Princess Adelaide; it falls clearly into two parts, the first doctrinal, the second more personal. The image of motherhood recurs through all the prayer, and it is with this that the prayer begins.

After addressing Paul as mother and nurse of sons in the faith

Anselm discusses sin, in the setting of the Last Judgement, where the sinner is accused by his own sins, by good and by evil spirits, and by the whole creation which he has misused. In this condemnation he finds himself too hardened by sin to pray, and because he cannot pray he loses hope. The virtue of faith also is lacking to him (here there is surely a reference to 1 Corinthians 13), and he has nothing to show. Thus in coming to Paul, he finds he has a deeper need than he thought – he is dead in sins and needs to be given life again. Once more the humility of self-knowledge is the turning point of the prayer. The idea of life from the dead leads him to refer to Elijah and Elisha and the raising of the son of the Shunammite; this leads into the second half of the prayer, which is a meditation on the motherhood of Paul and even more of Jesus.

This second half of the Prayer to St Paul contains one of the most famous texts in Christian spirituality about the motherhood of God. It is interesting that this reflection of the re-creative love of Christ, the maternal aspect of the second person of the Trinity, comes in the Prayer to St Paul rather than in the Prayers to St Mary.

He refers to Paul as his mother in the faith, and this leads him to speak of Christ as mother of both Paul and himself, 'Jesus, are you not also a mother?' and he goes on to use the words of the Lord to justify this, in the text from Matthew 23, 37, 'Are you not the mother who, like a hen, gathers her chickens under her wings?'

This idea goes back to the Old Testament references to God as a mother. Especially in Isaiah God is compared to a mother in his love for Israel (Isaiah 49, 15, and 66, 13). It is an important concept in the predominantly male idea of God in the Old Testament, and one that has been too little used in Christianity. Anselm here presents the idea of God as Father too, and works out the interplay of male and female aspects of the nature and work of God in a way that goes deep into the understanding of things, and which has a curiously modern ring.

The idea of Christ as mother had a steady though not copious history after Anselm. Aelred of Rievaulx wrote of 'the maternal breasts of Jesus',[2] and the idea is found in Margaret of Oyngt (d. 1310) and St Mechtild of Hackeborn (d. 1298). It also found expression in the Middle English prayers collected by the author of *The Talkyng of the Luv of God* and in the *Ancren Riwle*,[3] where it is connected with the thought of Christ giving suck to his redeemed by the blood flowing from his wounds. In painting and devotion this idea had a certain popularity later. The development which is closer to Anselm, however, is that contained in the *Revelations of the Divine Love*, where Julian of Norwich makes the Motherhood of Christ one of the central points of her teaching: 'Moreover I saw that the Second Person who is our Mother with regard to our essential nature, that same dear person has become our Mother in the matter of our sensual nature ... in our Mother, Christ, we grow and develop,' which she continues to expand in chapters 59, 60, and 61.[4]

The prayer ends with this theme of the Christ-mother, who gathers sinners like a hen gathering her chickens under her wings, and Anselm prays for his mercy and grace, by the knowledge he has of his compassion.

11. Prayer to St John the Evangelist (1)

The two prayers to St John the Evangelist form a dyptich, one showing the compunction that comes with fear, the other the compunction of love. They may have been among the collection sent to Adelaide.

In the first prayer John is addressed as the beloved disciple, and the 'reclinatio pectorum' is given a prominent place. Perhaps this is one of the earliest instances of this picture of Christ with the beloved disciple being detached from the whole setting of the Last Supper, and used as an instance of friendship. Anselm approaches John as 'the friend of God', but he finds that very intimacy daunting; anyone who loved God must hate the enemies of God, even God's creation must reject such. Yet he still asks John and the other friends of God to pray for him, not to defend or minimize his sin, but to reconcile him to his Creator and lord. He then turns to Jesus, as the friend of John, with the same request.

12. Prayer to St John the Evangelist (2)

This follows on from the first prayer, although the two can be used independently. This is a prayer of desire, a long petition for an increase in the love of God. The central image, taken from I John, 3, 17, is of the beggar who is in need and the rich man who can give. The ending of the prayer is a true theology, a true praising, where the soul rejoices in the love and redemption of Christ.

13. Prayer to St Stephen

This was among the prayers sent to Adelaide in 1071, and it and the Prayer to St Mary Magdalene are mentioned in Anselm's covering letter as prayers that 'tend more to the increase of love'.

Love is indeed the theme of the prayer, but it is neither easy nor sentimental love. The last part of it contains a deeper meditation on the joy of God and the bliss of heaven than any other of the prayers, but it is the love that is the other side of martyrdom. It is therefore no contradiction to find in the first half of the prayer one of Anselm's most stern and austere descriptions of sin and judgement. He is following the familiar way of compunction – the piercing of fear and shame leading on to the love and desire for God.

The first part of the prayer is this realization of sins that are 'too great' and all-pervasive. He is a sinner before the 'intolerably strict judge', aware of his own guilt and its deserts. He cannot ask to be 'let off', or to have the sentence changed; it is the same problem as that of all mankind, seen here in the person of one man, which he deals with in the *Meditation on*

Human Redemption and the answer is the same: the mercy of God and the love of the Redeemer.

The second part of the prayer is a meditation on the martyr-dom of St Stephen and more particularly on the love that made him pray for his enemies. Like the Prayer to the Cross these paragraphs about love and suffering set out the deepest truth about the evil men do and the way it is redeemed. Evil men crucified the Lord, and stoned Stephen, but the very things that were meant to harm were turned into the means of salvation for them. From the sight of such love Anselm argues that Stephen, who showed such kindness to his enemies, will show at least as much to his friends. He asks therefore for his prayers, that God 'lay not my sins to my charge', and concludes with a passage as joyful as the first part of the prayer was severe. He considers the words about Stephen's death, 'He fell asleep in the Lord', and draws from it a meditation on the bliss of heaven. The prayer ends with longing to share in that bliss, and a lament that the 'body of this death' still holds him back.

14. Prayer to St Nicholas

This prayer is mentioned in the letter Anselm wrote to Prior Baudry and the monks of Bec in 1093. He was in England as abbot of Bec on business of the monastery, which he found William Rufus slow to regulate. This was his fourth journey to England and it began on 7 September 1092; in the letter he fore-sees that he will be in England for Lent, but in fact it was ten years before he returned to Bec. He was made Primate of England in March 1093, and when he came again to his monas-tery it was as an exile. In this letter he asks them to send him 'the prayer to St Nicholas that I composed'.

It seems probable that the prayer had been occasioned by the translation of the relics of Nicholas of Myra to Bari on 9 May 1087, in which Bec seems to have taken a special interest.

The prayer occurs in all collections of the prayers, though in a few it is directed to St Martin. It is addressed to one who is not a biblical saint nor a martyr, but an Eastern confessor, around whom legends grew apace. The image of the three deeps, of sin, judgement, and mercy, is carefully worked out, and indeed this is one of the greatest of the prayers for its balance of the sense of the holiness of God and the peril of sin.

15. Prayer to St Benedict

This seems to have been written while Anselm was Prior of Bec, but there is no direct information about its composition. It was included in the collection sent to Mathilda, and it would hardly have been composed specially for that purpose. On the other hand it makes no mention of the cares of office, which seems to indicate a date before he became abbot. It follows the teaching of Anselm on the monastic life as a conversion, a continual turning to God, and uses the *Rule of St Benedict* as its basis. He does not so much quote the *Rule* as speak its language; the doctrine of reminiscence applied as much to the *Rule* as to scripture – to know both was to have made them a part of life.

The main part of the prayer is built around three images, all of which can be found in the *Rule*: the king and his knight, the master and his pupil, the abbot and his monk. The monastic life is described as a warfare in which the soldier is pledged 'to fight under your leadership': it is a training, for 'you have placed me under your tuition'. And in each case the relationship is based on complete and wholehearted obedience. The contrast is made throughout the prayer between the 'name and habit' of the monk and the reality of the life. The false monk is one who does not fulfil what he has promised, and he is bound by 'the ropes of sin'; the obedient, genuine monk is the one who is truly free. Balancing this awareness of falling short there is also delight in the monastic life and in Christ. The end echoes the penultimate chapter of the *Rule*, 'Let them prefer nothing whatever to Christ and may he bring us all alike to life everlasting.'

16. Prayer to St Mary Magdalene

This prayer was also sent to Adelaide, and this too, Anselm says, tends 'to increase love, . . . said slowly and from the depths of the heart'.

It is a prayer of love and tears – the title it is given in some manuscripts, 'Recalling the love between her and Christ', is one of love, and it begins in tears: 'You came with springing tears to the spring of mercy, Christ.' This leads at once to the biblical setting of Mary as the woman who was a sinner and washed the Lord's feet with tears in the house of Simon the Pharisee. Next Anselm, also a sinner, comes into the picture and the prayer revolves around the three relationships. The setting is mostly in the garden of the resurrection, when Mary was outside the tomb weeping.

This is most of all a prayer of compunction – there is sorrow for sin, grief at the suffering of the Lord, out of which come tears of love and longing and joy. In this passionate and lyrical prayer there is nonetheless a plain and unexpected piece of theology where Anselm asks Christ, 'Have you put off compassion now you have put on incorruption . . .?'

The prayer ends with longing to share in the penitent love of Mary Magdalene; it asks 'my most dear Jesus' for the 'bread of tears and sorrow' in order to come to 'the everlasting sight of your glory'. There is a reference to 'the greater Mary' also, presumably because they stood together at the Cross, which is the only reference to St Mary in the prayers, apart from the passage in the Prayer to Christ and the three prayers to St Mary herself.

17. Prayer by a Bishop or Abbot to the Patron Saint of his Church

This prayer may have been written after Anselm became abbot; it belongs to the monastic period of his life, and is about the responsibilities of office. As in the Prayer to St Benedict the contrast is made between what one is and what one seems to be, in this case, abbot. He asks for the prayers of the patron of the abbey and shares the responsibility with him.

The name of the patron is left blank, but it seems to suppose an apostle. (In the Littlemore Anselm the name of St Peter is inserted, and St Augustine substituted for St Benedict; canon replaces monk wherever it comes.) It seems likely that St Aelred knew this prayer before he wrote his *Pastoral Prayer*.

18. Prayer for Friends

The theme of friendship held an important place in the thought of the ancient world and the Middle Ages; from Cicero and Cassian, to Bernard and Aelred, the ideal of the union of the souls of good men in the pursuit of virtue grew and achieved a place in Christian theology.

In Anselm's letters from Bec the affection of friendship is very much stressed, but, as Professor Southern has shown, this was not an expression of personal or sentimental feeling: 'He (Anselm) bends his mind to the contemplation of an ideal image, he attaches himself to it with a passionate intensity, he defines its nature and he gives it a name. Here the name is that of friend. In his prayers and meditations, formed under the influence of a similar impulse, the name is that of a saint of God.'[5] This intellectual conviction formed the Prayer for Friends which Anselm was probably writing at the same time as the early letters of friendship. It is the love that God in Christ has for men that interests him, and it is from this that he draws his love for other men. Christ is 'the good friend' and it is in that friendship that men find fellowship with each other. Yet within this love Anselm recognizes quite simply that there are some whom Christ's love has impressed on his heart 'with a special and more intimate love', and so he prays specially for them. What he asks for them is in this objective, sober tone: 'Make them to love you with all their heart . . . and come at last to your glory.' This is not in the effusive tone of the letters but is closer to the description of friendship in heaven which comes at the end of the *Proslogion*: '. . . they will love God more than themselves, and each other as themselves; God will love them more than they love themselves, because it is through him that they have love for him and themselves and one another; and it is through his own self that God loves both himself and them.'

19. Prayer for Enemies

Anselm balances the Prayer for Friends with a Prayer for Enemies. That they do go together is proved by the last lines of the Prayer for Enemies, where the prayer widens out into a prayer for all men: 'I have prayed,' he says, 'for my friends, and for my enemies.'

There is a prayer for enemies in the *Manual of St John Gualbert*;[6] it prays simply for 'any who hate me' and asks for grace to love them. Anselm was at once more discerning and more hopeful. As in the Prayer to St Stephen he knows that enmity is only answered by the humility of love, and so he begins with an acknowledgement of his own failure to love. Then he prays for himself alongside his enemies on the pattern of the Lord's Prayer: 'Forgive us our debts as we forgive our debtors.' The end he looks towards is fellowship with them in Christ, 'that we may obey with one heart in love one Lord and one Master'. We know from Eadmer a few of the men who might be counted as 'enemies' of Anselm, and we know of many more whom he called 'friends', but these two prayers are not the limited petitions he might have made for these people he knew. They are universal because they are based on the truths about God's love and forgiveness and reconciliation.

4. Meditations 1 and 2

Meditation 1

This meditation is mentioned in a letter from Durandus, Abbot of Casa-Dei; he calls it a prayer which has caused much heart-searching and tears, and asks for others like it. In his reply

Anselm does not answer his request, and does not make much response to the somewhat effusive compliments of the abbot.

It may have been joined to Meditation 2 – Dom Wilmart calls them 'the two halves of a dyptych'[1] – but each is complete in itself and a distinct difference of style makes it possible to treat them separately.

The form of this meditation is a soliloquy, which ends in more direct prayer. Instead of an address to a saint it begins with a terse statement: 'I am afraid of my life.' Then follows a sober and searching consideration of the state of the soul before God, passing from the image of the barren tree to the more dramatic picture of the Last Judgement with its terrifying echoes of the Dies Irae. This analysis of the horror of sin and its punishment is meant to provoke repentance while there is time, but from this almost hysterical pitch of fear at this picture of judgement the prayer swings over into its remedy: 'But it is he . . . Jesus. The same is my judge, between whose hands I tremble.' The prayer concludes with a lyrical meditation on the name of Jesus, which was the forerunner of so much in later devotion, especially in St Bernard, Richard Rolle, and the author of *Dulcis Jesu Memoria*. The repeated use of the Name may derive from Celtic sources.

Meditation 2

This has the appearance of being one of the earliest of the prayers. The rhetoric is heightened and the emotion verges on the hysterical at times; the literary devices used become almost transparently artificial in places.

It is called a lament for the loss of virginity, and there are two senses in which this can be understood. Dr Pusey asserted firmly that the fornication referred to was any tendency of the soul to fall away from the love of Christ;[2] it was to be understood only in a spiritual sense, mostly, one feels, because Dr Pusey thought it was more edifying that it should be so. But there seems to be no reason for not taking it in its natural sense, as the lament of someone, not necessarily Anselm himself, who has in some way sinned sexually, and sees this in terms of estrangement from Christ. The language of the meditation seems to lead to this view when it is compared with the letters Anselm wrote to Gunhilda when he was upbraiding her for adultery with Count Alan. The picture of the hell prepared for fornicators in the meditation is described in words very like those in the letters: 'You loved Count Alan Rufus and he you; where is he now? What has become of the lover you loved? Go and lie now with him in the bed where he lies; gather his worms into your bosom; embrace his corpse; kiss his bare teeth from which the flesh has fallen. He does not now care for your love in which he delighted while he lived; and the flesh which you desired now rests.'[3]

This does not, of course, exclude the possibility of both interpretations of the prayer being used.

5. Meditation on Human Redemption and Proslogion

The Anselmian pattern of prayer is seen most clearly in the prayers to the saints, but there are two longer pieces by Anselm which are of special interest in this connection. The *Meditation on Human Redemption* and the *Proslogion* are like, and yet unlike, the *Prayers and Meditations*. They are written in the same heightened oratorical style, in rhymed prose, with the same literary skill and finish; they have the ardour of the prayers and they are as searching as the meditations; and above all, they have the same purpose; the knowledge of God, the *transitus* from the land of unlikeness to the vision of God in the land of the living. They both have, however, special claims to consideration. For one thing they are both much longer than any of the prayers or meditations; they are *libelli*, small books, on their own account, and deserve much fuller treatment than can be

given here. They are of great importance as the prayed framework of Anselm's greatest works: the discussion about the
existence of God in the *Proslogion*, and the restatement of the
doctrine of the Atonement in the *Cur Deus Homo*.

Nevertheless they are included here because they are prayers,
and show in a special way the connection between thought and
prayer which has been noticed in the other meditations and
prayers. Anselm was a theologian in the ancient sense of the
word, 'one whose prayer is true', and as Dr McIntyre says, 'We
dare not dismiss unthinkingly . . . anyone who prays as Anselm
prays . . . and who makes his theology a prayer.'[1] This combination of theological veracity and personal ardour is what most
distinguishes Anselm's writings from similar prayers, and makes
him both traditional and revolutionary. It is the ground of all
the prayers, but especially of the *Proslogion* and the *Meditation
on Human Redemption* where speculation is continually breaking out into prayer, dialectic turning into humility and praise.

Meditation on Human Redemption

The *Meditation on Human Redemption* was written much
later than the rest of the Prayers and Meditations. Eadmer, who
was there, says it was written at Lyons, when the archbishop
was in exile after the Council of Bari in 1099. He was living in
Liberi, a village 'which, being on the top of a mountain, has
always a healthy and cool air'.[2] He had completed the *Cur Deus
Homo*, and he now wrote a meditative summary of the longer
work. Eadmer calls it 'a small work (*opusculum*) which found
favour and gave joy to many, which he entitled a "*Meditation
on Human Redemption*"'.[3]

It is set in the form of a meditation, with a summary of
chapters 4 to 11 of the first book of the *Cur Deus Homo* inset as
the middle eight paragraphs. Out of his reasoning about the
why of the Crucifixion Anselm has created a deeply personal
meditation on the Cross of Christ, without losing theological
clarity. He begins by apostrophizing himself, 'Christian soul',

and urging himself to '*excita mentem*', to shake off torpor, in order to know the things of God. Then he puts forward the scandal of the Cross as the mystery of salvation, which must be not only understood but assimilated. The arguments from *Cur Deus Homo* follow, showing the relationship of man to God, the debt which man must but cannot pay, the free offering of one who is both God and man as the reconciliation in Christ. The next two paragraphs are a meditation on the Cross and the obedience of the Son of God, as the answer to the 'Christian soul': here is 'the strength of your salvation'. This is the turning point of the prayer, where the mind has been roused from lethargy and now comes to the piercing of the first compunction of sorrow, in realization of the need of man and the cost of his redemption. This part of the prayer takes the form of a dialogue between the soul and Christ which is unique in Anselm's prayers. This sorrow leads to a whole-hearted desire for dedication to Christ, and the prayer concludes with that longing for heaven and the vision of God which is the compunction of love.

It is the greatest of the meditations, and shows how Anselm himself prayed his theology till there was no difference between theology and prayer. It can be seen as an example of how the reasoning of the other treatises, like the *De Spiritu Sancto*, could become prayer, though they are not in fact written in that form.

Proslogion

In the Preface to the *Proslogion* Anselm makes it clear that his aim in writing it is theological and devotional rather than philosophical and speculative. Like the *Monologion* the *Proslogion* is to be an '*exemplum meditandi*', and it is written for 'someone trying to raise his mind to the contemplation of God, and seeking to understand what he believes'. For Anselm faith and love come first, 'seeking to understand' is the means to increase them, to bring them to fuller 'contemplation of God'. It is a matter of pondering the mysteries of the faith in order to understand them better and by them to come to an experiential knowledge of God, in so far as that is possible in this life. In the first chapter Anselm expands and explains his title for the work, '*Fidens quaerens intellectum*', in just this sense:

> but I do desire to understand a little of your truth
>   which my heart already believes and loves.
> I do not seek to understand so that I may believe,
>   but I believe so that I may understand;
>   and what is more,
> I believe that unless I do believe I shall not understand.

The *Proslogion* was written during Anselm's time as Prior of Bec, when he was writing the *Prayers and Meditations*; Eadmer says he gave it that title because 'in this work he speaks either to himself or God'.[4] He sent it to Lanfranc for his approval in 1078, by which time most of the *Prayers and Meditations* seem to have been completed. The situation in which it was written and the motive behind it is in a way much the same as that which inspired the prayers, especially perhaps the three prayers to Our Lady. Of the prayers in general Eadmer says they were written 'at the desire and request of his friends',[5] who knew him as a man of prayer; and of the prayers to St Mary, Anselm himself explains in the letter to Gundolf how 'a certain brother asked me, not once but many times, if I would compose a prayer to St Mary'. But the prayer which he wrote on request was followed by the third and greatest prayer to St Mary, proceeding out of Anselm's own interest and affection. So with the *Proslogion*: he wrote the *Monologion* 'at the pressing entreaties of the brethren',[6] but its sequel, the *Proslogion*, came from Anselm's own inspiration and thought. It came, in fact, against his will: when 'I had grown weary resisting its importunity',[7] and it was written down so that others might share his own pleasure in the work.

There is, however, a difference of approach in the prayers and the *Proslogion*: the prayers are centred around the response of man to God's work of salvation, and the *Meditation on Human*

Redemption is about the nature of that salvation which was wrought in Jesus Christ; in the *Proslogion*, the subject is the nature of God himself and, from that point of view, man's relationship to him. This is a different emphasis, shifting from the consideration of man's mean condition to the search for the vision of the everlasting God, and in this sense the *Proslogion* can be said to be more 'contemplative'. But the contrast should not be pressed. There is another difference between the prayers and the *Proslogion*, this time one of form – most of the prayers are addressed to the saints and ask their help: the meditations and the *Proslogion* are soliloquies of the soul directly addressed to God; but in both kinds of devotion prayer and meditation are constantly mingled, so that the difference is more one of emphasis than of kind.

The *Proslogion* is set in the form of a prayer and follows the Anselmian pattern of withdrawal, self-knowledge, and compunction. The first chapter is a long prayer, which goes through all the stages of compunction: there is, first, the withdrawal into solitude, both of place and of mind, in order to free himself for God; then there is the stirring up of the mind, and the compunction of sorrow, when the estrangement of man from God is first experienced:

I sought for peace within myself,
and in the depths of my heart I found trouble and sorrow.

Out of this experience there rises a longing for God, which is the second compunction of desire. This leads on to thanksgiving for all that God has done and promised, and a resolution to continue in this way of vision and faith.

In the next three chapters Anselm expounds his 'single proof' of the existence of God: 'God is that than which nothing greater can be thought.' This so-called 'ontological argument' is one of the great contributions of Western thought to philosophy, and one of the few ideas in medieval philosophy to be of interest today. It has provided Karl Barth with a basis for theological reinterpretation, and is still as capable of arousing argument and discussion as when it was first propounded. It is perhaps important here to see the 'argument' in its context, as part of a prayer, and as something 'given', rather than as an abstract and logical argument. Both Eadmer and Anselm say that it came into his mind as a gift, a sudden illumination, and that this happened during Matins, that is, during a period of corporate prayer: 'Suddenly one night during Matins the grace of God shone in his heart, the whole matter became clear to his mind, and a great joy and jubilation filled his inmost being.'[8] There is a quality in the 'argument' which defies logical definition; the more it is refuted, the more it seems to convince. It is a statement about what is beyond our thought; it is, in fact, a matter of the kind of knowledge of God which belongs to prayer and contemplation more than the narrower sense of knowledge. This kind of awe and wonder in expressing the inexpressible convinces despite itself; it is this quality that Dr Pusey found in the writings of Newman, and his comment on them seems applicable: 'These words exhibit God's works with a sort of wondering awe . . . and do in fact convince much more than those which make conviction their professed object and recall our minds from the contemplation of those works to reflect on their own convincingness. We are not framed to seek conviction but to have it.'[9] The *Proslogion* argument is convincing when the mind is concerned with the God about whom it speaks rather than with the details of the argument itself.

The rest of the *Proslogion* is about the nature and attributes of God: again and again, as Anselm understands more of the vision of God and his relationship to men, he breaks out into praise. The goodness and the mercy of God move him especially:

> Ah, from what generous love and loving generosity
> compassion flows out to us!
> Ah, what feelings of love should we sinners have
> towards the unbounded goodness of God![10]

In chapter 14 he returns to the theme of longing and seeking
for God, and the mystery of light inaccessible. The last chapters praise God and the bliss of heaven, where God is all in all;
and the whole concludes with the most moving of all Anselm's
prayers, which could also be taken as a summary of his life and
thought:

> God of truth,
> I ask that I may receive,
> so that my joy may be full.
> Meanwhile, let my mind meditate on it,
> let my tongue speak of it,
> let my heart love it,
> let my mouth preach it,
> my flesh thirst for it,
> and my whole being desire it,
> until I enter into the joy of my Lord,
> who is God one and triune, blessed forever. Amen

Conclusion

Anselm appeared to his contemporaries to be pre-eminently a
man of prayer, someone who walked with God and who could
guide others in the same way. He came to Normandy at a turning-
point in the spiritual life of northern Europe, where a growing
compassion for the Saviour and more personal emotion and
affection for his Mother were already finding expression in
hymns and prayers. He gave impetus to these trends in a unique
and powerful way, till it could be said that the dialectic he
fathered and the affective devotion he developed changed the
whole atmosphere of Western spirituality for the rest of the
Middle Ages and beyond. But Anselm himself was no revolutionary theologian; rather he was a bridge, a link with the
tradition of the undivided church. In many ways his clear and
independent mind gave new life to traditional teaching, and

carried it through into a new age. He prayed in the tradition of the Fathers, but he gave this received teaching expression in the concepts and language of his times, with the result that the later outpouring of devotion to the humanity of the Saviour had its roots in the tradition of the church.

The form of the prayers meant that they would be imitated, taking on the colour of other men's devotion, but it is significant that Anselm's imitators caught only parts of his thought and style (see Appendix). The prayers themselves proved inimitable, the products of supreme genius, and they stand out clearly from their successors. Today they do not yield their riches at a casual reading, nor can they be easily appreciated; the affective devotion and ardour of the eleventh century is at a discount in this age. Yet there is here a unique combination of theological veracity and personal ardour that has value at any time. They are ultimately prayers that are meant to be prayed; that is, they are ways to come to God, preparations for that silence of soul which is prayer.

Notes

The Liturgy

1. *The Book of Cerne*, ed. Kuyper, A. B., Cambridge University Press, 1909, Liturgical Note V, by Bishop, Edmund, p. 234.
2. *Rule of St Benedict*, ed. McCann, J., Orchard Books, London 1952, chapter 8.
3. *Constitutions of Lanfranc*, ed. Dom David Knowles, Nelson, 1967.
4. Augustine, *Enarrationes in Psalmos*, PL 136, 123.
5. Wilmart, A., *Prières pour la Communion, en 2 psaltiers du Mont-Cassin*, Ephemerides Liturgicae, 1929.
6. *Pilgrimage of Etheria*: Latin text printed in Duchesne, L., *Christian Worship*, S.P.C.K., 1904.
7. *The Dream of the Rood*, translated by Kennedy, Charles W., Mills and Carter, 1952.
8. VA, II, iii.

9. cf. Wilmart, *Prières médiévales pour l'Adoration de la Croix*, Ephemerides Liturgicae, 1932; and Gjerløw, Lilli, *Adoratio Crucis*, Norwegian University Press, 1961.

10. Barré, H., *Prières anciennes de l'Occident à la Mère du Sauveur*, Paris, 1962.

11. Saxer, Victor, *Le culte de Marie Madeleine en Occident des origines à la fin du moyen âge*, Paris, 1959.

The 'Preces Privates'

1. Alcuin, PL 101, 465-6.

2. *Canones Hippolyti* 233-5, Appendix 6, in Duchesne, op. cit.

3. Brou and Wilmart, *The Psalter Collects of the V-VI Centuries*, Henry Bradshaw Society, London, 1949

4. MS. D'Orville 45; text also printed in Bianchini, *Thomasii Opera*, vol. 2, 526-8.

5. *Precum Libelli*, pp. 82-85.

6. ibid., pp. 14-16.

7. ibid., pp. 11-13.

8. ibid., p. 44.

9. cf. MS. D'Orville 45, 40-41.

10. Genesius of Rome, in Hamaan, A., *Early Christian Prayers*, Longmans, 1961, p. 54.

11. PL 142, 934.

12. *Precum Libelli*, p. 140.

13. PL 158, 946.

14. *Book of Cerne*, prayer 52. For discussion of this prayer see Wilmart, *Auteurs spirituels et textes dévots du moyen âge latin*, Paris, 1932, pp. 474-564.

15. PL 158, 959.

16. *Book of Cerne*, prayer 60.

17. *Rouen Psalter*, prayer 13 in Gjerløw, *Adoratio Crucis*, op. cit., appendix.

18. *Book of Cerne*, prayer 59.

19. *Rouen Psalter*, prayer 15.

20. cf. *Liber de Beatitudine Caelestis Patriae*, chapter 10, PL 159, 638.

21. Julian of Norwich, *Revelations of Divine Love*, Penguin Books, 1966, ch. 43, pp. 129-30.

22. *Precum Libelli*, p. 56.
23. Wilmart, *Le Manuel de Prières de S. Jean Gualbert*, Rev. Bén., July–December 1936, pp. 259–99.

'*Meditari aut Legere*'

1. *Meditation on Human Redemption*.
2. *Apostolic Constitutions*, trans. Donaldson, J., in Ante-Nicene Christian Library, XVII, 1870, Part 2.
3. Origen, *Patrologiae Graecae*, 13, 235D.
4. Hilary, *de Trinitate*, PL 10, 49.
5. Augustine, *Confessions*, Penguin Books, 1961, p. 21.
6. Butler, C., *Benedictine Monachism*, Longmans, 1919, pp. 61–7.
7. Cassian, John, *Conferences*, English trans. Gibson, E. C. S., Library of Nicene and Post-Nicene Fathers, 2nd Series, vol XI, Oxford 1894; 1st Conference of Abbot Nestorius, p. 440.
8. ibid., Conference of Abbot Isaac, pp. 387–409.
9. *Rule of St Benedict*, ed. cit., ch. 52.
10. ibid., ch. 20.
11. ibid., ch. 49.
12. ibid., ch. 48.
13. Anselm, Prayer to St Paul, line 273.
14. Anselm, Prayer to St Mary (3), line 148.

John of Fécamp

1. *Confessio Fidei*, III, xi. The text of the works of John of Fécamp have been published by Leclercq and Bonnes, *Jean de Fécamp, un maître de la vie spirituelle au moyen âge*, Paris, 1956.
2. *Confessio Theologica* II, iv.
3. Wilmart, *Revue d'Ascétique et de Mystique*, 1937, p. 338.
4. *Confessio Theologica*, III, xi.
5. Leclercq and Bonnes, op. cit., Introduction, p. 80.
6. ibid., Letter to Agnes, pp. 211–17.
7. Introduction by Wilmart to Dom Castel's translation of *Les Prières et Méditations*, Paris, 1923, p. lxii.

Introduction

The Anselmian Pattern

1. *Proslogion*, ch. 1.
2. Cassian, Conference IX, on Prayer, trans. Gibson, op. cit., pp. 387–409.
3. *Prayers and Meditations*, Preface.
4. Augustine, *Confessions*, ed. cit., p. 188.
5. Augustine, ibid., p. 232.
6. Butler, op. cit.
7. Gregory the Great, *Moralia in Job*, book XXIII, PL 76, 292.
8. ibid., book XXIII, PL 76, 296.
9. ibid., PL 76, 277.
10. Anselm, Prayer 16.
11. Gregory the Great, op. cit., PL 76, 277.
12. Anselm, Meditation 1.
13. Gregory the Great, loc. cit.

The Prayers

1. See Young, K., *The Drama of the Mediaeval Church*, Oxford, 1933, vol 1, pp. 239 ff.
2. Aelred of Rievaulx, *Speculum Caritatis*, Part 2, 19, PL 195, 568C.
3. *Ancren Riwle*, ed. Salu, M. B., Burns Oates, 1955.
4. Julian of Norwich, *Revelations of Divine Love*, op. cit., ch. 58 ff.
5. Southern, R. W., *St Anselm and His Biographer*, Cambridge University Press, 1963, p. 73.
6. *Le Manuel des Prières de S. Jean Gualbert*, Prayer 89, ed. Wilmart, Rev. Bén., July–December 1936, p. 293.

Meditations 1 and 2

1. Wilmart, Introduction to *Prières et Méditations*, trans. Castel, Paris, 1923, p. xxiv.
2. *Meditations and Prayers to the Holy Trinity and Our Lord Jesus Christ by St Anselm of Canterbury*, Innes and Co., 1856; see note on p. 31: 'Sin is continually in Holy Scripture spoken of as adultery against God and is so below.'
3. Letter 157, Schmitt, vol. 4, p. 24.

Meditation on Human Redemption and Proslogion

1. McIntyre, J., *St Anselm and his Critics*, Edinburgh, 1954, p. 16.

(Meditation on Human Redemption)

2. VA II, xxx.
3. VA II, xliv.

(Proslogion)

4. VA I, xix.
5. VA I, viii.
6. *Proslogion*, Preface.
7. ibid.
8. VA I, xix.
9. Dr Pusey, quoted by Allchin, A. M., in *The Rediscovery of Newman*, Coulson and Allchin, S.P.C.K., 1967, p. 62.
10. *Proslogion*, ch. 9.

THE PRAYERS AND MEDITATIONS
OF ST ANSELM

Preface

The purpose of the prayers and meditations that follow is to stir up the mind of the reader to the love or fear of God, or to self-examination. They are not to be read in a turmoil, but quietly, not skimmed or hurried through, but taken a little at a time, with deep and thoughtful meditation.

The reader should not trouble about reading the whole of any of them, but only as much as, by God's help, he finds useful in stirring up his spirit to pray, or as much as he likes. Nor is it necessary for him always to begin at the beginning, but wherever he pleases.

With this in mind the sections are divided into paragraphs, so that the reader can begin and leave off wherever he chooses; in this way he will not get bored with too much material but will be able to ponder more deeply those things that make him want to pray.

Letter of Anselm to the Countess Mathilda of Tuscany

(Schmitt, vol. 3, p. 4, before the Preface to the Prayers and Meditations)

Anselm, the unworthy bishop of the Church of Canterbury, sends salutations to the reverend Countess Mathilda.

It has seemed good to your Highness that I should send you these prayers, which I edited at the request of several brothers. Some of them are not appropriate to you, but I want to send them all, so that if you like them you may be able to compose others after their example. They are arranged so that by reading them the mind may be stirred up either to the love or fear of God, or to a consideration of both; so they should not be read cursorily or quickly, but little by little, with attention and deep meditation. It is not intended that the reader should feel impelled to read the whole, but only as much as will stir up the affections to prayer; so as much as does that, think it to be sufficient for you.

Second Letter to Countess Mathilda

(Schmitt, vol. 5, end of Letter 325, p. 256)

Your Highness has told me that you have not got the Prayers and Meditations which I myself have copied and I thought you had got. I send them to you by my son, Alexander. The Almighty God rule and protect you always; with my blessing.

1. Prayer to God

Almighty God, merciful Father, and my good Lord,
    have mercy on me, a sinner.
    Grant me forgiveness of my sins.
Make me guard against and overcome
all snares, temptations, and harmful pleasures.   5

May I shun utterly in word and in deed,
    whatever you forbid,
    and do and keep whatever you command.
Let me believe and hope, love and live,
    according to your purpose and your will.   10

Give me heart-piercing goodness and humility;
discerning abstinence and mortification of the flesh.
Help me to love you and pray to you,
    praise you and meditate upon you.
May I act and think in all things according to your will,   15
    purely, soberly, devoutly,
    and with a true and effective mind.
Let me know your commandments, and love them,
    carry them out readily, and bring them into effect.
Always, Lord, let me go on with humility to better things   20
    and never grow slack.

    Lord, do not give me over
either to my human ignorance and weakness
    or to my own deserts,
or to anything, other than your loving dealing with me.   25
Do you yourself in kindness dispose of me,
my thoughts and actions, according to your good pleasure,
    so that your will may always be done
    by me and in me and concerning me.

Deliver me from all evil
and lead me to eternal life
through the Lord.

2. Prayer to Christ

Lord Jesus Christ,
my Redeemer, my Mercy, and my Salvation:
   I praise you and give you thanks.
They are far beneath the goodness of your gifts,
   which deserve a better return of love;   5
   but although I requite so poorly
   the sweet riches of your love
   which I have longed to have,
   yet my soul will pay its debt
   by some sort of praise and thanks,   10
   not as I know I ought, but as I can.

*

Hope of my heart, strength of my soul,
   help of my weakness,
   by your powerful kindness complete
   what in my powerless weakness I attempt.   15
   My life, the end to which I strive,
although I have not yet attained to love you as I ought,
   still let my desire for you
   be as great as my love ought to be.

*

My light, you see my conscience,   20
because, 'Lord, before you is all my desire',
and if my soul wills any good, you gave it me.
   Lord, if what you inspire is good,
or rather because it is good, that I should want to love you,
   give me what you have made me want: 25
grant that I may attain to love you as much as you command.

I praise and thank you for the desire that you have inspired;
    and I offer you praise and thanks
    lest your gift to me be unfruitful,
which you have given me of your own accord.   30
    Perfect what you have begun,
and grant me what you have made me long for,
not according to my deserts but out of your kindness
    that came first to me.

        *

    Most merciful Lord,   35
turn my lukewarmness into a fervent love of you.
    Most gentle Lord,
    my prayer tends towards this –
that by remembering and meditating
    on the good things you have done   40
    I may be enkindled with your love.
    Your goodness, Lord, created me;
Your mercy cleansed what you had created
    from original sin;
    your patience has hitherto borne with me,   45
    fed me, waited for me,
when after I had lost the grace of my baptism
    I wallowed in many sordid sins.
    You wait, good Lord, for my amendment;
My soul waits for the inbreathing of your grace   50
    in order to be sufficiently penitent
    to lead a better life.

        *

    My Lord and my Creator,
you bear with me and nourish me –
    be my helper.   55
I thirst for you, I hunger for you, I desire you,
    I sigh for you, I covet you:

I am like an orphan deprived of the presence
    of a very kind father,
who, weeping and wailing, does not cease to cling to   60
    the dear face with his whole heart.
So, as much as I can, though not as much as I ought,
    I am mindful of your passion,
your buffeting, your scourging, your cross, your wounds,
    how you were slain for me,   65
    how prepared for burial and buried;
and also I remember your glorious Resurrection,
    and wonderful Ascension.
All this I hold with unwavering faith,
    and weep over the hardship of exile,   70
hoping in the sole consolation of your coming,
ardently longing for the glorious contemplation of your face.
    Alas for me, that I was not able to see
    the Lord of Angels humbled to converse with men,
    when God, the one insulted,   75
    willed to die that the sinner might live.
    Alas that I did not deserve to be amazed
in the presence of a love marvellous and beyond our grasp.
    Why, O my soul, were you not there
    to be pierced by a sword of bitter sorrow   80
    when you could not bear
the piercing of the side of your Saviour with a lance?
    Why could you not bear to see
the nails violate the hands and feet of your Creator?
    Why did you not see with horror   85
the blood that poured out of the side of your Redeemer?
    Why were you not drunk with bitter tears
    when they gave him bitter gall to drink?
    Why did you not share
    the sufferings of the most pure virgin,   90
    his worthy mother and your gentle lady?

*

95

My most merciful Lady,
what can I say about the fountains
  that flowed from your most pure eyes
when you saw your only Son before you,   95
  bound, beaten and hurt?
What do I know of the flood
  that drenched your matchless face,
when you beheld your Son, your Lord, and your God,
  stretched on the cross without guilt,   100
when the flesh of your flesh
  was cruelly butchered by wicked men?
How can I judge what sobs troubled your most pure breast
  when you heard, 'Woman, behold your son,'
and the disciple, 'Behold, your mother,'   105
  when you received as a son
  the disciple in place of the master,
    the servant for the lord?

John [handwritten annotation]

*

Would that I with happy Joseph *Arimathea* [handwritten annotation]
might have taken down my Lord from the cross,   110
  wrapped him in spiced grave-clothes
    and laid him in the tomb;
    or even followed after
    so that such a burial
might not have been without my mourning.   115
Would that with the blessed band of women
I might have trembled at the vision of angels
and have heard the news of the Lord's Resurrection,
  news of my consolation,
  so much looked for, so much desired.   120
Would that I might have heard from the angel's mouth,
'Fear not, Jesus who was crucified, whom you are seeking,
  is not here; he is risen.'

*

Kindest, gentlest, most serene Lord,
will you not make it up to me for not seeing   125
the blessed incorruption of your flesh,
for not having kissed the place of the wounds
    where the nails pierced,
for not having sprinkled with tears of joy
the scars that prove the truth of your body?   130
O wonder, beyond price and beyond compare,
'how will you comfort and recompense me for my grief?'
For it cannot cease while I am a pilgrim, far from my Lord.
    Alas, Lord, alas, my soul.
You have ascended, consoler of my life,   135
and you have not said farewell to me.
Going up on your way you blessed your own,
    but I did not say good-bye;
    'lifting up your hands'
you were received by a cloud into heaven,   140
    and I did not see it;
angels promised your return; and I did not hear it.

*

What shall I say? What shall I do? Whither shall I go?
Where shall I seek him? Where and when shall I find him?
    Whom shall I ask? Who will tell me of my beloved?   145
      'for I am sick from love'.
'The joy of my heart fails me';
    my laughter 'is turned to mourning';
    'my heart and my flesh fail me';
'but God is the strength of my heart, my portion for ever.'   150
    'My soul refuses comfort,' unless from you, my dear.
      'Whom have I in heaven but you,
    and what do I desire upon earth beside you?'

I want you, I hope for you, I seek you;
'to you my heart has said, seek my face';   155
'your face, Lord, have I sought;
    turn not your face from me.'

*

    Most kind lover of men,
'the poor commits himself to you,
        for you are the helper of the orphan'.   160
    My most safe helper,
    have mercy upon the orphan left to you.
I am become a child without a father;   *lost someone dear*
    my soul is like a widow.
Turn your gaze and behold my tears   165
    which I offer to you till you return.
almost begging? Come now, Lord, appear to me and I will be consoled;
    show me your face and I shall be saved;
    display your presence and I have obtained my desire;
    reveal your glory and my joy will be full.   170
'My soul thirsts for you, my flesh longs after you,'
    my soul thirsts for God, the fountain of life;
    'when shall I come to appear before the presence of God?'
My consoler, for whom I wait, when will you come?
    O that I might see the joy that I desire;   175
that I might be satisfied with the appearing of your glory
        for which I hunger;
that I might be satisfied with the riches of your house
        for which I sigh;
that I might drink of the torrent of your pleasures   180
        for which I thirst.

*

Lord, meanwhile, let my tears be my meat day and night,
    until they say to me, 'Behold your God,'
    until I hear, 'Soul, behold your bridegroom.'

Meanwhile, let me be fed with griefs, 185
and let my tears be my drink;
   comfort me with sorrows.
Perhaps then my Redeemer will come to me,
   for he is good;
he is kind, he will not tarry, 190
to whom be glory for ever. Amen.

3. Prayer Before Receiving the Body and Blood of Christ

Lord Jesus Christ
by the Father's plan and by the working of the Holy Ghost
  of your own free will you died
and mercifully redeemed the world
  from sin and everlasting death.   5
  I adore and venerate you
  as much as ever I can,
though my love is so cold, my devotion so poor.
  Thank you for the good gift
  of this your holy Body and Blood,   10
which I desire to receive, as cleansing from sin,
  and for a defence against it.

*

Lord, I acknowledge that I am far from worthy
  to approach and touch this sacrament;
    but I trust in that mercy   15
  which caused you to lay down your life for sinners
    that they might be justified,
    and because you gave yourself
  willingly as a holy sacrifice to the Father.
  A sinner, I presume to receive these gifts   20
  so that I may be justified by them.
I beg and pray you, therefore, merciful lover of men,
let not that which you have given for the cleansing of sins
  be unto me the increase of sin,
  but rather for forgiveness and protection.   25

*

Make me, O Lord, so to perceive with lips and heart
   and know by faith and by love,
that by virtue of this sacrament I may deserve to be
planted in the likeness of your death and resurrection,
   by mortifying the old man,   30
   and by renewal of the life of righteousness.
May I be worthy to be incorporated into your body
   'which is the church',
so that I may be your member and you may be my head,
   and that I may remain in you and you in me.   35
Then at the Resurrection you will refashion
   the body of my humiliation
   according to the body of your glory,
   as you promised by your apostle,
   and I shall rejoice in you for ever   40
      to your glory,
who with the Father and the Holy Spirit
lives and reigns for ever. Amen.

4. Prayer to the Holy Cross

Holy Cross,
which calls to mind the cross
whereon our Lord Jesus Christ died,
to bring us back from that eternal death
    to which our misery was leading us,   5
    to the eternal life we had lost by sinning.
I adore, I venerate, and I glory in that cross
    which you represent to us,
and by that cross I adore our merciful Lord
and what he has in mercy done for us.   10
Cross, worthy to be loved, in whom is our salvation,
    our life, and resurrection.
Most precious wood, by whom we are saved and set free,
sign to be reverenced, by which we are sealed for God,
    glorious cross, we ought to glory only in you.   15

*

We do not acknowledge you because of the cruelty
that godless and foolish men prepared you to effect
    upon the most gentle Lord,
    but because of the wisdom and goodness of him
    who of his own free will took you up.   20
    For they could not have done anything
    unless his wisdom had permitted it,
and he could not suffer except that in his mercy he willed it.
    They chose you
that they might carry out their evil deeds;   25
    he chose you
that he might fulfil the work of his goodness.

They that by you
   they might hand over the righteous to death;
    he that through you he might save sinners from death.   30
They that they might kill life;
   he that he might destroy death.
They that they might condemn the Saviour;
   he that he might save the condemned.
They that they might bring death to the living;   35
   he to bring life to the dead.
They acted foolishly and cruelly; he wisely and mercifully.
   Therefore, O Cross to be wondered at,
     we do not value you
   because of the intention of their cruel folly,   40
   but according to the working of mercy and wisdom.

*

In what way, then, shall I praise you,
   how shall I exalt you,
  with what love shall I pray to you,
   and with what joy shall I glory in you?   45
    By you hell is despoiled,
by you its mouth is stopped up to all the redeemed.
   By you demons are made afraid and restrained,
   conquered and trampled underfoot.
By you the world is renewed and made beautiful with truth,   50
   governed by the light of righteousness.
   By you sinful humanity is justified,
    the condemned are saved,
  the servants of sin and hell are set free,
  the dead are raised to life.   55
   By you the blessed city in heaven
  is restored and made perfect.
By you God, the Son of God willed for our sakes
'to become obedient to the Father, even unto death',

because of which he is exalted and has received   60
   'the name which is above every name'.
By you 'his throne is prepared' and his kingdom established.

*

O Cross, chosen and prepared for such ineffable good,
   the work that was accomplished on you exalts you more
than all the praises of human or angelic thought and tongue.   65
In you and through you is my life and my salvation;
in you and through you is the whole and all my good;
   'forbid that I should glory save in you'.
   For why was I conceived and born, and given life,
      if afterwards I am to descend to hell?   70
   If that is to be my fate it were better for me
      if I had never been conceived.
And it is certain that it would have been so
   if I had not been redeemed by you.

*

With what love shall I glory in you, O Cross,   75
     when without you
  there would be nothing for me to glory in,
and in eternity I should have the grief and misery of hell.
   With what delight will I rejoice in you,
when by you the servitude of hell which I inherited   80
   is exchanged for the kingdom of heaven.
   With what jubilation shall I laud you,
    when without you I faced that future
which horrifies me, even if it had lasted only a moment,
and through you I now expect to rejoice in eternity.   85
Though now I serve God between hope and fear,
I am sure that if I give thanks, love, and live to your glory,
   through you I shall at last come to that good.

*

So let my glory be through you and in you;
let my true hope be through you and in you.   90
By you my sins are wiped out,
by you my soul is dead to its old life
and lives to the new life of righteousness.
I beseech you, wash me by baptism from the sins
in which I was conceived and born,   95
and cleanse me again from those that I committed
    after I was reborn,
so that by you I may come to those good things
    for which man was created,
by the might of the same Jesus Christ our Lord   100
who is blessed for ever and ever. Amen.

*field prayer and request
    of the cross

A Letter to Gundolf at Caen

(Letter 28, Schmitt, vol. 3, pp. 135-6)

To the monk Gundolf, from Brother Anselm, who is Gundolf's Anselm.

There is no need for me to say much about how long our friendship has lasted, to one who I know is my other self in the bond of love. Let me say this briefly about us – my love for you has never diminished by any change in me from its first beginning, and I am careful that alteration shall always serve only to increase it.

A certain brother asked me, not once but many times, if I would compose a prayer to the great St Mary. What he asks me in person here you also urge upon me in your absence. For I realized that if I did do this, I could also send it to you, so I have been more ready to agree to what he asked. I composed one prayer, as I was asked to do, but I was not satisfied, knowing what had been asked, so I started again and composed another. I was not satisfied with that either, so have done a third which at last is all right.

So accept them, for they have been made with you in mind, and do not blame me for their length, which was made at the request of someone else. And would that they might be so long that, before whoever was reading them – or better still, meditating on them, since that is what they are meant for – came to the end, he might be pierced by contrition or by love, through which we reach a concern for heavenly things. You will find that I have divided the prayers up into paragraphs to prevent you from becoming bored, so that you can begin to read at any place you like.

5. Prayer to St Mary (1)

when the mind is weighed down with heaviness

Mary, holy Mary,
among the holy ones the most holy after God.
Mother with virginity to be wondered at,
Virgin with fertility to be cherished,
you bore the Son of the most High,   5
and brought forth the Saviour of the lost human race.
Lady, shining before all others with such sanctity,
    pre-eminent with such dignity,
it is very sure that you are not least in power and in honour.
Life-bearer, mother of salvation,   10
    shrine of goodness and mercy,
I long to come before you in my misery,
sick with the sickness of vice,
in pain from the wounds of crimes,
putrid with the ulcers of sin.   15
However near I am to death, I reach out to you,
and I long to ask that by your powerful merits
    and your loving prayers,
    you will deign to heal me.
        Good Lady,   20
    a huge dullness is between you and me,
so that I am scarcely aware of the extent of my sickness.
    I am so filthy and stinking
that I am afraid you will turn your merciful face from me.
So I look to you to convert me,   25
    but I am held back by despair,
    and even my lips are shut against prayer.

*

My sins, my wicked deeds,
since you have destroyed my soul with your poison,
    why do you make it a horror with your filth,   30
    so that no one can look on my misery?
If your weight is so great that I have no hope of being heard,
why by your shame do you block the voice of my prayer?
    If you have made me mad with love for you,
why have you made my senses unfeeling with your torpor? 35
Alas, what a shameful thing is the filth of sin
    before the brightness of holiness.
Alas, what confusion there is for an impure conscience
    in the presence of shining purity.

*

You are blessed above all women,   40
    in purity surpassing the angels,
    in goodness overpassing the saints.
Already dying I long to be seen by such kindness,
but I blush before the gaze of such purity.
    What I want to ask you, Lady, is   45
    that by a glance from your mercy
you will cure the sickness and ulcers of my sins,
    but before you I am confounded
    by the smell and foulness of them.
I shudder, Lady, to show you all my foul state,   50
lest it makes you shudder at the sight of me,
but, alas for me, I cannot be seen any other way.

*

How disturbed and confused is the state of sin!
How my sins tear my heart in pieces and divide it,
    gnaw at it and torment it.   55
    Because of these sins of mine, Lady,
    I desire to come to you and be cured,
    but I flee from you for fear of being cursed.

My sins cannot be cured unless they are confessed,
but to acknowledge them throws me into confusion.   60
If they are concealed they cannot be healed,
  if they are seen they are detestable.
They chafe me with sorrow, they terrify me with fear,
they bury me with their weight, they press upon me heavily,   65
  and confound me with shame.

*

Mary, powerful in goodness, and good in power,
  from whom was born the fount of mercy,
I pray you, do not withhold such true mercy
  where you know there is such true misery.
    The brightness of your holiness   70
  confounds the darkness of my sins,
but surely you will not blush to feel kindness
    towards such a wretch?
  If I acknowledge my iniquity,
surely you will not refuse to show kindness?   75
If my misery is too great to be heard favourably,
surely your mercy will be less than it ought to be?
Lady, before God and before you my sins appear vile;
  and therefore so much the more do they need
    his healing and your help.   80
  Most gentle Lady, heal my weakness,
and you will be taking away the filth that offends you.
    Most kind Lady, take away my sickness,
and you will not experience the dirt you shudder at.
    Most dear Lady, do not let what grieves you be,   85
and there will be nothing to defile your holiness.
    Hear me, Lady,
and make whole the soul of a sinner who is your servant,
  by virtue of the blessed fruit of your womb,
who sits at the right hand of his almighty Father   90
  and is praised and glorified above all for ever. Amen.

6. Prayer to St Mary (2)

when the mind is anxious with fear

Virgin venerated throughout the world,
  Mother dear to the human race,
  Woman, marvel of the angels,
    Mary, most holy.
By your blessed virginity you have made all integrity sacred,   5
  and by your glorious child-bearing
you have brought salvation to all fruitfulness.
    Great Lady,
to you the joyous company of the saints gives thanks;
to you the fearful crowd of the accused flee;   10
  and to you, Lady of might and mercy,
I flee, a sinner every way, beyond measure distressed.

*

    Lady, it seems to me as if I were already
  before the all-powerful justice of the stern judge
  facing the intolerable vehemence of his wrath,   15
  while hanging over me is the enormity of my sins,
    and the huge torments they deserve.
    Most gentle Lady,
  whose intercession should I implore
when I am troubled with horror, and shake with fear,   20
    but hers, whose womb embraced
    the reconciliation of the world?
Whence should I most surely hope for help quickly in need,
but from her whence I know came the world's propitiation?
Who can more easily gain pardon for the accused   25
    by her intercession,
    than she who gave milk to him
who justly punishes or mercifully pardons all and each one?

Most blessed Lady, it is not possible for you to forget
   that those merits which are so specially yours   30
      are very necessary to us.
Most gentle Lady, it is not credible that you should not **pity**
   such pitiable suppliants.
     Well the world knows,
and we sinners do not in any way hide it from the world,   35
we know well enough, Lady, who is 'the son of man',
   and to what sons of men 'he came
     to seek that which was lost'.
     Lady, mother of my hope,
   surely you will not forget in hatred of me   40
   what you so mercifully brought into the world,
   so happily revealed and lovingly embraced?
   The son of man in his goodness came
of his own free will to save that which was lost;
   how can the mother of God not care   45
     when the lost cry to her?
The son of man came to 'call sinners to repentance' –
   how can the mother of God despise
     the prayers of the repentant?
     The good God, the gentle man,   50
   the merciful son of God, the good son of man,
   came to seek the sinner who had strayed;
   and will you, good mother of the man,
     mighty mother of God,
     repel wretches who pray to you?   55

              *

     O human virgin,
of you was born a human God, to save human sinners,
   and see, before both son and mother
is a human sinner, penitent and confessing,
     groaning and praying.   60
     I beg you both,

good Lord and good Lady, dear son and dear mother,
by this truth which is the only hope of sinners,
that you will be her son and you will be his mother
    to save this sinner.   65
Thus, thus let this sinner be absolved and cared for,
    healed and saved.
  In this he shows himself to be your sinner,
    as indeed he is,
  for he knows you to be both son and mother   70
    for the salvation of sinners.
  Indeed I am the sinner who belongs to you both.

*

When I have sinned against the son,
  I have alienated the mother,
nor can I offend the mother without hurting the son.   75
  What will you do, then, sinner?
    Where will you flee?
Who can reconcile me to the son if the mother is my enemy,
or who will make my peace with the mother
  if I have angered the son?   80
Surely if I have offended you both equally
  you will both also be merciful?
So the accused flees from the just God
  to the good mother of the merciful God.
The accused finds refuge from the mother he has offended 85
  in the good son of the kind mother.
The accused is carried from one to the other
  and throws himself between
  the good son and the good mother.

*

Dear Lord, spare the servant of your mother;   90
dear Lady, spare the servant of your son.

Good son, make your servant's peace with your mother;
  good mother, reconcile your son to your servant.
When I throw myself between two
    of such unbounded goodness   95
I shall not fall under the severity of their power.
    Good son, good mother,
do not let me confess this truth about you in vain,
  lest I blush for hoping in your goodness.
  I love the truth I confess about you,   100
and I beg for that goodness which I hope for from you.

*

Tell me, judge of the world, whom you will spare,
tell me, reconciler of the world, whom you will reconcile,
  if you, Lord, condemn, and you, Lady, turn away
    your goodness and love from this little man   105
      who confesses his sin with sorrow?
Saviour of each one, tell me whom you will save,
mother of salvation, tell me for whom you will pray,
if it is by your command, Lord,
    and with your consent, Lady,   110
that torments vex the sinner
  who blames himself and prays to you,
that hell absorbs the prisoner
  who accuses himself and entreats you,
that Tartarus devours the poor man   115
  who despairs of himself and hopes in you.

*

God, who was made the son of a woman out of mercy;
  woman, who was made mother of God out of mercy;
    have mercy upon this wretch,
      you forgiving, you interceding,   120
or show the unhappy man to whom he may flee for safety
and point out in whose power he may more certainly confide.

If it is – or rather because it is –
  that my sin is so great and my faith so small,
    so cool my love, so feeble my prayer,   125
    so imperfect my satisfaction,
  that I deserve neither the forgiveness of sins
    nor the grace of salvation,
for this very reason I ask that in whatever way
you see that my merits are not sufficient for me,   130
there in your mercy you will not be found wanting.
  So I ask you to hear me
  by your own merits rather than mine,
  so that by the goodness you pour forth
  and the power in which you abound,   135
I may escape the sorrows of damnation which I deserve
  and enter into the joy of the blessed
    to praise you, God,
who are worthy to be praised and exalted for ever. Amen.

7. Prayer to St Mary (3)

to ask for her and Christ's love

Mary, great Mary,
most blessed of all Marys,
greatest among all women,
   great Lady, great beyond measure,
I long to love you with all my heart,   5
I want to praise you with my lips,
I desire to venerate you in my understanding,
I love to pray to you from my deepest being,
   I commit myself wholly to your protection.

*

Heart of my soul, stir yourself up as much as ever you can   10
   (if you can do anything at all),
and let all that is within me praise the good Mary has done,
   love the blessing she has received,
wonder at her loftiness, and beseech her kindness;
   for I need her defence daily,   15
and in my need I desire, implore, and beseech it,
   and if it is not according to my desire,
at least let it be above, or rather contrary to, what I deserve.

*

Queen of angels, Lady of the world,
Mother of him who cleanses the world,   20
   I confess that my heart is unclean,
and I am rightly ashamed to turn towards such cleanness,
   but I turn towards it to be made clean
      in order to come to it.
Mother of him who is the light of my heart,   25
nurse of him who is the strength of my soul,

I pray to you with my whole heart
   to the extent of my powers.
Hear me, Lady, answer me, most mighty helper;
   let this filth be washed from my mind,   30
let my darkness be illuminated, my lukewarmness blaze up,
   my listlessness be stirred.
For in your blessed holiness you are exalted above all,
   after the highest of all, your Son,
through your omnipotent Son, with your glorious Son,   35
    by your blessed Son.
   So as being above all after the Lord,
   who is my God and my all, your Son,
   in my heart I know and worship you,
   love you and ask for your affection,   40
   not because of my imperfect desires,
but because it belongs to your Son to make and to save,
   to redeem and bring back to life.

*

   Mother of the life of my soul,
   nurse of the redeemer of my flesh,   45
who gave suck to the Saviour of my whole being –
   but what am I saying?
My tongue fails me, for my love is not sufficient.
Lady, Lady, I am very anxious to thank you for so much,
but I cannot think of anything worthy to say to you,   50
and I am ashamed to offer you anything unworthy.
How can I speak worthily
   of the mother of the Creator and Saviour,
   by whose sanctity my sins are purged,
   by whose integrity incorruptibility is given me,   55
by whose virginity my soul falls in love with its Lord
   and is married to its God.
What can I worthily tell of the mother of my Lord and God
by whose fruitfulness I am redeemed from captivity,

by whose child-bearing   60
I am brought forth from eternal death,
by whose offspring I who was lost am restored,
and led back from my unhappy exile
   to my blessed homeland.

*

'Blessed among all women',   65
   all these things were given to me
   by 'the blessed fruit of your womb'
   through his baptism of regeneration,
   some in fact, others in hope;
   yet by sinning I put it all away from me   70
so that now I have nothing and scarcely any hope.
     What then?
   If they vanished because of my guilt
   surely I will not be ungrateful to her
   by whom so many good things came to me?   75
Stop, lest I add iniquity upon iniquity!
   I give great thanks for what I have had,
   I weep for what I have not,
   I pray so that I may have them again.
For I am sure that since through the Son   80
   I could receive grace,
I can receive it again through the merits of the mother.
     Therefore, Lady,
   gateway of life, door of salvation,
   way of reconciliation, approach to recovery,   85
I beg you by the salvation born of your fruitfulness,
   see to it that my sins be pardoned
   and the grace to live well be granted me,
   and even to the end keep this your servant
     under your protection.   90

*

Palace of universal propitiation,
  cause of general reconciliation,
vase and temple of life and universal salvation:
  I have made too little of your praises,
and in a little man like me it is especially vile   95
    to belittle your merits.
  For the world rejoices in your love
  and so proclaims what you have done for it.
O Lady, to be wondered at for your unparalleled virginity;
to be venerated for a holiness beyond all reckoning –   100
you showed to the world its Lord and its God
    whom it had not known.
You showed to the sight of all the world
  its Creator whom it had not seen.
You gave birth to the restorer of the world   105
  for whom the lost world longed.
You brought forth the world's reconciliation,
  which, in its guilt, it did not have before.
Through your fruitfulness, Lady,
  the sinner is cleansed and justified,   110
the condemned is saved and the exile is restored.
Your offspring, Lady, redeemed the world from captivity,
  made whole the sick, gave life to the dead.
  The world was wrapped in darkness,
surrounded and oppressed by demons under which it lay, 115
but from you alone light was born into it,
which broke its bonds and trampled underfoot their power.

*

Heaven, stars, earth, waters, day and night,
and whatever was in the power or use of men was guilty;
they rejoice now, Lady, that they lost that glory,   120
  for a new and ineffable grace
  has been given them through you.
They are brought back to life and give thanks.

For all things were as if dead,
since they had lost that inborn dignity by virtue of which   125
they were ruled and used to the praise of God
    for which they were made.
  They were buried by oppression,
and tainted by being used in the service of idols
    for which they were not made.   130
But see now, how they are raised to life, and praise the Lord,
for they are ruled by the power of those who confess God,
    and are honoured by the use they put them to.
And now they bound with joy,
    in a new and inestimable grace,   135
    for they know the very God, the Creator,
    not only ruling invisibly over them all
but visibly among them, sanctifying them by use.
    So much good has come into the world
    through the blessed fruit of Mary's womb.   140

*

  But, Lady, why do I only speak
of the benefits with which you fill the earth?
They go down to hell, they go up to heaven.
For through the fullness of your grace
    those in hell rejoice that they are delivered,   145
    and those in heaven are glad at that restoration.
By the glorious Son of your virginity,
    all just men who died before his birth exult
      that their captivity is broken down,
      and the angels wish each other joy   150
      in the rebuilding of their half-ruined city.

*

O woman, uniquely to be wondered at,
and to be wondered at for your uniqueness,
by you the elements are renewed, hell is redeemed,

demons are trampled down and men are saved,   155
even the fallen angels are restored to their place.
   O woman full and overflowing with grace,
     plenty flows from you
   to make all creatures green again.
   O virgin blessed and ever blessed,   160
   whose blessing is upon all nature,
not only is the creature blessed by the Creator,
but the Creator is blessed by the creature too.
   O highly exalted,
   when the love of my heart tries to follow you,   165
   whither do you escape the keenness of my sight?
   O beautiful to gaze upon,
   lovely to contemplate, delightful to love,
whither do you go to evade the breadth of my heart?
Lady, wait for the weakness of him who follows you;   170
     do not hide yourself,
   seeing the littleness of the soul that seeks you!
     Have mercy, Lady,
   upon the soul that pants after you with longing.

*

A thing to be wondered at –   175
   at what a height do I behold the place of Mary!
     Nothing equals Mary,
   nothing but God is greater than Mary.
God gave his own Son, who alone from his heart
was born equal to him, loved as he loves himself, to Mary,   180
   and of Mary was then born a Son
   not another but the same one,
that naturally one might be the Son of God and of Mary.
All nature is created by God and God is born of Mary.
God created all things, and Mary gave birth to God.   185
God who made all things made himself of Mary,
and thus he refashioned everything he had made.

He who was able to make all things out of nothing
   refused to remake it by force,
     but first became the Son of Mary.   190
So God is the Father of all created things,
  and Mary is the mother of all re-created things.
God is the Father of all that is established,
  and Mary is the mother of all that is re-established.
For God gave birth to him by whom all things were made 195
  and Mary brought forth him by whom all are saved.
God brought forth him without whom nothing is,
  Mary bore him without whom nothing is good.
O truly, 'the Lord is with you',
   to whom the Lord gave himself,   200
   that all nature in you might be in him.

*

Mary, I beg you, by that grace
through which the Lord is with you
  and you willed to be with him,
   let your mercy be with me.   205
Let love for you always be with me,
  and the care of me be always with you.
Let the cry of my need, as long as it persists,
   be with you,
and the care of your goodness, as long as I need it,   210
   be with me.
  Let joy in your blessedness be always with me,
and compassion for my wretchedness, where I need it,
   be with you.

*

O most blessed,   215
all that turns away from you, and that you oppose,
  must needs be lost,
and equally it is not possible that whatever turns to you
and you regard with favour, should perish.

For just as, Lady, God begat him   220
　　in whom all things live,
　　so, O flower of virginity,
　　you bore him by whom the dead are raised up.
And as God through his Son
　　keeps the blessed angels from sin,   225
　　so, O glory of purity,
through your Son you save unhappy men who have sinned.
For just as in some way the Son of God
　　is the bliss of the just,
　　so in some way, O rich in saving grace,   230
　　your Son is the reconciliation of sinners.
For there is no reconciliation
　　except that which you conceived in chastity,
there is no salvation
　　except what you brought forth as a virgin.   235
Therefore, Lady,
　　you are mother of justifier and the justified,
　　bearer of reconciliation and the reconciled,
　　parent of salvation and of the saved.

*

Blessed assurance, safe refuge,   240
the mother of God is our mother.
The mother of him in whom alone we have hope,
　　whom alone we fear,
　　is our mother.
The mother of him who alone saves and condemns   245
　　is our mother.

*

　　You are blessed and exalted
not for yourself alone but for us too.
What great and loving thing is this
that I see coming to us through you?   250

Seeing it I rejoice, and hardly dare to speak of it.
    For if you, Lady, are his mother,
    surely then your sons are his brothers?
    But who are the brothers and of whom?
Shall I speak out of the rejoicing of my heart,   255
or shall I be silent in case it is too high for me to mention?
    But if I believe and love
    why should I not confess it with praise?
So let me speak not out of pride but with thanksgiving.

*

For he was born of a mother to take our nature,   260
and to make us, by restoring our life, sons of his mother.
He invites us to confess ourselves his brethren.
    So our judge is our brother,
    the Saviour of the world is our brother,
and finally our God through Mary is our brother.   265
With what confidence then ought we to hope,
    and thus consoled how can we fear,
when our salvation or damnation hangs on the will
    of a good brother and a devoted mother?
With what affection should we love   270
    this brother and this mother,
with what familiarity should we commit ourselves to them,
    with what security may we flee to them!
For our good brother forgives us when we sin,
    and turns away from us what our errors deserve,   275
    he gives us what in penitence we ask.
The good mother prays and beseeches for us,
    she asks and pleads that he may hear us favourably.
She pleads with the son on behalf of the sons,
    the only-begotten for the adopted,   280
    the lord for the servants.

The good son hears the mother on behalf of his brothers,
the only-begotten for those he has adopted,
   the lord for those he has set free.

*

Mary, how much we owe you, Mother and Lady,   285
   by whom we have such a brother!
   What thanks and praise can we return to you?
   Great Lord, our elder brother,
   great Lady, our best of mothers,
teach my heart a sweet reverence in thinking of you.   290
   You are good, and so are you;
   you are gentle, and so are you.
   Speak and give my soul the gift
of remembering you with love, delighting in you,
rejoicing in you, so that I may come to you.   295
   Let me rise up to your love.
Desiring to be always with you, my heart is sick of love,
   my soul melts in me, my flesh fails.
   If only my inmost being might be on fire
   with the sweet fervour of your love,   300
so that my outer being of flesh might wither away.
   If only the spirit within me
might come close to the sweetness of your love,
so that the marrow of my body might be dried up.

*

   Lord, son of my lady,   305
   Lady, mother of my lord,
if I am not worthy of the bliss of your love,
certainly you are not unworthy of being so greatly loved.
So, most kind, do not refuse what I ask,
for though I confess I am not worthy of it,   310
   you cannot worthily refuse it.
Give me not according to my deserts when I pray,

but something that will be worth your loving.
   Give me, unworthy as I am,
   something that I can worthily give back to you.   315
If you are not willing to give according to my desire,
   at least do not refuse to give
   what I ought to give back to you.

*

Perhaps I am presumptuous to speak,
   but the goodness of you both makes me bold.   320
   So I speak thus to my lord and my lady,
   I, 'who am dust and ashes'.
Lord and Lady, surely it is much better for you to give grace
   to those who do not deserve it
   han for you to exact what is owing to you in justice?   325
The first is praise-worthy, the other is wicked injustice.
   Give us then your grace,
   so that you may receive what is owing to you.
Show me your mercy,
   for I need it and it is right for you to give it,   330
   lest I act towards you unjustly,
   which noone needs and is no good to anyone.
Be merciful to me because I ask it,
lest I be unjust towards you by whom I am cursed.
Kind Lord and Lady, do not make it difficult to pray to you, 335
   but give my soul your love,
which not unjustly it asks and you justly expect it to ask,
   lest I be ungrateful for your good gifts
because of that which in justice it shudders at
   and you not unjustly punish.   340

*

Surely Jesus, Son of God, and Mary his mother,
   you both want, and it is only right,
   that whatever you love, we should love too.

So, good Son,
I ask you through the love you have for your mother,   345
that as she truly loves you and you her
   you will grant that I may truly love her.
   Good mother,
   I ask you by the love you have for your Son,
   that, as he truly loves you and you him,   350
   you will grant that I may love him truly.
For see, I am asking what it is indeed your will to do,
for why does he not act as my sins deserve
   when it is in his power?
   Lover and ruler of mankind,   355
you could love those who accused you even to death,
and can you refuse, when you are asked,
   those who love you and your mother?
Mother of our lover who carried him in her womb
and was willing to give him milk at her breast –   360
are you not able or are you unwilling to grant your love
   to those who ask it?

                    *

So I venerate you both,
as far as my mind is worthy to do so;
   I love you both,   365
as far as my heart is equal to it;
   I prefer you both,
as much as my soul can;
   and I serve you both,
as far as my flesh may.   370
And in this let my life be consummated
that for all eternity all my being may sing
'Blessed be the Lord for ever. Amen.'

8. Prayer to St John the Baptist

St John:
you are that John who baptized God;
you were praised by an archangel
before you were begotten by your father;
   you were full of God   5
before you were born of your mother;
you knew God before you knew the world;
you showed your mother the mother bearing God
before the mother who bore you within her
   showed you the day.   10
It was of you that God said:
'Among them that are born of women
   there has not risen a greater'.
To you, sir, who are so great, holy and blessed,
   comes a guilty, creeping thing,   15
      a wretched little man
   whose senses are almost dead with grief,
and, what grieves him even more, a sinner with a dead soul.
   To you, so great a friend of God,
he comes, very fearful, doubtful of his salvation,   20
because he is sure of the greatness of his guilt,
   but hoping in your greater grace;
for your grace, sir, is greater than my guilt;
   what you are able to do before God
   will more than blot out all my wickedness.   25
   To you, then, sir,
whom grace has made such a friend of God,
   to you, in my distress, I flee.
I, the accused of God through manifold iniquities,
worth nothing because of so much misery,   30
come to you whom grace has filled with blessedness.

Truly, sir, I admit this:
    my sins have made me what I am,
but you have not made yourself what you are,
    but the grace of God with you.   35
So remember, sir,
    that as the grace of God made you so high,
    so your mercy can raise him up
    who is laid so low by his guilt.
Alas, what have I made of myself?   40
    What was I, O God, as you had made me –
    and how have I made myself again!
In sin I was conceived and born,
    but you washed me and sanctified me;
    and I have defiled myself still more.   45
Then I was born in sin of necessity,
    but now I wallow in it of my own free will.
In sin I was conceived in ignorance,
    but these sins I commit willingly, readily, and openly.
From them in mercy I was led forth by you;   50
    to these miseries I have led myself.
I was redeemed from them by goodness,
and I have broken with that redemption by wickedness.
You healed, good God, a soul wounded in its first parents;
    I, wicked man, have killed what was healed.   55
You set aside, merciful Lord, the old rags of original sin,
    and clothed me in the garments of innocence,
    promising me incorruptibility in the future;
    and casting off what you had given me,
    I busied myself with sordid sins;   60
    despising what you had promised,
I chose rather the sorrows of eternal misery.
You had made the son of your wrath
    into the son of your grace,
    and I, contemptuous of that,   65
    made myself the son of your hatred.

You refashioned your gracious image in me,
and I superimposed upon it the image that is hateful.
    Alas, alas, how could I?
How could I, miserable and crazy little man that I am,   70
  how could I superimpose that image
    upon the image of God?

*

O why did I not blush to do that which·I dread to speak of?
O why did I not loathe to imitate him
  at whose name I shudder?   75
He fell because it was his lot to do so;
  I chose to become vile.
Before him none had been punished for sin,
  and he fell through pride;
    but I, who had seen his punishment,   80
  was contemptuous of it,
    and rushed into sin.
He was created in innocence; I was restored to it.
He sinned against his maker;
  I against him who made me, and re-made me.   85
He deserted God, and God let him go;
  I fled from God, and God came with me.
He persisted in evil, cast off by God;
  I ran headlong into the same evil,
    when God was calling me back.   90
He hardened his heart when he was punished;
  I hardened mine when I was kindly treated.
So we are both set against God:
  he against him who does not want him;
  I against him who died for me.   95
O wretched man that I am –
  if indeed my humanity has not gone from me
  where such huge malice closes in.

See – I shuddered at the horror of his appearance;
and I see myself in many ways more horrible than he.   100

*

  Flee, flee,
you who are of I know not what horrible substance;
flee from yourself; be terribly afraid of yourself.
  But, alas, you cannot flee from yourself,
nor can you look at yourself, because you cannot bear it.   105
For if you could bear it, without a horror of grief,
  you would find your toleration intolerable.
Insofar as you can tolerate yourself
  you are like the first sinner,
  and thereby you are less tolerable to God,   110
  for to tolerate yourself is not courage,
  but the blunt edge of death;
  it is not health, it is hardened sin;
it comes not from consolation but from damnation.
I cannot bear the interior horror of my face   115
  without a huge groan in my heart.
  So then, I cannot fly from myself,
nor can I look at myself, for I cannot bear myself.

*

But see, it is worse still if I do not look at myself;
  for then I am deceived about myself.   120
  O too heavy weight of anguish.
If I look within myself, I cannot bear myself;
if I do not look within myself, I do not know myself.
If I consider myself, what I see terrifies me;
if I do not consider myself, I fall to my damnation.   125
If I look at myself, it is an intolerable horror;
if I do not look at myself, death is unavoidable.
  Evil here, worse there, ill on every side;
  but there is too much evil here,

too much that is worse there, 130
   too much ill on every side.
For he is very wretched whom his conscience torments,
   when he cannot flee from it;
and even more wretched is he
   who looks into his own damnation, 135
   when he is not able to avoid it;
very unhappy is he who is horrible in his own eyes;
   and more unhappy still will he be
   when he undergoes eternal death.
Very wretched is he who is continually afraid 140
   of the filthy horror of himself;
   but more wretched still will he be
whom anguish will torture eternally because of his sins.
   Evil here, and evil there;
   too much here, and too much there. 145

*

To sin – how evil and bitter that is.
Sins – how easy to commit, how hard to give up.
Sinners – so misled by sins – are caught by their fetters.
Understand, O understand how evil and bitter it is
   to have lost the Lord. 150
Sinner, turn back; refuse in your will to sin.
   Refuse, I say, refuse.
   It is evil and bitter – refuse.

*

   Truly it is evil and bitter;
   I am expert, in this I am expert indeed. 155
For either the sorrows of continual repentance
   torture my life,
or eternal torments will vex my soul to punish it.
   Both are evil, both are bitter,

and surely justly is the accused of God distressed   160
   between evil and worse,
     so much evil, among too, too much evil.
It is done justly, it is done rightly, my just judge;
   but at least you are yourself
     God, and Lord, and my Creator.   165

*

Take away, then, Creator,
   take away so much evil from your creature;
     if he is to give thanks that you made him;
Lord, snatch your servant away from so much evil,
   if he is to rejoice to have you as his Lord.   170
Spare, God, spare your sinner,
   if he is not to despair of your goodness.
For even if I have sinned more than the first sinner
I do not hate you as he does, nor detest your goodness.

*

Then, by the great merit of your Baptizer,   175
   renew in me the grace of your baptizing.
Go before me with your grace; follow me with your mercy.
Give me back through the sorrow of penitence
what you had given through the sacrament of baptism.
Give to me who asks,   180
   what you gave to him who knew you not.
Refashion the face that I have spoiled,
   restore the innocence that I have violated.
You, Lord, were not involved in that sin
   which you were born to bear.   185
Lord, take away the sin that I have contracted in living.
Take away, you who take away the sin of the world,
   these which are sins of the world,
     which I carry from living in the world.
Take away, you who take away the sin of the world,   190

by the merits of him who with that same word of witness
   pointed you out to the world,
take away the sins that I have contracted in the world;
   take from me whatever is not from you,
for I hate whatever is from me; and still I hope in you.   195
And you, St John,
   who showed to the world
   him who takes away the sin of the world,
   by the grace given to you
gain for me that mercy to take away my sins.   200

*

You, God, take away the sin of the world,
   and you, his friend, say,
   'Here is he who takes away the sin of the world.
Behold, before you,
   him who is burdened with the sin of the world.'   205
You bear the sin – and you proclaim that he bears it.
Behold me, whose sin you bear as John proclaims.
Behold, healer, and the healer's witness, here am I –
behold, the sick servant of the healer and his work
   petitions here the healer and his witness.   210
   True healer, I pray you heal me;
   true witness, I beg you to pray for me.
   Reconcile me to myself,
   you by your action, you by your words.
Let me prove what I hear, let me experience what I believe. 215
Jesus, good Lord,
   if you perform the work that he testifies of you,
John, revealer of God, if you witness to what he performs,
   be it to me according to your word.
Lord, from whom comes healing, heal me.   220
Do this for me, Lord, since you are able to do it,
     you are the great Lord,
and you, John, are 'great in the sight of the Lord'.

You can do all things by your own nature;
   you are very powerful before him.   225
You are the high and good God,
   and you are the very good friend
of him who is in eternity the merciful and blessed God.
                                Amen.

9. Prayer to St Peter

Holy and most kind Peter,
faithful shepherd of the flock of God,
chief of the apostles,
prince among such mighty princes.
You are able to bind and loose as you will;   5
you are able to heal and raise up as you will;
you can give the kingdom of heaven to whom you will.
    Great Peter,
rich with so many and such great gifts,
high in so many and such great dignities,   10
    here am I,
the poorest and weakest of men,
surrounded by many difficulties and hardships.
In my misery I need the help of your power and kindness,
but I have no words to express my need as it really is,   15
    and my love is not great enough to reach up
from such a depth as mine to such a height as yours.

*

Again and again I try
to shake the lethargy from my mind,
    to prevent my thoughts   20
    from being scattered among vanities,
but when I have gathered together all my strength
    I am not able to break out of the shadows
    of the torpor that holds me
    because of the filth of my sins.   25
Nor do I have the strength
    to remain for long of the same mind.
    I am the most wretched of wretches.
It really is so, it is not pretence, it is true.

Who is there to help a wretch   30
who has not the strength to express his trouble in words
    or show the sorrow of his heart?

                              *

    O great Peter,
if the cry of my trouble does not come up as far as you,
let the care of your goodness come down as far as me!   35
Shatter my hardness, shine on my darkness,
    look upon my wretchedness!
    Have a care, kind shepherd,
for the lamb of the flock committed unto you,
and have mercy on the misery in which he toils.   40
Do not make demands according to his wickedness,
but make allowance according to his prayer.

                              *

    See now, the sickly sheep,
lies groaning at the shepherd's feet;
he comes before the Lord of the shepherd and the sheep.   45
    The runaway returns
and asks forgiveness for his errors and disobedience.
He shows to the good and healing shepherd
    the gashes of wounds, and the bites of wolves,
    which he ran into when he strayed,   50
    and the neglected sore places
    that he has had for a long time.
He begs him to have mercy while there is still life in him,
and he prays more by showing his need
    to the merciful shepherd   55
    than by any beseeching.

                              *

    Peter, good shepherd,
do not be difficult of access;
do not turn away your merciful eyes.

Have a care, I pray you,   60
  lest you throw down the penitent,
  and delay to hear a suppliant.
Because his soul loathes the life-giving pasture,
  he grows weak for lack of strength;
  because he indulges in what is unhealthy,   65
  he attracts tormenting diseases.
  Full-grown ulcers, open wounds, putrid decay,
  draw him swiftly to death.
Wolves have tasted his blood and now they lie in ambush,
  watching, and plotting his overthrow.   70
  His enemy, 'as a roaring lion', goes about seeking him,
  so that he 'may devour him'.
Faithful shepherd, look upon him,
and recognize that he has been committed to you.
He may have strayed but at least it is not he   75
  who has denied his Lord and Shepherd.
Consider his appearance
  and see the sign of your Lord and his.
If, under so much filth, you do not recognize
a face washed and made white at the font of Christ,   80
see at least that he confesses the name of Christ.
Remember that Christ asked you three times
  if you loved him,
  and when three times you confessed it
  he said to you, 'Feed my sheep'.   85
  He is indeed a lover of the sheep
  who thus sifts the love of the shepherd
  before committing them to him.
When you had confessed that you loved him,
  then he confided his sheep to you.   90
  How, then, can his shepherd spurn his sheep?
Peter, shepherd of Christ,
  gather up the lamb of Christ.

Your Lord sought and found him,
and bore him on his shoulders, rejoicing;   95
do not repel him now he comes back and prays.
The Lord bought him with his own blood
  before he was born;
Christ's shepherd should not value him lightly
  now he is reborn   100
  and so diligently commended to him.
Alas, how long shall I not know
that I am received, healed, and cherished?

*

  St Peter,
if the names shepherd and sheep do not move you,   105
prince of the apostles, let the name of apostle
and the name of a Christian soul, do so.
The sheep I am offering you
  is my soul reborn by baptism in Christ.
Those wounds of which I spoke, those ulcers, those weals, 110
  are not in the flesh of a sheep but in a rational being.
This hunger, this lack of strength, these sufferings,
  are not in the belly of a sheep but in a human soul.
These wolves and lions are not animals but demons;
  these ills come from poverty in virtue and heaped up sins. 115

*

I do not feel that I have yet obtained a favourable hearing,
  so with urgent anguish
  I will repeat my story from the beginning,
  and begin my prayers over again.
To the door-keeper of the kingdom of heaven,   120
  the prince of the apostles,
I will show a faithful soul, unhappy in the kingdom of sin,
  longing for the kingdom of heaven;

138

and in this way I will call upon Peter,
door-keeper of heaven, prince of the apostles.   125

*

In your presence, merciful Peter,
I show you my soul, the strength of its virtue dissolved,
     bound by the chains of sin,
       weighed down by a burden of vices,
       stinking and dirty with misdeeds,   130
     torn by the wounds of devils,
       festering and filthy with the ulcers of crimes.
By these and other grave ills, which you see better than I,
     I am destitute, oppressed, surrounded,
       overwhelmed, and relieved of all good.   135
See, here is a soul needing mercy,
     and here is the merciful apostle Peter
       before the God of mercy,
     who had mercy upon the apostle Peter
and taught him what to do and gave him power to do it.   140
     See, here is misery, and there is mercy,
       the mercy of God and his apostle Peter,
and a soul in misery, confiding in God, and calling upon
     God and his apostle Peter.
This soul, weighed down for so long by its misery,   145
     looks towards God and Peter;
will it see now the mercy of God and of Peter?

*

O God, and you his greatest apostle,
     is this misery of mine so huge
that it cannot be met by the wideness of your mercy?   150
     Or if it can, but will not,
       what is the enormity of my guilt
       that exceeds the multitude of your mercies?
Is it that I have not confessed the whole of my sin?

Truly, I have confessed all that I know of my sins.   155
   Or is it because I do not make amends
     by sufficient penitence?
   Or because the good in me does not equal the bad?
I acknowledge that all this is true,
but this is the very misery by which I am tormented.   160
Is it true, then, that the more I am oppressed by misery,
   the more mercy will tarry?
That is an unheard-of word from one who is merciful
   to one who prays.

*

   And yet, just God,   165
I understand what reply you make to my soul:
   I deserve to suffer
because I have sinned of my own free will,
I do not deserve to be heard because I have disobeyed.
   Ah, how bitter it is to be without hope!   170
That, surely, is the sentence of justice, not of mercy,
   and who calls on justice in my cause?
   My talk was of mercy, not of justice.
In the wretched tribulation of my soul
   I beg of you, my God, the bread of mercy;   175
why do you press the stone of justice into my mouth?
   Let your mercy, merciful God,
and the intercession of your dear apostle, blessed Peter,
   hasten to free me, my sins being forgiven.
   St Peter, prince of the apostles,   180
   by the mercy shown you and the power given you,
   loose my chains, heal my wounds.
Free me from the misery of the kingdom of sin,
and lead me into the bliss of the kingdom of heaven,
   where rejoicing with you   185
I may give thanks and praise God for ever. Amen.

10. Prayer to St Paul

St Paul, great Paul:
one of the great apostles of God.
You followed after all the rest in time,
but you surpassed them in labours and in effect
    in the husbandry of God.   5
While you were still weighed down by the flesh
you were rapt 'even to the third heaven',
and heard 'things that cannot be said by men'.
Among Christians you were like a nurse
    who not only cared for her sons,   10
    but in some way brought them forth a second time,
    with careful and marvellous tenderness.
You were 'made all things to all men'
    so that 'you might gain all'.
Sir, you are known to the world   15
    by these and many other words and deeds
    to be of great power before God
    and of immense pity towards men:
to you I come, certainly a very great sinner
    and greatly accused before God,   20
    the powerful and strict judge.
Not by one, nor by a few am I accused,
    but by innumerable offences;
not by small ones, but by those that are very great;
    not in doubt, but quite certainly;   25
not by a short accusation, but by one that is long as life,
not by one accuser, but by as many as know my sins.
    For the judge himself is my stern accuser
    and I am clearly a sinner against him.
Moreover all spirits, good and evil, accuse me   30
    in the presence of God.

The good because they owe justice to God;
   the evil because they serve my injustice.
The good, because they bear witness
   to the truth that they look to;   35
the evil, because they seek my punishment
   which they look for.
They both judge my iniquity in this,
   because they know that according to justice
      I deserve to be damned.   40
Alas, how many judges, how many accusers
   over one miserable man!
Alas, how hard they are on a fool,
   how closely they look into what is manifest.
Alas, who will make excuse for him whom God accuses?   45
   Or which one will be an intercessor for him,
   if all are his accusers and judges?

*

But even more since I know my guilt,
   I will be my own accuser and judge.
For I confess that I have sinned more than enough   50
   and therefore deserve a heavy condemnation.
Even that which is irrational and insensible condemns me,
   if I am not insensitive.
For I understand that I ought to blush
   before the face of all creatures,   55
   for I have sinned against him
   who had the power to make them
   and the goodness to will to do so.
And I am condemned by myself, too,
   for I also was made by him.   60
Alas, whence have so many and so great evils poured in,
   that so rush down upon a wretch?

*

My evil sins, it is from you that all these ills flow into me.
You encourage those who would make accusation;
You discourage those that would make excuse.   65
   You lead on the ones who condemn;
   you shut out those who intercede.
   You call forth vengeance;
   you turn away pardon.
You lead me on by your enticements to fear and confusion;   70
you tear away from me hope and consolation;
   you push me on to eternal ruin;
   you keep away from me all help;
   and to increase my wretched state
   you add this crowning unhappiness –   75
that while it is all true, yet it does not seem so to me.

*

   In fact, if I did see the reality
   I should not feel it or be moved by it.
Reason teaches this, but my heart does not grieve.
   I see this because it is so,   80
   and alas that I do not dissolve entirely in tears
   because it is so.
If only I could do that, perhaps I might hope;
     hoping, I might pray;
     praying, I might obtain.   85
When truly, because of my wretchedness,
   feeling and grief are not in me,
   how can I hope?
   Without hope, how can I pray?
   And without prayer, what can I obtain?   90

*

   Unhappy little man that I am!
   What has become of my prayer?
   Where have my hope and faith vanished to?

143

I began to pray with the hope of rashness,
   and despair soon made me understand   95
   the truth of my state;
   my prayer itself slackened
because I could not hope in the goodness of anyone.
For if whatever is just is against me,
   whose goodness is with me?   100
If all things that are right are turned against me,
   who in pity will turn towards me?
If Creator and creatures rightly look down on me,
   who will turn his gaze towards me?
Unhappy sinner, if this is so, nothing is left to you   105
except to be inert about hope and silent about prayer,
and thus always to lie down in your misery.
Since of your own accord you have made yourself wretched,
in justice it is right that you should always be wretched.

*

Is it thus, unhappy sins, that you keep your promises?   110
   When you drew me on, you promised sweetness;
when it was done, and I was in your power,
   you filled me with bitterness.
When you were persuading, you were gentle with me;
   when you had persuaded, you stabbed my soul to death. 115
When you called me into your trap you showed me
   that it was easy to get out by the grief of penitence;
in fact, when I rushed in headlong I fell and was buried.
   Buried, I was blinded; blinded, I was hardened;
   when I was hardened, all ways out were closed against me. 120
And thus, the wretch you have deceived and captured
   you make fast in despair,
   to be silent and lie insensible,
   as if lost to God and forgetting God,
   until he is sold to the merchants of hell,   125
who collect their merchandise in the lake of death.

All this you have done to me;
    I am expert in all these matters,
even if I am not yet handed over to those merchants.
That is both what I expect at last in my miserable fear   130
    and what they wait for with wicked delight.
Alas, how evil it is to despair and to be silent like this;
and alas, how vain it is to cry out without hope,
        to strive without hope.

*

God, whose goodness is not exhausted,   135
    whose mercy is not emptied out,
    whose knowledge does not fail,
    whose power can effect what you will;
whence shall I ever be able to get back life,
who have thus been driven desperate by my sins?   140
    For if you are angry against sinners,
at least, kind Lord, you are accustomed to give counsel
    to those who plead with you.
Teach me, O Lord, whence I ought to hope,
    so that I can pray.   145
    For I long to pray to you;
    but I neither know how because of my ignorance,
    nor am I able to because of my hardness.
And I am forbidden to do it by despair because of my sins.
I seek for something that will excuse me,   150
    and there is nothing that does not accuse me.
I seek for someone who will pray for me,
    and I find whatever exists is against me.
I seek for someone to have mercy upon a wretch,
    and all that has being opposes the wretch.   155

*

    Jesus, good Lord,
why did you come down from heaven,
what did you do in the world,

to what end did you give yourself over to death,
unless it was that you might save sinners? 160
St Paul, what did you teach
   when you were passing through the world?
   God, and his apostles, and you most of all,
   invite us sinners to faith;
   you show us this as our only safe refuge. 165
How then should I not hope, if I believe this,
   and ask in this faith?
How can this hope be frustrated in me,
   if that faith does not fail me
   from which it was born? 170

*

Jesus, God, and you his apostle,
I, a sinner, believe in this faith by your command;
   on this I throw myself;
   indeed I have already thrown myself.
Thus clothed I have access to you when I pray. 175
   In this faith I ask, I seek, I knock,
   that you may both have mercy upon a sinner,
   that you, Lord, may spare, and you, Paul, may intercede;
   you save and you pray.
Before you both I wrap myself in this faith, 180
   so that I may be hidden
   from those who would search out my sins
   and exact their deserts,
   and from your buffeting, O God, my stern judge.
A sinner asks by your counsel to be concealed; 185
I beg you, do not reveal him, by your justice,
     to damnation.

*

But alas, I fall into yet another heavy ill.
   I thought to get hope through faith,
and lo, I see that I have no hold upon faith. 190

146

I had thought myself to be clothed in this faith,
   and I know myself to be without it.
I was confident that I was concealed in it,
   and I know myself to be far from it.
   For 'faith without works is dead';   195
   in truth, dead faith is not faith.
   He then who has dead faith has no faith.
Alas, the fertility of evil works forbids me to have hope;
and sterility of good works proves me to be without faith.
   Alas, the evil I have done!   200
   Alas, the good I have neglected to do!
   For if it is necessary that by evil works
   God should be displeased;
   then it is impossible without faith,
   which counts for nothing without good works,   205
      to please God.

*

But if 'the just man lives by faith',
   whoever has no faith is dead.
But those who are sterile in good are dead;
then how much more dead are those who are fertile in evil? 210
For if 'the tree that does not bear good fruit'
   is cut down, as being withered;
   that which bears bad fruit will even more
      be rooted up as evil.
For this is death, not of the flesh, but of the soul.   215
How great and how much worse it is to die that death
   than to die the death of the flesh.
For at the last all who die in human flesh rise again;
   but all who die in the spirit rise not.
And that death destroys more by taking away a life   220
   that perhaps can never be restored
than when it takes away life because necessity demands it.
It is worse to cease from a life of righteousness,

through which one loses the life of bliss,
    than to let go of this miserable bodily life.   225
Finally and much more miserably does he perish
    who goes forth from the life of the spirit,
        that, if it had been preserved,
could restore to the body a better life in place of the life lost,
and without which it were better not to have been born,   230
than he who only loses the life of the body,
without which nothing prevents the soul from being blessed.
    I live this unhappy life,
I am dead to that life of blessedness.
    I live in that which is vile to me,   235
and I am dead to that which is better.
    I am more dead than alive,
and I am worse dead than I shall be when I die in the flesh;
    for that death will not be evil to me
        unless the other precede it.   240

*

St Paul, I came to you as a sinner to be reconciled,
    and lo, when I am in your presence
    I find that I am a dead man to be raised.
I came as one accused, in need of an intercessor,
    and I find rather that I am a dead man   245
    needing to be restored to life.
As a wretch I came, and I find I am the most wretched of all.
    I came to you as one living and accused;
    and lo, before you I am dead and condemned.
Even if I am not yet handed over   250
    to the torments of eternal death,
    even now I am abandoned to the spiritual death
        that draws to the other.
Even if it is not yet permitted that I be thrust down
    into the prison of tortures,   255
    already I am confined in a trap of sins.

For however much up till now
I may not have been buried in hell,
I am even now wound in the grave-clothes of sin.

*

Certainly neither could I pray, nor did I know how.   260
  This was true, because I understood
  that I was cursed by all things,
  and I did not grieve, as if unfeeling.
  I knew through my rational nature,
    but I did not understand;   265
    death had made me insensitive.
Indeed I was dead, and as a dead man I have come to you;
  it is only now that I have realized that I am dead.

*

O God, who will pray for such a dead man?
St Paul, I have carried him before you;   270
  do not turn him away;
    pray on his behalf.
Lord, Elijah and Elisha brought the dead to life.
  They joined themselves to the dead limbs
  and brought the living from death.   275
Lord, these came to life by the living touching the dead,
  and the dead only came to life to your glory.
Sir, you once said yourself that you 'were made all things
    to all men, that you might gain all'.
Friend of God, the example of others makes me bold,   280
  your words draw me to have confidence.
So I say, 'Sir, sir, come down upon this dead man;
  stretch yourself upon this dead man;
make yourself not dead, but like the dead man.
  Let the caress of your compassionate touch   285
    make the dead man warm;

let the working of your power revive the dead man,
that the dead man may live to glorify God and you.'

*

Sir, you are not powerless to raise the dead,
   for by the witness of God   290
   the 'grace of God is sufficient for you'.
For if when you lived on earth it was sufficient for you,
   now that you stay in heaven
   it will not be insufficient for you.
Why, sir, should what is offered to you   295
   be any longer cast down,
   dead without life,
   when God attests your power
   and you could attest his goodness?
Lord God, you said to Paul, 'My grace is sufficient for you'. 300
   St Paul, you said, 'I can do all things';
   and see, the effect of your words is that this dead man
   waits for this hope to be realized.
You have spoken, and hearing you the dead man hopes.
You have promised, and the dead man desires to pray.   305
You have spoken and by you it will be accomplished.
I beg you, let me experience the granting of that
which the world rejoices to have known through you.
   If you do not refuse to speak,
   why do you refuse to grant what is asked?   310
Or is there anyone to whom the dead man can more safely
   be carried to be brought back to life,
   if when he is offered to you, he is brought back dead?
   To whom will you send him if you send him away?
   Whither shall he go if he is sent away from you?   315
O God, who can bring back to life if God does not?
From whom shall he receive back the life he has lost
if not from him from whom he first received it?
In whom is there hope if there is no hope in God?

St Paul, who will be good to the poor and sorrowful   320
  if he who promised to be weak with the weak be hard?
Who will deign to pray for sinners if he disdains it
  who proclaimed himself to be made all things to all men?
Or who will be heard if he is not heard,
  to whom the grace of God is sufficient?   325
If goodness and power are deficient in him,
  in whom is the grace of God sufficient?

*

O you two, what will move you if all this does not?
  Who will take up that which I offer you
  to excite your mercy if you do not?   330
Dead soul, what can you show about yourself
  that is not sinful and wretched?
  Yet I pray, repenting and grieving.

*

O, if he who came from heaven to call sinners to repentance,
and he who after him in this same thing   335
laboured more than all,
if these condemn a penitent soul because a sinner,
if he who came from the Father's heart to carry our sorrows,
and he who called himself weak with the weak,
if they despise sorrow because it is wretched,   340
if he who gave himself over to death
that dead souls might live,
and he who asserted that he was made all things to all men,
if they reject this prayer because it is dead –
  let it not be so, God, let it not be so.   345
  Keep that away, let it not be so.
  If it is so, compassion has perished,
  If it is so, pity is dead.

*

O soul, thrown backward and forward –
when you sin you are thrown forward,   350
when you pray you are thrown back,
    whither shall you turn?
Turn yourself to importunity.
To be importuned by one who suffers, this is what they seek.
They love those who lament unceasingly before them.   355
    Then do you seek this,
and show this to them without flagging.

*

O St Paul, where is he that was called
the nurse of the faithful, caressing his sons?
Who is that affectionate mother who declares everywhere   360
that she is in labour for her sons?
    Sweet nurse, sweet mother,
who are the sons you are in labour with, and nurse,
but those whom by teaching the faith of Christ
    you bear and instruct?   365
    Or who is a Christian after your teaching
who is not born into the faith and established in it by you?
    And if in that blessed faith we are born
    and nursed by other apostles also,
    it is most of all by you,   370
for you have laboured and done more than them all in this;
so if they are our mothers, you are our greatest mother.

*

So then, St Paul, your son is this dead man.
Mother, this dead man is certainly your son.
Dear mother, recognize your son   375
    by the voice of his confession;
    he recognizes his mother by her loving compassion.
Recognize your son by his confession of Christianity;
    he recognizes his mother by the sweetness of goodness.

O mother, you who again give birth to your sons,   380
   offer your dead son again, to be raised up by him
   who by his death gives life to his servants.
O mother, offer your son to him
   who by his death, which was not owing,
   called back his condemned ones   385
     from the death that was their due;
that he may call back to him the life he has lost.
   By baptism he was led out of death;
by barrenness and corruption he is led back into death.
   O mother, well known for your love,   390
   your son knows the heart of a mother's goodness.
     Show him to God,
you who have brought him back to life
     and cared for him living.
Pray to him for your son, who is his servant;   395
pray to him for his servant, who is your son.

                 *

And you, Jesus, are you not also a mother?
   Are you not the mother who, like a hen,
   gathers her chickens under her wings?
Truly, Lord, you are a mother;   400
   for both they who are in labour
   and they who are brought forth
     are accepted by you.
You have died more than they, that they may labour to bear.
   It is by your death that they have been born,   405
   for if you had not been in labour,
     you could not have borne death;
and if you had not died, you would not have brought forth.
   For, longing to bear sons into life,
     you tasted of death,   410
   and by dying you begot them.
You did this in your own self,

your servants by your commands and help.
You as the author, they as the ministers.
So you, Lord God, are the great mother.   415

*

Then both of you are mothers.
Even if you are fathers, you are also mothers.
For you have brought it about that those born to death
   should be reborn to life –
you by your own act, you by his power.   420
Therefore you are fathers by your effect
   and mothers by your affection.
Fathers by your authority, mothers by your kindness.
Fathers by your teaching, mothers by your mercy.
Then you, Lord, are a mother,   425
   and you, Paul, are a mother too.
If in quantity of affection you are unequal,
   yet in quality you are not unalike.
Though in the greatness of your kindness
   you are not co-equal,   430
   yet in will you are of one heart.
Although you have not equal fullness of mercy,
   yet in intention you are not unequal.

*

Why should I be silent about what you have said?
Why should I conceal what you have revealed?   435
Why should I hide what you have done?
   You have revealed yourselves as mothers;
      I know myself to be a son.
   I give thanks that you brought me forth as a son
      when you made me a Christian: 440
   you, Lord, by yourself, you, Paul, through him;
      you by the doctrine you made,
      you by the doctrine breathed into you.

You by the grace you have granted to me,
　　you by the grace you accepted from him.　　　445
　Paul, my mother, Christ bore you also;
so place your dead son at the feet of Christ, your mother,
　　because he also is Christ's son.
Rather, throw him into the heart of Christ's goodness,
　　for Christ is even more his mother.　　　450
　Pray that he will give life to a dead son,
　　who is not so much yours as his.
St Paul, pray for your son, because you are his mother,
　that the Lord, who is his mother too,
　　may give life to his son.　　　455
Do, mother of my soul,
　what the mother of my flesh would do.
At least, if I may hope, I may pray as much as I can;
　nor cease until I obtain what I can.
Certainly, if you will, you need not despair;　　　460
　and if you pray, you are able to obtain.
Ask then, that this dead soul which you brought to life,
　may be restored to life,
nor cease until he is given back to you, living.

*

And you, my soul, dead in yourself,　　　465
run under the wings of Jesus your mother
and lament your griefs under his feathers.
Ask that your wounds may be healed
and that, comforted, you may live again.

*

　Christ, my mother,　　　470
you gather your chickens under your wings;
this dead chicken of yours puts himself under those wings.
For by your gentleness the badly frightened are comforted,
　by your sweet smell the despairing are revived,

your warmth gives life to the dead,   475
your touch justifies sinners.
Mother, know again your dead son,
both by the sign of your cross and the voice of his confession.
Warm your chicken, give life to your dead man,
    justify your sinner.   480
Let your terrified one be consoled by you;
despairing of himself, let him be comforted by you;
and in your whole and unceasing grace
let him be refashioned by you.
For from you flows consolation for sinners;   485
to you be blessing for ages and ages. Amen.

11. Prayer to St John the Evangelist (1)

by a man fearful of damnation

Holy and blessed John,
  chief of the evangelists of God,
  best beloved of the apostles of God.
You were pre-eminent in the love of God
  among so many who were eminently loved,   5
  so that outstanding love
  was your characteristic sign amongst them all.
John, who reclined familiarly
  on the glorious breast of the Most High;
God gave you to his mother as her son in place of himself   10
  when he left her at bodily death.
To you, blessed one, so loving and so loved of God,
  this little man who is accused of God
    appeals with prayers,
  so that by the intercession of one so loved   15
he may turn from himself the threat of the wrath of God.
  For, sir, because of his sins he needs must
  seek someone to intervene for him,
and he runs to that well-known friendship of yours
  with him whom he fears as an avenger.   20
I know, sir, what power you have
  through that same friendship
  by which you can do what you wish before God.
I hope in your goodness,
  for you will not turn away from a sinner   25
  who calls to you in anguish.
I turn to you, although I am so dull,
  yet with all the love of my heart,
and I presume to ask your powerful intercession
    for my sinful soul,   30

so that you may draw it back from those torments
   to which it is being drawn away
      by evils of every kind.

            *

But alas for my wretched state,
   how my sins cry out against me!   35
For lo, when I try to find comfort
   in your friendship with God,
I am compelled to hold back from that very friendship
   because of my sin against God.
Beloved of God,   40
   because I have sinned against your beloved,
I am certain that I have deserved your hatred also.
O immoderate offence, offence against God,
      that offends not only him,
but also those who are able to intercede before him.   45
Indeed an offence against God deserves to be hated
   by the friends of God,
   and not only by his friends,
   but by himself and all his creatures.
Sins, sins, the more considered,   50
   the more horrible you become!
Where are you carrying him away to, whither do you take
   this miserable little man whom you have seduced?
Where does he fall to, where will he be cast down to,
   this unhappy soul who follows you?   55
What does he lose, I say, what hardships does he endure,
who is forced away by your malice from the love of God
   to which he could hold by innocence,
to become abhorred of God and all his creatures?

           *

If sins draw down upon themselves   60
   such universal execration
   for those whom they drag away from God,

where can he hide himself, to whom can he show himself,
this little man weighed down by the pack of his sins
    which he is not able to put off,   65
with horrible and stinking wounds and sores of his sins
    which he is not able to heal?
It is such a one that appeals to you, John, beloved of God.
    Such is my soul that appeals openly to you.
No – rather, this is my misery,   70
that I am on such friendly terms with the world,
    and weighed down by so many sins,
    that I have made myself an enemy of God.

*

    Alas, that is a name abhorred by all things,
        the name of 'enemy of God'!   75
How evil draws it to me, how justly it is imputed to me!
Alas, the truth of the matter convicts me
    as an enemy of God,
but a great horror prevents me from avowing it.
Alas, I have provoked God and all things to vengeance,   80
and there is nothing left that is not offended
    to intercede for me.
    Grief, sorrow, groans, sighs,
where are you present if here you are absent?
Where are you fervent if here you are tepid?   85
Let my limbs be wrenched apart by torments,
    let my inside be consumed with dryness,
    let there be uproar in my inmost being,
if only he will look upon my misery with compassion!
    O you compassionate friends of God,   90
    have compassion upon one so needy,
by that same compassion that God had towards you!
      Come to my help,
lest the wrath of God overwhelm me with his enemies!

I refuse, I detest, I loathe, being or being called   95
   an enemy of God,
although I confess that I have sinned against him.
  If only someone would help me!

*

  John, that disciple whom Jesus loved,
if you will acknowledge that as your title,   100
I will pray to you by that same love:
I acknowledge my great need of your help.
  John, John,
if you are that disciple whom Jesus loved,
  I pray you, by that very thing,   105
let me, by your prayers,
  be that sinner whom Jesus forgives.
  If that glorious breast
  was a familiar place for you to lean upon,
  I ask that through you it may become to me   110
  a place of salvation.
I confess, sir, beloved of God, that you are right to be angry
with one who has sinned against your beloved God,
but it is certain that the Lord will spare a suppliant servant
  for the sake of his friend.   115
  Therefore, O blessed John,
  endowed with so much love before God,
his accused servant implores you to reconcile him to him.
Beloved of God, it is not contrary to the love of God
  if you help one of his accused,   120
not by defending him, but by interceding for him.
  I do not ask you to defend my iniquity,
  nor do I want it defended,
but I make confession of it and seek for intervention.
  Friend of God   125
  do not count him God's enemy or yours
who, with as much love as he can, confesses and believes

God to be your friend.
  I believe and confess it,
and I want to love such a great love   130
  as was granted you by God.
I ask you, by the grace that was given you,
  turn away from me the hatred of God which is my due.
Do this, sir, for the sake of that love of yours.
Do this because I am his handiwork,   135
  his servant, and his redeemed.
Do this therefore for his sake and in his presence,
  lest what he has created be lost,
  lest what he has redeemed perish.
Do this as you truly love his work,   140
  and confess his blessed name.

*

Jesus, against whom I have grievously sinned,
  Lord, whom I have wickedly despised,
Omnipotent God, whose anger I have stirred up by pride;
  you are the lover of John, your blessed apostle,   145
  and to him your terrified accused flees.
Your sinner, your offender, however great his wickedness,
  however great his disgrace,
  holds the name of your beloved
between him and the threatening sentence   150
  of your just judgement.
By that blessed love spare him who seeks John's protection.
Lord, by what name will you have mercy upon sinners
  if you condemn someone who prays
  by the name of your beloved?   155
  Lord, under what cover is there protection,
if under the name of your beloved there is punishment?
Where is there refuge if with your beloved there is peril?
Lord, do not feel hatred for him who flees to your beloved.
Lord, Lord, do not let my iniquity avail for damnation   160

more than his grace avails for mercy!
Good Lord, do not let your hatred of me
mean the loss of the work of your hands,
    but let your beloved avail
      to spare the servant you have redeemed.   165
Most kind God, who 'hatest nothing that you have made',
    behold what you have made and redeemed.
Why then will you damn him, Lord, who accuses himself
    and calls upon you, if you do not hate him?
Do this then, Lord, on behalf of him whom you loved most 170
    among your disciples,
    so that you may not condemn me,
    for you only are the Saviour,
    may you be blessed for ever. Amen.

12. Prayer to St John the Evangelist (2)

to ask for the love of God and those near him.

St John,
one of the great apostles of God,
one of the great lords of the kingdom of God,
one of those who are very rich in love,
loving God, and loved by him,   5
the richest in love of those whom God loves.
John, wealthy with such blessed riches,
and rich with such blessed wealth.
See, here is a soul that is wretched but Christian,
poor, and in need of those riches with which you are rich.   10
Hungry, I plead at the gate of your clemency,
a beggar, I ask alms of your rich store.
Out of that which is able to satisfy you and many
without being diminished
at least share with me as much as will enable me to live.   15
Rich friend of God,
grant to the soul of a poor servant of God who loves you
from the wealthy store-room of your heart
that which is little to you but great to me,
easy to you, vital to me;   20
give me alms, that my Lord who has been pleased
to enrich you in order to make many rich
may deign through you to revive even this dying life.
My soul is poor, my lord, beloved of our Lord;
I am forced to confess it and I blush to do so.   25
It is poor in the love of God in both ways –
it loves God so much less than it ought,
and it has so much less of the love of God than it needs.
Of course, I confess that on the one hand I am most unjust
and on the other that God is just;   30

in both ways I know myself to be very wretched
 in the just judgement of God.

*

 Just and merciful God, when I say this,
I am not forgetting the many good gifts of your love
 from the beginning of my creation,   35
 nor am I ungrateful for them,
but my soul will always call itself poor and needy
until it is filled with your love in both ways.
 Indeed that is in itself the best,
the most gracious of all your benefits to me,   40
that the sweet taste of you here has aroused desire in me,
 so that 'my soul refuses to be consoled'
 except by your fullness.
It is not enough to pray for this
 by the poor love of this sinner of yours;   45
 to obtain this I call upon the merits of one
 who loves you much and is loved by you.
Therefore you who are good with sweetness
 and sweet with goodness,
 from whom all good things do come,   50
make him favourable to me and you to him,
 or rather may you both hear my entreaties,
 so that through you both I may follow on
 to be filled with the good that I desire.
Lord, I know and admit that I am not worthy of your love, 55
but surely you are not unworthy of my love?
Therefore grant to me, Lord,
by the merits of him from whom you have honour,
that I may be made worthy out of my unworthiness.
But he prays for me more powerfully,   60
 for he is able to do more,
 he whom you love, Lord Jesus.
 Leaning on your dear heart he prays for me,

and there you hear my desire,
through him who is close to you.   65

*

St John, dear to Jesus Christ, my Lord,
   the servant of your friend begs you,
according to the name of his Lord, your beloved,
to obtain for him that two-fold love of God.
   Get for me, I beg you, grace   70
   so that I may be worthy to love him
   as I am loved by him.
For surely, friend of God, if he loves us because of you,
   he will pay out mercy to us;
and if we love him through you,   75
   he will repay that with grace.
Surely, sir, if you turn him to loving us,
   you make us that much more your debtors,
   and if you bring us near to loving him,
   you yourself repay all our debt.   80
And surely, blessed John, however much you do
   to make him love others,
   there will be no less love for you;
   and whatever you do to make others love him,
   so much the more you repay that debt.   85
   Then have mercy, sir, upon your suppliant,
so that I may be indebted to you for so much good
   and you may restore to God a soul.
   Do this, sir, I beseech you, do this,
for if you refuse, nothing but damnation will result;   90
   but save your servant by your grace
   that he may come to the glory of God.

*

   Good and most dear disciple,
why should you, so rich, refuse one so poor,

165

you, so powerful, refuse this request 95
   which brings evil to no one
   and is liable to lead to so much good?
For if my sins stand in the way of that which I desire,
why do not your merits assist my prayers the more?
Are my sins potent for ill, and your merits impotent to help? 100
Let it not be so, sir, lest I be compelled to realize
   that which I shudder even to say.
Why should my petition be refused
   on account of my sins,
when I ask not trusting in my own deserts but yours? 105
Why, I say, when the merits that are offered to him
   are greater than the sins that offend him?
   For I am sure, sir, that if you will
your grace will count for so much before God who loves you
   that he will forgive my sins 110
   and by loving me he will make me his beloved.

*

So do this, blessed John,
so that he who loves you may also love me,
through the wideness of that love which you taught,
   and which you have, 115
   and by which you envy no one,
but rather wish that the good you rejoice in
   may belong to all men.
Do this in exchange for the love that you owe him,
so that you may set free for him even my love with yours, 120
   for you owe him not only your love
   but that of many more.
   Therefore, blessed John,
you are experienced in that blessedness of yours,
for just as no one is able to give to God 125
   before he is in debt,
so no one can give back more than he is in debt for.

So however many love God, your lover, through you,
they will not be able to balance the debt.
I beg you, sir, do not reject one who asks   130
    to be numbered among them.
Kindle love in my darkness and make me glow.
    Help me to shine, hear my prayer.

*

Lord Jesus, by whom I long to be loved,
John, whose intercession I ask,   135
    my desire constrains me thus
    so that my heart desires to constrain you;
indeed not against your own will but of your own accord,
    not unwillingly but willingly.
    Therefore suffer me and spare me,   140
    if what love plans, love may enforce.
Sustain me, I say,
    because the love of the love of God constrains me.
    Jesus and John,
    I believe and know that you love each other,   145
      but how can I experience this
      if you do not grant what I ask of you both?
    Jesus, how can I prove
your love for him, or for me, or my love for you both
unless through him you grant me what I long for –   150
    to be loved of you and to love you?
    John, how can I know that he loves you
    if you do not grant me to be loved also?
      Or that you love him
    if you do not help me to love him too?   155
    (Excuse my daring, beloved of God,
for it is this love of yours that urges me to speak so.)

*

So you, Lord God, and you, his beloved John,
do not love only yourselves in your blessedness,

but also us sinners in our misery.　　　　　　　160
We share your joy – do you share our sufferings.
Do not keep to yourselves the enjoyment of so much good,
　　but let some of it flow down to us
　　to be spread abroad among us,
　　and enrich and rejoice our souls.　　　　　165

*

John, lover and beloved of God,
you are secure in that blessed fullness of glory
　　which is your mutual love.
Behold this poor man,
　　a beggar for the two-fold love of God;　　170
　　grant it to him liberally,
　　for you know you have it in great abundance
　　and you see me in great need.
You know, sir, what you yourself have written
　　in your Epistle　　　　　　　　　　175
　　of whosoever has this world's goods
　　and sees that his brother has need,
　　and shuts up his bowels of compassion to him;
what then, sir, if anyone has the goods of eternal life
　　and sees a soul near him have need?　　180
Will he shut up his bowels of compassion to him?
Merciful teacher, if you have wished
　　that the bowels of compassion
　　of those that have this world's goods
　　should not be shut to the needs of sufferers,　　185
　　surely this is much more true
　　of those who have better goods,
　　　to those whose need is even greater?
I hear you teach that we must open our hearts
and I see that you have the riches of loving God　　190
　　and being loved by him,
　　and you see in what need my soul is.

Lo, here is the one who teaches this, and has this wealth,
   in the presence of one who is in need,
    and they gaze at each other.   195
If then, sir, your gaze has more good in it
   than my prayer has devotion,
    let your gaze become my prayer.
    For you have not written
'If any see his brother have need and praying,   200
   and shuts his heart against him',
but 'If any sees his brother have need!'
Act, then, sir, seeing my need; for indeed you see just that.

*

    O soul, my soul,
   draw together all your love,   205
    and bring it before him.
Cry, groan from the depths of your soul in his sight,
   'You see me',
and a second time repeat the words with importunity,
   'You see me – see me!'   210

*

John, you see me; there is no doubt that you see me.
   Then look on me!
  Sir, see me, and know me,
  look and have pity upon me!
   You see and you know.   215
  See in order that I may know it.
You see and know my need,
  see that I may know your goodness.
  Look, look on me, since you do see me!
At once I know, even now I experience that you see me.   220
  I know, I experience it.
How my intellect charges me with what it hears.
  I know well, sir, that you have ordained
that one should open one's heart to one's brother,

but whether I am that brother or that neighbour   225
   I dare not assert though I long to be.
I do not want to claim that which is not right for me.

*

   Jesus, John's master, look on us.
Near to the waters my soul longs with thirst;
   but there is nothing for it to drink   230
   unless something flows from the fount.
Fount of mercy, flow from yourself through John
   so that I may drink of you in him.
   Good Lord, make answer on my behalf.
I go back to the fount itself, I can do no other.   235
Near to the fount of life no thirsting soul perishes.
Do not block the way of the thirsty to drink.
The one who is full of love hears your thought
and your thirsty one drinks your mercy through him.
Say to him, 'John, who seems to you to have been neighbour   240
   to him that fell among thieves?'
   And, blessed John, do you answer
in the words the human race applied to the Samaritan
   and give thanks to him –
   reply, 'He that had mercy upon him.'   245
Good Jesus, you have begun to help my prayer,
   now into your hands I commend it,
so that your perfect goodness may perfect it.
Speak, I pray you, to your beloved John
   to show him me, your servant,   250
and say to him, 'Go and do thou likewise.'

*

   Hope and rejoice,
   rejoice and love, O my soul!
He whom so doubtfully you asked to hear you
himself prepares for you an intercessor.   255

As a beggar I prayed through another
because I had no confidence before him myself;
 and lo, he himself takes care of me,
 and prays where I myself failed.
 What goodness, piety, and love!   260
 See, he shows how much he loves me –
he comes near to me so that I may love him!
 So I press on and I hope,
 not in myself but in him,
for he listens to my desire who thus crowns my prayer.   265
'My heart and my flesh' rejoice in him and love him,
'and all that is within me' bless him. Amen.

A Letter from Anselm to the Princess Adelaide, Accompanying a Collection of Prayers and Selections from the Psalms

(Schmitt, vol. 3, Letter 10, pp. 113-4)

To the worthy and royal lady, Adelaide, who is noble by birth but more noble still by a holy life; greetings from her brother, Anselm. May you add to the lustre of your earthly nobility the glory of virtue, so that in everlasting bliss you may be united to the King of Kings.

I send herewith the 'Flowers from the Psalms' which from your high estate you deigned to command me to choose for you, for the love of God. I have executed the task, out of my low estate, as well and quickly as possible. Insofar as your order was a result of your devotion to God, just so far has my obedience been successful. I hope and pray that God Almighty will so preserve and nourish that same devotion in you, that on earth your heart may be filled with his dearest love and in heaven be fulfilled with the sight of his face. It is a poor and mean gift that I am sending to you who are rich and noble; do not despise it, coming from my poverty and insignificance. It is not encrusted with gold and jewels, but it has been made with loving faithfulness and it is given with faithful love.

After the 'Flowers from the Psalms' I have added seven prayers. The first of them is not so much a prayer as a meditation, in which briefly the soul shakes itself free from sin, despises it, is humbled by it, is troubled by fear of the Last Judgement and concludes by breaking out in tears and sighs. In the prayers proper, those to St Stephen and St Mary Magdalene tend more to the increase of love, if they are said from the depths of the heart and at a slow pace. And indeed in all seven I beg you, as your servant and loving friend, to give them your whole attention, and to do it as well as you are able, so that with humility of mind and the feeling of fear and love the sacrifice of prayer may be offered.

Farewell, now and in eternity, in God.

Farewell, and receive this little book which I am sending as a pledge of my faithfulness before God, with my prayers, for what they are worth.

At the end of my letter I add what I urge on you in them all: despise everything that will have to be left behind, even while you have it, with your whole mind set on things above; and strive only for that which can be kept for ever, as long as you have it not, with a humble mind. I pray the Holy Spirit to persuade you of all I want to urge upon you, in whom I say for the third time, farewell.

13. Prayer to St Stephen

Holy Stephen, blessed Stephen, loving Stephen,
  mighty soldier of God,
first of the blessed army of the martyrs of God,
powerful prince, one of the great lords of heaven.
  I call upon you, sir, with joy,   5
  because I believe this of you:
  when you were on earth
  such light of holiness glowed within you
that your venerable face shone with the nobility of an angel,
  for purity made your heart so clear   10
  that your blessed eyes saw God in his glory;
  and you were on fire with so much love
that in your goodness you prayed for the evil men
  that surrounded you.
  It was so, good Stephen, it was indeed so,   15
and I rejoice, praise, and exult that I know this of you.
    For I am fearful,
  knowing the wrath of the strict judge,
  for I am a sinner, a prisoner deserving punishment,
  and I need someone to help me.   20
In love and assurance I send you as my intercessor,
  that you may make peace
  between me and your powerful friend,
  the Lord and Creator of both you and me.
For I am quite certain, sir,   25
  that by your great merits you can do this,
and I am sure that out of your great charity you will do this.
  I hope in the immense mercy of the Judge
  that he will not refuse you.
So anxious and trembling I come to you for refuge   30
  only too well aware that I am a sinner.

So, good Stephen, behold my wretchedness
and pour over it your love.

*

For see, the accused stands before the tremendous Judge.
He is accused of many and great offences.   35
He is convicted by the witness of his own conscience
    and by the witness of the eyes of the Judge himself.
He has done no good deeds
    that can be weighed against the bad ones.
He has not deserved to have a friend of the Judge   40
to act as his advocate because of some former service;
having offended everyone, he deserves to be accused.
    Terrible is the severity of the Judge,
intolerably strict, for the offence against him is huge,
    and he is exceedingly wrathful.   45
    Once given, his sentence cannot be changed.
    A prison with no remedy gapes;
    in that prison lie great torments,
    tormentors are ready, to snatch away to torment
    those upon whom sentence of condemnation is given.   50
Torments without end, without interval, without respite,
horrible tortures which never slacken,
    on which no one has pity.
Fear shakes the accused, his conscience confounds him,
    thoughts beset him and he cannot flee.   55
      Thus he stands,
    with the heaviest of sentences hanging over him.
The wretch is in peril because of his distress
    and in distress because of his peril.
See how much such a man is in need of swift aid!   60
Where now is the help of the one
    who under the weight of stones
    had pity on those who were stoning him?
    He it is who will pray for him,

for he appeared before the severe Judge   65
to intercede for his murderers.

*

   Stephen, Stephen,
indeed you are 'Stephen', for you are truly crowned!
   Stephen, Stephen, I say:
here is a place for goodness, here is a time for mercy,   70
here at least is an opportunity to show charity!
   For I stand continually in danger
   although I do not always recognize this,
and I am the more miserable and wretched
   when I forget that it is so.   75
   For God always sees me and my sins,
always his severe judgement threatens
   the sinfulness of my soul,
always hell gapes and its torments are ready
   to snatch my wretched soul away to that place.   80
Thus am I placed when I wake, thus when I sleep;
   I am thus when I smile, thus when I jest;
   thus when I am proud, thus when I am humiliated;
   thus when angry, thus when vindicated;
   thus, thus I am when I miserably love   85
   the delights of the flesh.
   Thus am I then always and everywhere.
So I pray you, Stephen, make haste
   before I am condemned,
   before the enemies of the human race   90
   snatch me away to torment,
   before the prison of hell swallows me up,
   before the torments of gehenna consume me.

*

   But you, O my sins,
you are too great, you are too many,   95
and rightly is pardon refused to my soul.

It really is so, I acknowledge that it is so.
But however grave my unhappiness,
   however bitter my need,
how much more wonderful will be   100
  the goodness of him who forgives,
how much greater will appear
   the grace of the one who intercedes
   in the presence of the one who forgives!
I know well enough, sir, Stephen, beloved of God,   105
  that in offending God
  I have offended you also and all the saints.
   Truly my need is great
  when it impels me to ask for the help
  even of those by whom I deserve to be punished.   110
But you and all the saints are so full of such wealth
  from the unending fount of all goodness,
  that you delight rather to free by your goodness
  those whom by justice you are able to condemn.

*

  Great Stephen,   115
  your merits are so great
  that they suffice for both you and for me,
and if they are used for me, they are not diminished for you.
  See, blessed Stephen, before God and before you,
   are all my sins   120
  which terrify, distress, and weigh down my soul.
Do you, as a man of love, say to your best and dearest friend,
  'Lord, lay not these sins to his charge.'
Speak up for someone in need who asks it of you,
  as you did for those who killed you.   125
If in your goodness and love you ask this, I am sure
the most loving God will remit the whole of my evil deeds.
  For he is merciful and my creator,
  I am wretched and his workmanship,

and you are the beloved friend of him who is   130
'blessed for ever. Amen.'

*

When those who in their folly were your enemies
pressed upon you, O friend of God,
– this is what the truth of scripture testifies –
on your knees you cried with a loud voice,   135
'Lord, lay not this sin to their charge.'
O heart, rich with the treasures of charity,
from which when it was afflicted
such copious mercy poured!
O mind, vehemently ablaze with love,   140
filled with the oil of charity,
from which when it was in tribulation such sparks shone,
sweetly burning and burning with sweetness!
O honeycomb, rich with the honey of love,
from which when it was pressed   145
such rich and joyous drops were distilled!

*

'Lord, lay not this sin to their charge.'
    Blessed man,
what hope you give to sinners who are your friends
when they hear that you were so concerned   150
    about the wicked men who were your enemies!
Vessel of love, overflowing with fullness,
how richly will you give drink to those
who desire to hold you in their heart,
when you poured out so much   155
on those who cast you out of their city.
If you gave so much to your neighbours
who ran upon you, panting with fury,
how kindly will you deal with those
who run towards you, panting with fear?   160

*

'Lord, lay not this sin to their charge.'
If this was the way he responded when he was provoked,
   what will he do when he is invoked?
Now he is lifted up,
   how will he cherish those who are cast down,   165
   who, when he was cast down,
went to the help of those who thought themselves lifted up?
   Now he is free and powerful
how swiftly will he free those who are afflicted,
if when he was afflicted he helped those who afflicted him? 170
   They hastened to take away your life,
   and you paid your creditors
   by giving your life for their souls.
Stiff-necked, they raged furiously that you might perish,
and you on your knees prayed with a loud voice   175
   that they might not perish.
Certainly you prayed with a great voice
     for love is great,
   and on your knees, for truth is simple.
Their pride vexed your humility with sharp stones,   180
   and there came out a fragrant smell of charity.
Their hatred threw stones at your love,
   and it gave back the ringing sound of goodness.
Their evil pressed stones on your goodness,
   and the oil of mercy flowed out.   185

*

If only I could ever call forth by prayer
   this oil of the love of Stephen
   which they were able to force out with stones!
But my soul is weary with a very heavy languor
   that nothing can heal except the oil of mercy.   190
If only someone would suggest to God
   for me and all my sins,
   that he 'lay not these sins to his charge'.

Teach me, blessed soul of the blessed Stephen,
in what tasting you rejoice, in what fullness you burn,   195
  when your heart 'rejoices in such a good word'.
How sweet is your word in the jaws of my soul,
  above honey and honeycomb in the mouth.
Eaten, it grows in sweetness,
  and when that sweetest sap is sucked   20c
  it flows more and more within.
The more this word is seen, the brighter it looks.
  In whatever way one examines it,
  it always grows in delight.
It carries the form of faith, it has the solidity of patience,   205
  it shines with the purity of simpleness,
  it glows with the colour of kindness,
  its taste is charity, its smell is goodness;
  touched, it gives back gentleness;
  sounded, it responds with mercy.   210

*

Then tell us, blessed Stephen,
  what it was you cherished within you
  that broke forth outwardly in such a sweet mixture?
Undoubtedly you were full of all these things,
you were adorned with and reckoned with all these things.   215
I ask you, loving Stephen, by all these virtues
  in which you abounded,
to pray that 'love, rich and full' may 'fill my hungry soul'.
Help me, so that my hungry soul
  may be satisfied with the bread of love.   220
Do this, so that my frigid soul
  may flame with the fire of love
  in the presence of God its maker.

*

'And having said this, he fell asleep in the Lord.'
  Ah, he fell asleep!   225

Sleep with rest, rest with security, security with eternity.
 Happy man, to rest in joy, and joy to rest.
 Safe home, you are glorified in fullness
 and you are filled with glory.
Your joy does not change, your light does not fail.   230
 Whatever you could not do, being far away,
 you can do now you are present to those who pray.
Your soul is 'athirst for the fount of the living God'.
  You have come to him
 and you drink of the torrent of his pleasures,   235
 as much as you want, whenever you want it,
 and as long as you want it.
Always filled, always you drink,
 because always you delight to drink,
 and you are never wearied.   240
You do not drink to make yourself full,
 as if you were not full,
 but always you drink
 so that the fullness you have may endure always.
For you always desire what you always have,   245
 and what is always secured to you, you have always.
Of course you desire incessantly and delightfully
  that delightful desire,
 and always you drink with delighted ardour
 what you desire, with the rich fullness of it.   250
O sufficient blessedness, and blessed sufficiency!
How happy to fall asleep, to fall asleep in the Lord.
 In how much peace do they fall asleep
 who fall asleep in the Lord.
For the heavy weight of the flesh does not oppress them, 255
 nor do the sorrows of corruption afflict them.
They do not fight against the sting of temptation,
 nor does the consciousness of sin terrify them.
 'God wipes away all tears from their eyes.'

*

O rich and blessed peace, how far I am from you!   260
  For see, when I try even slightly
  to savour the taste of alien happiness,
  I am compelled to swallow in full measure
  the bitter draught of my wretchedness.

The good that I cannot reach reminds me to be silent   265
  and weep for the heavy evils that I suffer
    and am able to touch.

Alas for my unhappiness, where I am not, where I am,
  and alas that I know not where I shall be.

How miserably my soul is in discord   270
  when it joins itself to my flesh;
the soul cannot follow the flesh without fear,
  it dares not, nor does it want, to leave it without grief;
  it wants to draw it after itself,
  and cannot do so except with labour.   275
      Unhappy man that I am,
who will free me from the body of this death?

*

    I pray you, blessed Stephen,
have compassion on me for I am poor and in misery,
for I rejoice with you in your bliss that knows no lack.   280
  Free me from the body of this death
  by your merits by the grace of God
  through Jesus Christ our Lord,
  so that some day in peace and the self-same
  I will be at rest and sleep in the Lord,   285
  who lives and reigns, God, for all ages. Amen.

Brother Anselm, to the Lord Prior Baldric and those who are brethren with him, in the desire that all may be well with you, within and without.

I am not yet able to tell you anything about the outcome of my journey to England on the business of the community, for the King still delays in answering my petition, however much he and the other English nobles show me love and honour.

The monk of the Lord Abbot Gislebert will be able to tell you more about my safety than a letter could. I hope you will receive him with kindness. I have no hope of returning any sooner than Lent. Send me letters with any news that you think I ought to know about.

Send me the prayer to St Nicholas which I composed, and the letter which I began against Roscelin, and any other letters of mine, if Dom Maurice has any he has not sent. Salute my mothers in the Lord, the Lady Eve and the Lady Basilia. Farewell.

14. Prayer to St Nicholas

Sinful little man, in such great need,
you have grieved God very much.
   Stir up your mind,
look inwards at what really matters for you,
and call down pity upon your pitiable state.   5
My soul, be watchful; my wretchedness, rouse yourself;
my wickedness, call upon the God you have angered,
that he may by chance soften his regard towards you.

*

But he is Most High, and I am weak;
   how can my voice reach up to him?   10
I will lift up my soul above myself,
   that it may come before him who is above it,
   perhaps he will hear me when I call.
But then he is Most Just, and I have greatly sinned;
   how should he hear my cry?   15
I will enter into my inmost being,
   exclude everything except him and myself,
and before him I will pour out my soul and all that is in me.
   I will stir up my mind to grieve,
   and with grieving love   20
I will spread out my hardship before him
and perhaps his great goodness may move him.

*

But my sins are without bounds or limits,
   my prayer will not be heard,
all this is not enough without an intercessor.   25
I will pray to one of the great friends of God
and perhaps God will hear him on my behalf.

I will call upon Nicholas, that great confessor,
whose name is honoured throughout the world.
    Nicholas!   30
  If only he will hear me!
    Great Nicholas!

*

But if God looks down on me, who will look up to me?
If God turns his face from me, who will look towards me?
If God hates me, who will dare speak on my behalf?   35
    O God, 'merciful and pitiful',
do you indeed ward off one who would return to you,
so that you cannot bear to have mercy
    upon one who cleaves to you?
Will you curse one who has grieved you so much   40
that you will not hear any of your friends on his behalf?
You are called 'kind and merciful'
    and 'set above all malice';
are you so inflamed against a penitent sinner
    that you forget your own nature?   45
Either hear me yourself, or let someone else hear me
    whom you will listen to on my behalf.
Lord, if it is my sins that hold you back from hearing me
    you are within your rights,
but do not forbid another to hear a miserable suppliant,   50
    because you are also good.
Kind Lord, your mercy goes beyond any understanding;
    I feel this no less than I presume to hope it.
Your servant, created and re-created by your goodness,
    has such confidence in you, Lord,   55
    that when you accuse him
    he dares to ask you for an intercessor.
For no one will pay attention to me, unless you order it,
    nothing helps me without you,

and so I have a good hope that what you refuse me   60
   on account of my sins,
you will grant me because of the merits of your friend.
Good Lord, do not show yourself to be an avenger
   when I ask you for an intercessor,
      for you do not give stones for bread,   65
a serpent for a fish, or for an egg a scorpion.
Give me then, Lord, Nicholas as my intercessor,
your great confessor whom you have glorified
with the name of blessed throughout the world.

*

St Nicholas, I pray to you through him   70
who has made your name venerated throughout the world;
   do not refuse to help a needy suppliant.
Why, sir, are you called upon by all men in all the world
unless you are to be the advocate of all who pray to you?
   Why does this sound in all ears,   75
'My lord, St Nicholas', 'My lord, St Nicholas',
   unless it means,
'My advocate, St Nicholas', 'My advocate, St Nicholas'?
Why is your name poured forth everywhere
   except that the world may have   80
   some great good poured into it?
      Your fame calls to me,
your miracles send me to your intercession,
   your works draw me to seek your help.

*

But why do I speak about your miracles,   85
when your power now is greater than them all?
   Why do I recount what you have done,
when before God you now have supreme grace?

Why recount the help that you gave to many
  when you are able to give spiritual help   90
    now that you live in heaven,
  of more value than the corporal help
  that you gave during your pilgrimage upon earth?
For it is not as if you were able to do those things then
  and can no longer do them.   95
No, I say, you could not have power only in those things
  that come to nothing,
  and be powerless in those that go on into eternity.
Indeed, you did not only accomplish the former,
  you did not ascend merely that you might grant them.   100
Bestow upon us the spiritual things in which you glory,
  the joys of eternity in which you rejoice,
pour upon us the heavenly things to which you have turned.
Through you we needy ones come to know that abundance
  which you receive fully in a perpetual stream.   105

*

O your plenitude of goodness,
and my abundance of badness!
How far they are from each other!
How vehemently the first makes you happy,
  how greatly does the latter make me unhappy.   110
The first comes down from the plenitude of God,
  the latter goes up from the need of myself;
the first flows from the abundance of God,
  the latter surges up from my poverty.
O if only that super-abundance would overflow   115
  and flood into my abundant ills!
O if only that full plenitude would fill
  the emptiness of my need!
I do not doubt, sir, that you can do this for me,

if you are willing to ask that much for me of my judge   120
  who is your beloved friend.

*

Do not wait, sir, to hear my importunities,
because you know my weakness
  when praying for a long time.
I fall away quickly, but do you be more swift to help.   125
  Certainly if my heart was contrite,
  if my heart was moved within me,
  if my soul was turned to water,
  if rivers of tears flowed from my eyes,
then I might hope that Nicholas would hear my prayers.   130
Therefore, my lord, St Nicholas, stir up my spirit,
    excite my heart,
move my mind to love according to my need,
so that I may feel the effect of your compassion
  according to your power.   135

*

But, alas, how long my tepid soul languishes,
  how hardened is my heart with stupor,
  how buried in torpor is my spirit.
Holy Nicholas, what is it that thus holds me back?
What is it that seems to be constricting my neck?   140
Whence is it that my gaze is darkened?
Whence comes it that my horizon is thus closed in?
My soul wants, sir, to turn towards God and to you,
and it is weighed down in a curve by a heavy weight.
It desires to direct its gaze towards you,   145
  and it is obscured by dark shadows.
It makes efforts to release itself,
  but it is held in bonds of iron.
It tries to come out,
  and it is held in a metal prison.   150

*

What are these things, O God, what are these things
   which thus darken my soul, weigh it down,
      enclose and bind it?
   Perhaps these are my sins?
Yes, indeed they are my sins; certainly they are.   155
Fleshly love weakens the sap of the spirit within me;
   attention to earthly things
bends my soul away from knowledge of things above;
earthly love extinguishes in me delight in heavenly things.
The habit of vice has wiped away in me   160
   the knowledge of true good.
I am far away from good, I am absorbed in evil.
I am excluded from those, I am included in these.
From those I have devolved, in these I am involved.
Here are darkness and chains,   165
   there are shadows and weights.
My sins, for what end do you keep me in these chains,
in this prison, under this shadow and this weight?
   For whom, unless for the strict judge,
and for your tortures and torments in eternity?   170
For what, if not for the prison of hell and eternal chains?
For what, if not for the darkness of perpetual night
   and the weight of unending death?
Certainly these are the evils you keep me for,
   this is the evil you are dragging me towards.   175
Certainly in these I will be involved
   if before then I am not absolved.
Truly at that hour I will be their bond slave
if I am not set free from them earlier.
At any rate, the day is near, near I say, and yet unknown. 180
   It comes suddenly and it may be today.

*

My sins, how can you be such an evil in the future,
   when here and now you make my soul
   drunk with your sweetness,
when you anoint my heart with your pleasures?   185
   Why did you hide these things from me?
   Why have you betrayed me?
   In fact you have not betrayed me,
but I have betrayed myself by believing in you.
You did not deceive me, but I have deceived myself   190
   because I have received you into myself.
      O unheard-of insanity!
   I knew there was no faith in you,
   and yet I had faith in you.
Indeed I had no faith and I did not believe you,   195
but how horrible the way in which I saw this:
like a blind man I committed myself to you.
   I saw, because I recognized you,
   and I understood what evils come after you.
     Yet I was blind,   200
   because I did not guard against what I knew.

*

   Alas! – sin; a name to be shuddered at,
a thing to be detested, no misfortune can be compared to it.
The blind man did not see the trench into which he fell,
the fool thought he ought to do what he did.   205
But he who sins willingly, seeing and knowing,
   throws himself over a precipice.
Death and torments, however great such torments may be,
   in them is no dishonour, because they are ordained.
But sin has in itself its own dishonour,   210
   and brings with it eternal unhappiness.
For it were better to choose eternal torment,
   which in itself does not bring eternal dishonour,
   than sin, which joins dishonour to eternal sorrow.

And certainly, unhappy man,   215
you ought to avoid the dishonour of sin in itself,
more than whatever torments there are in eternity.
For in sinning, by a most dishonourable perversity,
   you prefer yourself to God your Creator,
   than which nothing is more unjust;   220
whereas in bearing torments,
   according to a most perfect pattern,
the creature submits himself to the one who created him,
   than which nothing is more just.

*

O man, where has your humanity vanished to?   225
   You have been taught
   that 'whoever sins is the servant of sin';
of what great evil are you the slave in committing sins?
Did you know
   that 'the spirit goes forth and does not return'?   230
You have thrown yourself into the abyss of sin,
   which is irredeemable and bottomless.
   Truly my sins are an abyss,
because their weight and depth cannot be understood,
and their number cannot be gauged or bounded.   235
That abyss cannot be redeemed
   because out of its depths nothing returns
   unless drawn out by grace,
and it is bottomless, because whoever sins willingly
merits to fall infinitely, if he is not held back by mercy.   240

*

'Abyss calls to abyss.'
My sins, whatever torments you reserve for me are an abyss,
   for they are infinite and incomprehensible.
Alas, prisons and chains,
   darkness and the weight of sin, terrify me,   245

but I am made a slave to an evil
  to which no other is comparable
  and so I am drowned in an abyss,
  and with this sorrowful servitude
  I am buried in one abyss after another.   250
Woe upon woe; fear upon fear; sorrow upon sorrow.

*

Lo, there is a third abyss and that is yet more terrible.
  'The justice of God is very deep,'
  and at the voice of the cataracts
  my abyss calls to that abyss.   255
The cataracts are dark, the justice of God is dark.
  Therefore abyss calls to abyss
  in the voice of the cataracts of God,
where the abyss of sin meets the abyss of torment,
  and they proclaim the justice of God.   260
If my sins were not an abyss, I would still fear greatly
  the abyss of the great judgements of God,
  for that is dark beyond human understanding.

*

Truly there is the abyss of the judgements of God,
  the abyss of my sins,   265
  and the abyss of torments that are my due.
  The abyss of judgements above me,
  the abyss of hell below me,
the abyss of the sin in which I am, and which is in me.
I fear that which threatens me from above,   270
  lest it fall upon me,
  so that I may be thrown into myself
and buried with my abyss in that which is revealed below,
  where the torment of sin never ceases,
  and sin is always torment.   275

*

Unhappy man that I am, against whom have I sinned,
    to whom shall I reach out?
Whither shall I flee from God,
    where can I be lost to him?
Who will seek me in the abyss of abysses?   280
    Or who will look for the lost of God?
Who, outside the abyss of sin,
    will hear the cry out of the deep?

*

    But you, Lord, behold the depths.
    Whither shall I go then from your spirit,   285
    or where shall I flee from your presence?
Certainly, where I now am, you are not absent,
    for when I descend into hell you are there.
And therefore if in my wickedness I flee from you
    and hide myself in my abyss as one who is damned,   290
    even there you behold me.
For who, except you, can move my soul to penitence,
    and how could you move it,
    if in the abyss you could not see it?

*

    Good Lord,   295
you have roused and stirred me from the abyss of my sin
    like one sleeping in a bed.
    You have stirred up my torpor,
you have had a care to rouse my negligence,
you have made me repent of that which I rejoiced in,   300
and sorrow for that by which I was delighted.
You gave me counsel to ask for an intercessor,
    you have shown me who he is to be.
Good God, you have done all this while I was in the abyss,
and do you not hear my cry out of the deep?   305
In all this you have gone before him who fled from you,

193

and will you not take him back when he wants to return
   to perfect what you have begun?
   Good Lord, thank you.
Truly you have sought out your lost one in the abyss,   310
   and brought out him
whom you had driven there in fear because of his sin.
By the merits of St Nicholas, your beloved,
   lead out from the abyss of sin
   your lost one whom you have sought and found.   315
Do not lose your servant whom you have sought and found
   in the abyss of hell, where no one is found.
I hear, Lord, that you order me to come forth,
   but I cannot get out,
miserably bound and weighed down with so great a weight.   320

*

But, St Nicholas, why do I pray to God by your merits,
when you are in his presence and can do this better?
   I pray you, sir, through his name,
   do not turn away from one
   whom he has already looked upon,   325
   however much his accused slave he may be.
I ask you to plead for me in the presence of God,
I do not ask you to defend me, but to pray for me.
Before his face I cannot defend my sins;
I show them, not to excuse but to accuse.   330
   I am the accused; I am under him,
   and before him I am myself my accuser.
He who made me does not accuse me.
   Alone I was sufficient for sinning,
   alone I will be sufficient for accusing.   335
If he is Judge to pass sentence on his accused,
he is also Lord, to protect his servant,
Creator to watch over his handiwork,

and God, to save him who believes in him
    and is his baptized.   340
For how will he judge that sinner to deserve condemnation,
    who knows his wretched sins and is penitent?
Or how can he damn a sinner as an adversary,
    when he grieves over his sin,
    and flees to his friend as an intercessor?   345

                    *

    God, in you have I trusted,
St Nicholas, to you I entrust my prayers,
    upon you both I cast my care,
    even on you I throw my soul.
    This is what you exact from me,   350
you by your commands, you by your counsels.
Receive him who throws himself upon you both,
    have him who is prostrate before you.
Keep me when I sleep, help me in whatever I do,
    inspire me in whatever I think,   355
you, Lord, by your grace,
you, Nicholas, by your intercession;
you for the merits of your so loved confessor,
you according to the name of your and my Creator,
    'who is blessed for evermore'. Amen.   360

15. Prayer to St Benedict

Holy and blessed Benedict,
  the grace of heaven has made you rich
  with such full blessing of goodness
not only in order to raise you to the glory you desire,
to the rest of the blessed, to a seat in heaven,   5
but that many others be drawn to that same blessedness,
    wondering at your life,
  stirred by your kind admonitions,
  instructed by your gentle doctrine,
  called on by your miracles.   10
  Benedict, blessed of God,
whom God has blessed with such wide benediction,
  to you I flee, in anguish of soul.
  I fling myself down before you
  with all the humility of mind possible;   15
  I pour forth my prayer to you
  with all the fervour possible;
and implore your help with all the desire possible;
  for my need is too great; I cannot bear it.

*

For I profess to lead a life   20
  of continual turning to God,
as I promised by taking the name and habit of a monk;
  but my long life cries out against me
  and my conscience convicts me,
  as a liar to God, to angels, and to men.   25
  Holy Father Benedict
  hear what I ask of you;
  and I beg you not to be scandalized

by so many faults and such deceit,
    but hear what I acknowledge before you,   30
and have more pity on my sorrows than I deserve.

*

    At least, peerless leader
among the great leaders of the army of Christ,
you have pledged me to serve under your leadership,
    however feeble a soldier;   35
    you have placed me under your tutorship,
        however ignorant a pupil;
    I have vowed to live according to your Rule,
        however carnal a monk.
My perverse heart is dry and as cold as a stone   40
when it comes to deploring the sins I have committed;
but when it comes to resisting occasions of sin
    it is indeed pliant and soon defiled.
My depraved mind is swift and untiring
    to study what is useless and vile;   45
    but even to think of what is for its good
    makes it weary and stupid.
My blind and distorted soul is swift and prompt
to throw itself into vices and wallow in them,
    but how slowly and with what difficulty   50
    do I even call to mind the virtues.
It would take too long, dearest Father,
    to recall each thing separately.
It would be too long a story to tell
    of all the gluttony, sloth, inconstancy, impatience,   55
    vainglory, detraction, disobedience,
and all the other sins which my wretched soul commits,
    deriding me each day.
Sometimes my sins drag me here and there,
mocking at this wretched and tattered little man;   60
    and at other times they come in a mob

and trample me underfoot in triumph,
and triumph that they can trample me underfoot.

*

   See then, blessed Benedict,
   how bravely fights this soldier   65
   who is under your leadership;
see how much progress your pupil is making
     in your school;
   see what a marvellous monk this is,
dead to sin and the desires of the flesh,   70
   fervent and living only for virtue!
No, you see rather a false monk, lost to all virtue,
   dominated by a crowd of vices,
   burdened with a weight of sin.

*

For shame! Shameless monk that I am!   75
How dare I call myself a soldier of Christ
   and a disciple of St Benedict?
     False to my profession,
   how have I the effrontery to let people see me
   with the tonsure and habit of profession   80
   when I do not live the life?
Alas, 'anguish closes me in on every side,'
   for if I deny my sovereign king,
   my good teacher and my profession,
     it is death to me;   85
but if I profess myself a soldier, scholar, monk,
   my life argues that I am a liar
   and I am judged thereby.
'Faint within me, my spirit; be appalled, my heart;
   break forth and cry, O my soul.'   90

*

Jesus, good Lord,
  'consider my affliction and my trouble
  and forgive me all my sins.'
'Hear, O Lord, do not cast me off or forsake me',
but 'lead me and help me to do your will',   95
  so that my life may attest
what my heart and mouth confess so freely.
'Hear the voice of my prayer, my King and my God,'
by the merits and intercession of holy Benedict,
your dear friend, my master, and my leader.   100

*

And you, my good leader, my gentle master,
  my dear father, blessed Benedict –
    I pray and beseech you,
  by the mercy you have shown to others
and by the mercy that God has shown to you,   105
  have compassion on me in my misery,
  for I rejoice with you in your bliss.
Help me! I beg you to be my protector.
Dig me out from the mass of sin that buries me,
  free me from the ropes of sin that bind me,   110
  loose me from the wickedness that entangles me.
Lift up him who is cast down, strengthen the wavering,
  prepare the helpless with spiritual weapons of virtue,
  lead and protect him who is fighting in the battle.
Bring me to the victory and lead me to the crown.   115

*

Do this, advocate of monks, of that charity
  which you were so anxious for us to take
    as our rule of life.
Make it your care that we may be sufficiently willing
  and effectively able to do whatever we ought;   120

so that both you, on account of our discipleship,
and we, on account of your leadership,
   may glory before the face of God
   who lives and reigns for ever and ever. Amen.

16. Prayer to St Mary Magdalene

St Mary Magdalene,
  you came with springing tears
  to the spring of mercy, Christ;
from him your burning thirst was abundantly refreshed;
  through him your sins were forgiven;   5
  by him your bitter sorrow was consoled.
   My dearest lady,
  well you know by your own life
how a sinful soul can be reconciled with its creator,
  what counsel a soul in misery needs,   10
  what medicine will restore the sick to health.
It is enough for us to understand, dear friend of God,
to whom were 'many sins forgiven, because she loved much'.
   Most blessed lady,
  I who am the most evil and sinful of men   15
  do not recall your sins as a reproach,
  but call upon the boundless mercy
  by which they were blotted out.
This is my reassurance, so that I do not despair;
this is my longing, so that I shall not perish.   20
   I say this of myself
  miserably cast down into the depths of vice,
  bowed down with the weight of crimes,
thrust down by my own hand into a dark prison of sins,
  wrapped round with the shadows of darkness.   25

*

Therefore, since you are now with the chosen
  because you are beloved
  and are beloved because you are chosen of God,
  I, in my misery, pray to you, in bliss;

in my darkness, I ask for light; 30
in my sins, redemption;
impure, I ask for purity.
Recall in loving kindness what you used to be,
how much you needed mercy,
and seek for me that same forgiving love 35
that you received when you were wanting it.
Ask urgently that I may have
the love that pierces the heart; tears that are humble;
desire for the homeland of heaven;
impatience with this earthly exile; 40
searing repentance; and a dread of torments in eternity.
Turn to my good that ready access
that you once had and still have to the spring of mercy.
Draw me to him where I may wash away my sins;
bring me to him who can slake my thirst; 45
pour over me those waters
that will make my dry places fresh.
You will not find it hard to gain all you desire
from so loving and so kind a Lord,
who is alive and reigns and is your friend. 50

*

For who can tell, belov'd and blest of God,
with what kind familiarity and familiar kindness
he himself replied on your behalf
to the calumnies of those who were against you?
How he defended you, 55
when the proud Pharisee was indignant,
how he excused you, when your sister complained,
how highly he praised your deed, when Judas begrudged it.
And, more than all this,
what can I say, how can I find words to tell, 60
about the burning love with which you sought him,
weeping at the sepulchre,

and wept for him in your seeking?
How he came, who can say how or with what kindness,
　to comfort you, and made you burn with love still more;　65
how he hid from you when you wanted to see him,
　and showed himself when you did not think to see him;
how he was there all the time you sought him,
　and how he sought you when, seeking him, you wept.

*

But you, most holy Lord,　70
　why do you ask her why she weeps?
　　Surely you can see;
her heart, the dear life of her soul, is cruelly slain.
　O love to be wondered at;
　O evil to be shuddered at;　75
　you hung on the wood, pierced by iron nails,
stretched out like a thief for the mockery of wicked men;
　and yet, 'Woman,' you say, 'why are you weeping?'
She had not been able to prevent them from killing you,
but at least she longed to keep your body for a while　80
　with ointments lest it decay.
No longer able to speak with you living,
　at least she could mourn for you dead.
So, near to death and hating her own life,
　she repeats in broken tones the words of life　85
　which she had heard from the living.
　　And now, besides all this,
even the body which she was glad, in a way, to have kept,
　she believes to have gone.
And can you ask her, 'Woman, why are you weeping?'　90
　Had she not reason to weep?
For she had seen with her own eyes –
　if she could bear to look –
　what cruel men cruelly did to you;

[handwritten marginalia: body taken away = resurrection]

and now all that was left of you from their hands   95
　　she thinks she has lost.
　　All hope of you has fled,
for now she has not even your lifeless body
　　to remind her of you.
　　And someone asks,   100
'Who are you looking for? Why are you weeping?'
　　You, her sole joy,
　　should be the last thus to increase her sorrow.
But you know it all well, and thus you wish it to be,
for only in such broken words and sighs   105
can she convey a cause of grief as great as hers.
The love you have inspired you do not ignore.
　　And indeed you know her well,
the gardener, who planted her soul in his garden.
　　What you plant, I think you also water.   110
　　Do you water, I wonder, or do you test her?
In fact, you are both watering and putting to the test.

*

　　But now, good Lord, gentle Master,
　　look upon your faithful servant and disciple,
　　　so lately redeemed by your blood,   115
and see how she burns with anxiety, desiring you,
　　searching all round, questioning,
　　and what she longs for is nowhere found.
　　Nothing she sees can satisfy her,
since you whom alone she would behold, she sees not.   120
　　What then?
How long will my Lord leave his beloved to suffer thus?
　　Have you put off compassion
now you have put on in-corruption?
　　Did you let go of goodness   125
when you laid hold of immortality?

Let it not be so, Lord.
You will not despise us mortals
  now you have made yourself immortal,
for you made yourself a mortal   130
  in order to give us immortality.

*

And so it is; for love's sake
he cannot bear her grief for long or go on hiding himself.
  For the sweetness of love he shows himself
    who would not for the bitterness of tears.   135
The Lord calls his servant by the name she has often heard
and the servant knows the voice of her own Lord.
  I think, or rather I am sure,
    that she responded to the gentle tone
    with which he was accustomed to call, 'Mary'.   140
What joy filled that voice, so gentle and full of love.
He could not have put it more simply and clearly:
  'I know who you are and what you want;
    behold me;
    do not weep, behold me;   145
    I am he whom you seek.'
At once the tears are changed;
  I do not believe that they stopped at once,
  but where once they were wrung
  from a heart broken and self-tormenting   150
  they flow now from a heart exulting.
How different is, 'Master!'
  from 'If you have taken him away, tell me'; ·
  and, 'They have taken away my Lord,
  and I do not know where they have laid him,'   155
  has a very different sound from,
'I have seen the Lord, and he has spoken to me.'

*

But how should I, in misery and without love,
dare to describe the love of God
and the blessed friend of God? 160
Such a flavour of goodness will make my heart sick
if it has in itself nothing of that same virtue.
But in truth, you who are very truth, you know me well
and can testify that I write this for the love of your love,
my Lord, my most dear Jesus. 165
I want your love to burn in me as you command
so that I may desire to love you alone
and sacrifice to you a troubled spirit,
'a broken and a contrite heart'.
Give me, O Lord, in this exile, 170
the bread of tears and sorrow
for which I hunger more than for any choice delights.
Hear me, for your love,
and for the dear merits of your beloved Mary,
and your blessed Mother, the greater Mary. 175
Redeemer, my good Jesus,
do not despise the prayers of one who has sinned against you
but strengthen the efforts of a weakling that loves you.
Shake my heart out of its indolence, Lord,
and in the ardour of your love 180
bring me to the everlasting sight of your glory
where with the Father and the Holy Spirit
you live and reign, God, for ever. Amen.

17. Prayer by a Bishop or Abbot to the Patron Saint of his Church

St N, Holy N, Blessed N,
   one of the glorious apostles of God,
   one of the blessed friends of God,
this sinner, this needy one, this one of yours,
although unworthy, although incapable,   5
although so unsuitable a substitute,
   again and again comes back to you,
doubtful, ignorant, anxious about your people,
your congregation, and about his own peril.
Obviously I am a useless person,   10
   adorned with no good works,
   but darkened by a profound ignorance,
   deformed by countless vices, burdened by huge sins.
   I, I say, whom God and you after God,
either ordered or permitted (I know not which)   15
to be called abbot of this church under your patronage,
under your leadership, constituted under your name;
anxious about myself and those committed to me,
   I beg to consult you, I pray you to listen,
and I expect you through all to work on my behalf.   20

*

For I am called master, but I do not know it is so;
I am named shepherd, but I deny that it is so;
they say that I am abbot, but I am not.
   For they see me seated where the abbot sits,
but I see that I do not do the works that an abbot does.   25
   They behold me preceded like an abbot,
but I do not behold that I live like an abbot.

They show me honour like an abbot,
   but I do not show them the way of life of an abbot.
Scarcely have I led the life of a good layman,   30
   and yet they expect me to live like a monk.
What have I done, a little man,
   a creeping and decaying thing,
   what have I done, to what have I presumed,
   to what have I consented?   35

*

But you, God, and you, N, his apostle,
   what have you done?
   For you have done this,
either by commanding it or by permitting it.
So it is you, who have in some way done this thing,   40
   who must act – you by praying, and you by giving –
so that what you have done
   may hold back neither me nor others,
   but may lead forward me and many others.
You have made an ignorant doctor, a blind leader,   45
   an erring ruler:
   teach the doctor you have established,
   guide the leader you have appointed,
   govern the ruler that you have approved.
    I beg you,   50
   teach me what I am to teach,
   lead me in the way that I am to lead,
   rule me so that I may rule others.
Or rather, teach them, and me through them,
   lead them, and me with them,   55
   rule them, and me among them.

*

Jesus, good shepherd, they are not mine but yours,
   for I am not mine but yours.

I am yours, Lord, and they are yours,
because by your wisdom you have created   60
   both them and me,
   and by your death you have redeemed us.
So we are yours, good Lord, we are yours,
   whom you have made with such wisdom
   and bought so dearly.   65
Then if you commend them to me, Lord,
   you do not therefore desert me or them.
You commend them to me:
   I commend myself and them to you.
Yours is the flock, Lord, and yours is the shepherd.   70
Be shepherd of both your flock and shepherd.

*

Lord, by the merits of blessed N, your friend,
favourably hear the prayer of your sinner.
   Lord, let him care for us,
   whom you have given us as an advocate.   75
   We know he prays for us,
   and by him we daily entreat your help.
   Through him we obtain your grace,
and through him we daily implore your majesty.
We confess that he is our advocate, Lord,   80
and by him we know you to be our Saviour.
Do not let our deserts prevail over his merits, Lord,
   but blot out our sins by his prayer.

*

And you, O holy and blessed N, you are my advocate;
   be my intercessor to God.   85
   I pray you, entreat him,
   I beg you, beseech him.
Offer him my prayer,
   and bring his favourable answer back to me.

I intimate to him through you my sufferings,   90
and through you he gives back to me his consolation.
   Show him my peril, and show me his aid.

*

For I have undertaken to rule the church of God under you,
   I who can scarcely begin to rule my own soul.
For myself therefore I am timid,   95
   and for others I am forced to be solicitous.
Weighed down by a weight of sins,
   I am ordered to relieve others,
bowed down by a weight of crimes, I must put others right.
So holy, blessed and good N, recognize me   100
   as in some kind of way your deputy,
   and always go before me with your counsel,
   and follow me with your help,
   ruling me, and the flock committed to me.
For they are committed more to you than to me,   105
and those who are committed to me
   are not taken away from you,
but I am the more greatly committed to you.
So what is enjoined upon me about them
   do you perform for me and for them.   110
Do on my behalf what is enjoined upon me
   to do in your place.
   Act, sir, act for me,
for you see that I have neither the knowledge nor the ability
   to act in your place.   115
   Rather, act not for me but for yourself,
for this pertains first and more greatly to you than me,
and if it pertains to me, it is after and under you.
So you, sir, have more obligation, more knowledge,
   and more power than I have,   120
   so act more powerfully than me.

*

Let me not be weighed down, sir,
   by anxiety about their care,
for I am weighed down quite enough
   with the pack of my own sins.   125
Let me not be weighed down by them,
   for I am too much weighed down by myself.
Let them not weigh upon me,
   but neither let me be a burden to them,
   nor let my sins impede them,   130
   nor my evil deeds do them harm.
Let not my wrong-doing block the way of those
   who ought to benefit by my well-doing.
Let them not be held back by me, sir,
   by whom they ought to be led forward.   135
Let me not delay them whom I ought to urge on.
   For my sins are more than sufficient for me;
   do not let them be a drag on others.
   It is too much for me if my sins damn me;
   do not let them involve others with me.   140

*

But you, O apostle of God,
   you can raise up me and them.
Carry me and them, excuse me and them!
   Help us all, rule and protect us all,
   so that I may rejoice in their salvation with me,   145
   and they in mine with them,
   so that with you, his blessed apostle,
we may always praise our good Lord Jesus Christ,
who is the blessed God, for ever and ever. Amen, Amen.

18. Prayer for Friends

Jesus Christ, my dear and gracious Lord,
you have shown a love greater than that of any man
   and which no one can equal,
   for you in no way deserved to die,
   yet you laid down your dear life   5
for those who served you and sinned against you.
You prayed for those who were killing you
that you might make them just men and your brothers
and restore them to your merciful Father and to yourself.
Lord, who showed such love to your enemies,   10
you have also enjoined the same love upon your friends.

*

   My good Lord,
with what affection should I think of your love
  which is beyond measure?
What return shall I make for your boundless gifts?   15
For your loving kindness is beyond all telling,
the greatness of your gift surpasses all return.
   Then what return shall I make
to him who created me and re-created me?
To him who has had mercy on me and redeemed me?   20
   O God, you are my God,
   my goods are nothing unto you,
for the whole world is yours and all that is in it.

*

Then what shall I, a beggar and poor,
   a creeping thing of dust,   25
   what return can I make to my God,
   except to obey his commandment from my heart?
For this is your commandment, that we love one another.

Good man, good God, good Lord, good friend –
  you are whatever good there is.   30
Your humble and contemptible slave
  desires to obey your commandment.
You know, Lord, that I prize this love which you command,
  I hold this love dear, and long for this charity.
    This I ask, this I seek.   35
  For this your poor man, your beggar,
  beats and clamours at the gate of your mercy.
And now, insofar as I have already received
  the sweet alms you freely give,
  I love all men, in you and for your sake,   40
  though not so much as I ought or as I desire.
I pray your mercy upon all men,
yet there are many whom I hold more dear
since your love has impressed them upon my heart
  with a closer and more intimate love,   45
  so that I desire their love more eagerly –
I would pray more ardently for these.

*

  My good Lord,
as your servant I long to pray to you for my friends,
but as your debtor I am held back by my sins.   50
  For I am not able to pray for my own pardon,
  how then can I dare to ask openly
  for your grace for others?
I anxiously seek intercessors on my own behalf,
how then shall I be so bold as to intercede for others?   55
What shall I do, Lord God, what shall I do?
You command me to pray for them
  and my love prompts me to do so,
  but my conscience cries out against me,
saying that I should be concerned about my own sins,   60
  so that I tremble to speak for others.

Shall I then leave off from doing what you command
   because I have done what you have forbidden?
No, rather since I have presumed so greatly
   in what is forbidden,   65
   all the more will I embrace what is commanded.
So perhaps obedience may heal presumption,
   and charity may cover the multitude of my sins.

*

So I pray you, good and gracious God,
   for those who love me for your sake   70
      and whom I love in you.
   And I pray more earnestly for those
whom you know love me and whom I do most truly love.
I am not doing this, Lord,
   as being righteous and free from sin,   75
but as one urged on by some kind of love for others.
   So love them, you source of love,
      by whose command and gift I love them;
and if my prayer does not deserve to avail for them
   because it is offered you by a sinner,   80
let it avail for them because it is made at your command.
   Love them, Author and Giver of love,
      for your own sake, not for mine,
and make them love you with all their heart,
   all their soul, and all their mind,   85
      so that they will and speak and do
only what pleases you and is expedient for them.

*

My prayer is but a cold affair, Lord,
   because my love burns with so small a flame,
   but you who are rich in mercy   90
   will not mete out to them your gifts
   according to the dullness of my zeal,

but as your kindness is above all human love
so let your eagerness to hear
be greater than the feeling in my prayers.   95
Do this for them and with them, Lord,
so that they may speed according to your will,
and thus ruled and protected by you,
always and everywhere,
may they come at last to glory and eternal rest,   100
through you who are living and reigning God,
through all ages. Amen.

19. Prayer for Enemies

Almighty and tender Lord Jesus Christ,
  I have asked you to be good to my friends,
and now I bring before you what I desire in my heart
    for my enemies.
  For you see, O God, the reins and the heart,   5
  you penetrate the secrets of my mind.
If you have sown in the soul of your servant
  something that can be offered to you,
    you see it there;
  nor can it lie hid from you   10
  if I and the enemy of mankind have sown there
  that which will have to be consumed by fire.
    Most gracious God,
  do not despise what you have sown,
but cherish and increase it, perfect and preserve it.   15
  I can begin nothing good without you,
  neither can I bring anything to fruition
  nor maintain it, without you.
Merciful God, do not judge me
  according to that which displeases you in me,   20
  but root up that which you have not sown
  and save the soul you have created.
For without you I cannot amend,
  because whatever is good in us you have made
    and not we ourselves.   25
My soul would not be able to bear it
  if you should judge it according to its sins.

*

  You alone, Lord, are mighty;
  you alone are merciful;

whatever you make me desire for my enemies, 30
give it to them and give the same back to me,
    and if what I ask for them at any time
    is outside the rule of charity,
whether through weakness, ignorance, or malice,
    good Lord, do not give it to them 35
    and do not give it back to me.

*

You who are the true light, lighten their darkness;
you who are the whole truth, correct their errors;
you who are the true life, give life to their souls.
For you have said to your beloved disciple 40
    that he who loves not remains dead.
So I pray, Lord, that you will give them love for you
    and love for their neighbour,
as far as you ordain that they should have it,
lest they should sin before you against their brother. 45

*

    Tender Lord Jesus,
let me not be the cause of the death of my brothers,
    let me not be to them
    a stone of stumbling and a rock of offence.
    For it is more than enough, Lord, 50
    that I should be a scandal to myself,
    my sin is sufficient to me.
Your slave begs you for his fellow slaves,
    lest because of me they offend
against the kindness of so good and great a lord. 55
Let them be reconciled to you and in concord with me,
according to your will and for your own sake.

*

This is the punishment
that in the secret of my heart
   I want to exact   60
for those who serve with me and those who sin with me –
   this is the punishment that I ask
   for those who serve with me and hate me –
   let us love you and each other
   as you will and as is expedient for us,   65
   so that we may make amends to the good Lord
   for our own and for each other's offences;
   so that we may obey with one heart in love
      one Lord and one Master.
   This is the revenge your sinner asks   70
on all who wish him evil and act against him.
   Most merciful Lord,
   prepare the same punishment for your sinner.

*

Do this, my good Creator and my merciful Judge,
according to your mercy that cannot be measured.   75
   Forgive me all my debts
as I before you forgive all those indebted to me.
   Perhaps this may not be so
because in your sight I have not yet done this perfectly,
   but my will is set to do it,   80
   and to that end I am doing all I can.
   So I offer this to you here, Lord,
   so that you may perfectly forgive my sins
   and deal with me as gently as you can.

*

Hear me, good and great Lord,   85
for my soul hungers and longs
to feed upon the experience of your love,
but it cannot fill itself with you;

for my heart can find no name to invoke
that will satisfy my heart.   90
  For no words have here any taste to me
when my love receives from you that which you give.
  I have prayed, Lord, as I can,
  but I wish I could do more.
  Hear me, and answer as you are able,   95
  for you can do all that you will.
  I have prayed as a weak man and a sinner;
you who are mighty and merciful, hear my prayer.

*

  Fulfil my prayer, Lord, not only for my friends
and the enemies for whom I have prayed,   100
  but distribute the healing of your mercy
  wherever you know it may help anyone
  and not be contrary to your will,
  both to the living and the departed.
  Hear me always with your favour,   105
not according as my heart wills or as my mouth asks,
but as you know and will that I ought to wish and ask,
  O Saviour of the world,
  who with the Father and the Holy Spirit
    lives and reigns God   110
    throughout all ages. Amen.

Letter from Durandus, Abbot of Casa-Dei, to Anselm

(Schmitt, vol. 3, Letter 70, pp. 190–1)

Durandus, Abbot of Casa-Dei, by the sole grace of God, to the Lord Anselm, the venerable prior of Bec – eternal salutations.

Two visitors have come to us from Bayeaux, with letters, young men of outstanding ability in every way: the younger is called Roger, and the other is William. They, and many others too, but mostly these two, have poured into our ears the sweet oil of your name and goodness.

'I am afraid of my life, for however I look at it . . .', with all that follows, was uttered and written, out of the goodness of your contrite heart. When we read these words, your pious tears were before us, drawing the same from us, so that we marvelled in every way, both that such a dew of blessing should overflow from your heart, and that from thence without a murmur such a stream should descend into our hearts. For this is in fact what happened. The goodness of the prayers you have written stirs this up in us, loving this in you, or rather you in them, and above them and through them loving God and you. Pray for us, for you are able to intercede, pray for us who pray for you as we are able, and if you have any more prayers that you have written beyond what we have, send them, for we have heard of them and ask for them in the love that lies between us.

(In his reply Anselm does not mention the *Prayers and Meditations* at all.)

Meditation 1

A meditation to stir up fear

I am afraid of my life. For when I examine myself carefully, it seems to me that my whole life is either sinful or sterile. If anything in it seems to be fruitful, it is either imperfect or it is a pretence, or even in some way corrupt, so that either it fails to please or it actually displeases God. So, sinner, now not almost the whole, but certainly the whole of your life, is either sinful and damnable, or unfruitful and contemptible. But what is the difference between unfruitful and damnable? Whatever is unfruitful is also damnable, for what the truth said remains true: 'Every tree that does not bear good fruit is hewn down and cast into the fire.' And even if I do something that is beneficial, in no way can I weigh it in the balance against the things of the body which I have wasted. Who pastures a beast unless he is worth as much as he consumes? Yet you, kind God, nourish and wait for this useless creeping thing, this foul smelling sinner. The rotting corpse of a dog smells more tolerable than the soul of a sinful man to God, it is less displeasing to men than that other is to God. Alas, a sinner is not a man, but 'the scorn of men', more vile than a beast, worse than a corpse. 'My soul is weary of my life', I blush to be alive, I am afraid to die. Nothing is left for you, sinner, but to deplore your whole life all your life long, so that the whole may deplore the whole. Yet it is in this that my soul in its misery is to be wondered at, and is miserable in being wondered at: it does not grieve at what it knows about itself, but it sleeps in security, as if it did not know anything was wrong with it.

Barren soul, what are you doing? Sinful soul, why are you lying still? The day of judgement is coming, 'that great day of the Lord is nigh, it is near and comes quickly, day of wrath and day of mourning, day of tribulation and anguish, day of calamity

and misery, day of darkness and shadows, day of clouds and
eddies, day of trumpets and noises'. O bitter voice of the day of
the Lord. O man, luke-warm and worthy to be spewed out,
why are you sleeping? He who does not rouse himself and
tremble before such thunder, is not asleep but dead.   35

Barren tree, where is your fruit? You deserve to be cut down
and burnt, cut up and put on the fire; where is your fruit? At
least you bear the sharp and bitter thorns of sins. Would that
they might so prick you to repentance that they might be broken,
or become so bitter that they might disappear. Perhaps you   40
think of some sin as small? Would that the strict judge would
regard any sin as small. But, alas for me, surely all sin dis-
honours God because it disobeys his laws? Where then is the
sinner who dares to call any sin small? To dishonour God:
how small a thing is that?   45

Barren and useless wood, deserving eternal burning, what
reply will you make in that day when at the twinkling of an
eye an account is demanded of you for all the time that has been
dealt out to you? How have you expended it? Whatever then is
found in you that has not been directed according to the will of 50
God, whether in work or leisure, speech or silence, to the
smallest thought, even all your living, will be condemned. How
many sins will then rush forward as from an ambush, which at
present you do not see at all. They are surely many, and probably
more terrible than those that you do see. How many things that 55
you thought were not evil, how many that you believed to be
good, will there with naked face appear as darkest sins? There
beyond doubt you will be recompensed according to what you
have done in the body; it will be no longer the time for mercy.
Then your penitence will not be received, then you will not be 60
able to promise amendment. Think on your deeds here, and what
you deserve to receive for them. If there is much good and little
evil, be very glad; if there is much evil and little good, be very
sorrowful.

Useless sinner, is not this sufficient to draw from you a great 65

groan? Is it not enough to draw forth your blood and marrow
in tears? Here is hardness to be wondered at; such heavy
hammers as these are too light to break it up. Here is dullness
with so little feeling that even such sharp points are too blunt
to stir it. What a sleep of death is this, that such harsh and   70
terrible thunder cannot disturb? Useless sinner, there is enough
here to keep you continually mourning, there is enough here for
you to be able to drink continual tears.

Why should I keep hidden from the eyes of my soul any of the
gravity and greatness of the misery that threatens it? So that   75
unforeseen sorrows may rush in unexpectedly, so that an
intolerable tempest may suddenly overwhelm it? That would
be no help to a sinner. But even if I say whatever I can think of,
it cannot be compared to the reality. Therefore let my eyes flow
with tears day and night and cease not. O sinner, increase the   80
weight of wretchedness, add fear to fear, wailing to wailing. For
your judge will be he who has seen the shame of whatever sin you
have committed, in disobedience to God, or in treachery. He
returned to me good for evil and I have repaid him with evil for
good. He who is now most patient will then be most severe; now   85
most kind, then he will be most just. Alas, how greatly I have sinned; I have dishonoured God, I have provoked the Almighty. A
sinner, what have I done, to whom have I done it, how wickedly
have I behaved! Alas, wrath of the Almighty, do not fall upon
me. Wrath of the Almighty, where will you find a place in me?   90
There is nothing in the whole of my being that can endure you.

Alas for me, here are sins accusing me – there is the terror of
judgement. Below the horrible chaos of hell lies open – above is
the wrath of the judge. Inside is the burning of conscience – outside is the burning of the world. Scarcely shall the just be saved,   95
– and thus overtaken, where can a sinner turn? I am bound
fast, where shall I turn? How can I show myself? It will be
impossible to hide, it will be intolerable to appear. I shall desire
to hide and there will be nowhere to go; I shall curse being
seen, and I will be exposed everywhere. What will happen then?   100

Who will deliver me out of the hands of God? Where shall I find counsel, where safety? Who is he who is called Angel of mighty counsel, who is called Saviour, that I may call upon his name?

But it is he himself, he himself is Jesus. The same is my judge, between whose hands I tremble. Take heart, sinner, and do not 105 despair. Hope in him whom you fear, flee to him from whom you have fled. Without ceasing invoke him whom you have provoked by pride. Jesus, Jesus, for your name's sake, deal with me according to your name. Jesus, Jesus, forget the pride which provoked you, see only the wretchedness that invokes you. Dear name, 110 name of delight, name of comfort to the sinner, name of blessed hope. For what is Jesus except to say Saviour? So, Jesus, for your own sake, be to me Jesus. You have made me, do not let me perish. You have redeemed me, do not condemn me. You created me by your goodness, do not let the work of your hands perish by 115 my wickedness. I pray you, dearest Lord, do not let my sin destroy what your goodness has made. Most kind Lord, acknowledge what is yours in me, and take away anything that is not yours. Have mercy, Jesus, while the time of mercy lasts, lest in the time of judgement you condemn. For what profit is 120 there for you in my blood, if I go down to eternal corruption? 'For the dead praise you not, Lord, nor those that go down into hell.' If you take me into the wide heart of your mercy, Lord, it will not be the narrower on my account. O most desired Jesus, admit me to the number of your elect, so that with them I may 125 enjoy you, with them I may praise you, and glorify you with 'all those that love your name', who with the Father and the Holy Spirit shall be glorified for ever. Amen.

Meditation 2

A lament for virginity unhappily lost

My soul, my wretched soul, wretched soul of a wretched little man, shake off your lethargy, put away your sin, and pull yourself together. Let your heart break with the enormity of sin and let a huge groan break out of your heart. Unhappy man, turn your thoughts to the horror of your wickedness, and turn yourself to horrible terror and terrible grief. Once I was washed with the whiteness of heaven, given the Holy Spirit, pledged to the profession of Christianity; I was a virgin, I was the spouse of Christ.

Too well I remember it. And who is it I have named? He is not now the kind spouse of my virginity, but the terrible judge of my impurity. Alas, why does the memory of lost rejoicing thus make worse the weight of my present unhappiness? How wretched is the state of wicked men, for they are punished equally by both bad and good. I am tormented by a bad conscience and its tortures in which I fear I shall burn; I am tormented by a good conscience, and the memory of its rewards which I know I have lost and cannot freely regain. Ah, the misery of loss, the grief of loss: to have lost irreparably what ought to have been preserved forever. Alas, to have lost inconsolably that which is not only the loss of good, but the gain of torment.

O virginity, now not my delight but my loss, not my joy but my despair, whither have you gone? In what a stink, in what bitter filth have you abandoned me? O fornication, by which my mind is defiled, and my soul betrayed, whence have you crept up on me in my misery? From what brightness and joy in which I stood have you cast me down? It is a bitter grief which burns me, to have lost virginity; but it is anguish and heavy sorrow, and fear of heavier yet, to have committed fornication. The one is an inconsolable loss; the other is intolerable torment.

There is deep sorrow either way. Thus do good and bad equally and justly punish miserable sinners while they are still alive. Deserved, yes, indeed it is.

For, O my soul, you are unfaithful to God, false to God, an adulterer from Christ; it is of your own free will that you are 35 miserably cast down from highest virginity into the lowest pit of fornication. You were once the spouse of the king of heaven and with alacrity you have made yourself the whore of the tormentor of hell. Cast off from God, you are cast forth to the devil. Even more, you have cast off God and embraced the 40 devil. Wretched and obstinate harlot, you have offered to divorce your God who first loved and created you, and of your own accord you have given yourself to the devil, who betrays and destroys you.

Most wretched, more than wretched exchange. Alas, from 45 what a height are you fallen, to what depths have you sunk? Alas, what kindness have you cast away, to what merciless evil have you joined yourself? Demented mind, mindless of defilement, defiled by sin, what have you done? You have abandoned your chaste lover in heaven and gone after your hateful corrupter 50 in hell, and in the lower world you have prepared for yourself not a marriage chamber but a brothel. Marvellous horror, that you have perverted your will; horrible marvel, that you willed your perversity. Where, my God, shall I find amendment for such depravity? How can I make satisfaction to you, Lord, for 55 such wickedness?

Miserable little man, throw yourself into the dark depths of boundless grief, for of your own will you fell into the dark depths of horrible iniquity. Unhappy man, let the weight of terrible sorrow bury you, for you freely sank into the mud of stinking 60 hell. Wrap yourself round, wretch, in the horrible darkness of inconsolable mourning, for you were willing to roll into the pit of sordid lust. Plunge into the whirlpool of bitterness – you have wallowed in the trough of moral corruption.

Fear to be shuddered at, grief to be afraid of, mourning that 65 cannot be comforted – heap yourselves upon me, rush on me, bury me, trouble me, wrap me round, possess me! It is just, indeed it is just! With shameless daring I despised you all, and provoked you with my stinking delights. I provoked God even more than you and now in unhappy repentance I long for you. Torment the guilty and vindicate God! Let the fornicator feel beforehand the torments of hell that he has deserved, give him a foretaste of what he has to look forward to, let him become accustomed to what he will have to suffer. Immoderate sinner, show the mourning of repentance; too long have you been showing the evil of your impurity. Spin round and round in the whirlpool of bitterness as you have spun round so often in the giddiness of lust.

Consolation, security, joy – I will have none of you, unless the forgiveness of my sins brings you back. Be far from me before death, so that perhaps mercy will give you back to me after death. Let continual penitence be the bitter companion of my life, let sharp grief be the insatiable tormentor of my existence, may sorrow and sour mourning trouble my youth and my age without tiring. Would that it might be so! I choose, pray and desire that it may be so! I am not worthy to lift up my eyes to heaven to pray, but I am not too unworthy to make them blind with weeping. My mind is confounded by the shame of my conscience when I pray – let it be equally confounded by a crowd of mournful sorrows and griefs. I fear to show myself before the presence of God, so it is just that I should live with the torments of my wickedness.

My heart considers and reconsiders what it has done and what it deserves. Let my mind descend into 'the land of darkness and the shadows of death', and consider what there awaits my sinful soul. Let me look inwards and contemplate, see and be disturbed; O God, what is this that I perceive, the land of 'misery and darkness'? Horror! horror! What is this that I gaze upon, where they live without order, in eternal horror? Ah, a confusion of noises, a tumult of gnashing teeth, a babble of groans. Ah, ah, too much, ah, too much woe! Sulphurous flames, flames of hell, eddying darknesses, swirling with terrible sounds. Worms living in the fire, is it not marvellous that such a greediness of burning should gnaw you, and that you should be burnt up by the flame of fire? Devils that burn 105 with us, raging with fire and gnashing your teeth in madness, why are you so cruel to those who roll about among you? These torments of every kind are restrained by justice, not by suffering. Can they be in no way tempered, have they no remedy or end? Is this indeed the end, great God, prepared for fornicators and 110 despisers of your law, of whom I am one?

Even I myself am one of them! My soul, be exceedingly afraid; tremble, my mind; be torn, my heart. Exactors of my wickedness, whither are you bearing me away? Whither are you pushing me, O my sins? To what have you delivered me up, my God? I 115 have acted in such a way that I am your accused, but surely you cannot act in such a way that I am no longer your creature? My chastity has gone from me, but you have surely not lost your mercy? Lord, my Lord, I have done that for which you are able to condemn me, but surely you have not lost that by which 120 you are able to save? Lord, in remembering my wickedness, do not forget your goodness. God of truth, where is it written that 'as I live I do not desire the death of a sinner but rather that he be converted and live'? Lord, you do not lie; would it be truly not to 'desire the death of a sinner' to bury in hell a sinner 125 who cries out to you? Is to thrust down a sinner into hell to 'desire not the death of a sinner'? Surely it is rather that 'I will "that the sinner" "turn and live"'. Lord, I am indeed the sinner. What is it that forces you to do what you do not will, in handing me over to death? If you will that the sinner 'be con- 130 verted and live', what prevents you from doing what you will, that is, converting me that I may live? Can the hugeness of my sin force you to do what you would not and prevent what you would, when you are the omnipotent God? Not so, my God, not so, my Lord; let not the wickedness of the sinner who 135 confesses and grieves prevail over the will of the Almighty.

Just and loving God, remember that you are merciful and my Creator and Redeemer. Good Lord, do not recall your just claims against your sinner, but remember mercy towards your creature. Do not remember wrath against your accused, but have 140 compassion on one who needs mercy. Of course my conscience deserves damnation and my penitence is not enough for satisfaction; but it is certain that your mercy outweighs all offences.

Good Lord, of whom comes salvation, and who does not will the death of a sinner, spare my sinful soul. In terror I flee from 145 the dread of your justice to the comfort of your mercy. However much the treasure of virginity is, alas, corrupted irreparably, at least let not the punishment of the fornicator who is penitent be unavoidable; this is not impossible to your power, nor unbecoming to your justice, nor unwonted to your mercy; for you 150 are good and your mercy is everlasting, who are blessed for ever. Amen.

calls it out by name

Christian soul, brought to life again out of the heaviness of death, redeemed and set free from wretched servitude by the blood of God, rouse yourself and remember that you are risen, realize that you have been redeemed and set free. Consider again the strength of your salvation and where it is found. Meditate upon it, delight in the contemplation of it. Shake off your lethargy and set your mind to thinking over these things. Taste the goodness of your Redeemer, be on fire with love for your Saviour. Chew the honeycomb of his words, suck their flavour which is sweeter than sap, swallow their wholesome sweetness. Chew by thinking, suck by understanding, swallow by loving and rejoicing. Be glad to chew, be thankful to suck, rejoice to swallow.

What then is the strength and power of your salvation and where is it found? Christ has brought you back to life. He is the good Samaritan who healed you. He is the good friend who redeemed you and set you free by laying down his life for you. Christ did all this. So the strength of your salvation is the strength of Christ.

Where is the strength of Christ? 'Horns are in his hands, there is his strength hid.' Indeed horns are in his hands, because his hands were nailed to the arms of the cross. But what strength is there in such weakness, what height in such lowliness? What is there to be venerated in such abjection? Surely something is hidden by this weakness, something is concealed by this humility. There is something mysterious in this abjection. O hidden strength: a man hangs on a cross and lifts the load of eternal death from the human race; a man nailed to wood looses the bonds of everlasting death that hold fast the world. O hidden power: a man condemned with thieves saves men condemned with devils, a man stretched out on the gibbet draws all men to himself. O mysterious strength: one soul coming forth from torment draws countless souls with him out of hell, a man submits to the death of the body and destroys the death of souls.

Good Lord, living Redeemer, mighty Saviour, why did you conceal such power under such humility? Was it that you might deceive the devil, who by deceiving man had thrown him out of paradise? But truth deceives no one. He who is ignorant or does not believe the truth, deceives himself, and whoever sees the truth and hates or despises it, deceives himself. But truth itself deceives no one. Or was it so that the devil might deceive himself? No, even as truth deceives no one, so it does not mean anyone to deceive himself, although when it permits this it might be said to do so. You did not assume human nature to conceal what was known of yourself, but to reveal what was not known. You declared yourself to be true God; by what you did you showed yourself to be true man. The thing was itself a mystery, not made mysterious. It was not done like this so that it might be hidden, but so that it might be accomplished in the way ordained. It was not secret to deceive anyone, but secret so that it might be carried out. If it is said to be mysterious, this is only to say that it was not revealed to everyone. The truth does not show itself to all, but it refuses itself to no one. So, Lord, you did not do this to deceive anyone, or so that anyone might deceive himself, but only so that you might carry out your work, in all things established in the truth. So let anyone who is deceived about your truth complain of his own falsehood, not of yours.

Or has the devil in justice anything against either God or man, that God had to act in this secret way for man, rather than openly by strength? Was it so that by unjustly killing a just man the devil should justly lose the power he had over the unjust? But clearly God owes nothing to the devil except punishment, nor does man owe him anything except to reverse the defeat which in some way he allowed himself to suffer by sinning; and this he does by preserving his integrity intact even through the hardness

35

40

45

50

55

60

65

231

of death. But that also man owed to God alone, for he had not sinned against the devil but against God, and man was not of the devil, but both man and devil were of God. When the devil vexed man, he did it with the zeal of wickedness not of justice, and God did not order him to do it, but only permitted it; the justice of God not of the devil exacted this. So then there is nothing on the side of the devil to cause God to hide or dissemble his strength in saving mankind. 70

Was it then another kind of necessity that made the highest humble himself so, and the mighty one labour so much to do this work? But all necessities and impossibilities are subject to his will. What he wills, must be; what he wills not, cannot be. Therefore this was done by his will alone. And because his will is always good, he did this solely out of goodness. 75

God was not obliged to save mankind in this way, but human nature needed to make amends to God like this. God had no need to suffer so laboriously, but man needed to be reconciled thus. God did not need to humble himself, but man needed this, so that he might be raised from the depths of hell. The divine nature did not need nor was it able to be humiliated and to labour. It was for the sake of human nature that all these things needed to be done, so that it might be restored to that for which it was made. But neither human nature nor anything that was not God could suffice for this. For man cannot be restored to that state in which he was first established unless he is made like the angels in whom there is no sin. And that could not be done unless he received forgiveness for all his sins, and that could not be unless he first made entire satisfaction. *how it needed to happen* 80 85 90

To make such satisfaction it was necessary that the sinner, or someone for him, should give to God of his own something that he does not owe him, and something more valuable than all that is not God. For to sin is to dishonour God, and this no man ought to do, even if it means that all that is other than God should perish. Immutable truth and plain reason then demand that whoever sins should give something better to God in return for 95 100 the honour of which he has deprived him, that is more than the supposed good for the sake of which he dishonoured him.

Human nature alone could not do this, nor could it be reconciled without the satisfaction of the debt, nor could the justice of God pass over the disorder of sin in his kingdom. The good- 105 ness of God came to help, and the Son of God assumed manhood in his own person, so that God and man should be one and the same person. He had what was above all beings that are other than God, and he took on himself all the debt that sinners ought to pay, and this when he himself owed nothing, so that he could 110 pay the debt for the others who owed it and could not pay.

More precious is the life of that man than all that is not God, and it is more than all the debt that sinners owe in order to make satisfaction for their sins. For his death was more than all that can be thought outside the person of God. It is clear that such a 115 life is more good than all sins are bad. This man, who was not obliged to die for a debt, because he was not a sinner, gave his life of his own accord to the Father, when he allowed his life to be taken from him, for the sake of righteousness. This gave an example to others not to reject the righteousness of God because 120 of death, which of necessity they would all at some time have to undergo, for he who was not obliged to suffer death and could have avoided it with justice, willed to give himself up to death and underwent it for the sake of righteousness. Thus in him human nature gave to God something it had of its own, willingly, 125 and not because it was owed. So through him human nature might be redeemed in the other men who had not got that which would pay the debt that they owed.

In all this, divine nature was not humbled but human nature was exalted. God was not made any less, but mankind was merci- 130 fully helped. In that man, human nature did not suffer anything as of necessity, but solely of free will. He did not submit to violence, but freely embraced it out of goodness, to the honour of God and the benefit of other men. For praise and mercy he bore what evil brought upon him, and he was not coerced by 135 obedience, but he ordained it to be so by the power of his wisdom.

For the Father did not order that man to die and compel him to do so, but what Christ understood would please the Father and benefit man, that he did of his own free will. In this matter 140 the Father could not force him, for it was something that he had no right to exact from him. Such honour could not but please the Father, when the Son freely offered it with such good will. So the Son freely obeyed the Father, when he willed freely to do what he knew would please him. But since the Father gave 145 him that good will (which nevertheless was free), it is not undeservedly said that he received it as a command of the Father. In this way he was made 'obedient to the Father', 'even unto death', and 'as the Father gave him commandment, even so he did', and 'the cup that the Father gave him, he drank'. This 150 is the perfect and free obedience of human nature, in that Christ freely submitted his own free will to God, and perfectly used in liberty the good will he had received, without any compulsion.

So that man redeemed all others in that what he freely gave to God paid for the debtors what they owed. By this price man was 155 not only redeemed from blame but whenever he returns with genuine penitence he is received, though that penitence is not promised to sinners. Because of that which was done on the cross, by the cross our Christ has redeemed us. Then whosoever wills to come to this grace with the love it deserves, will be saved. And 160 those who despise it are justly damned, because they do not pay the debt they owe.

See, Christian soul, here is the strength of your salvation, here is the cause of your freedom, here is the price of your redemption. You were a bond-slave and by this man you are free. By him 165 you are brought back from exile, lost, you are restored, dead, you are raised. Chew this, bite it, suck it, let your heart swallow it, when your mouth receives the body and blood of your Redeemer. Make it in this life your daily bread, your food, your way-bread, for through this and not otherwise than through this, 170

[margin handwritten note:] Almost imploring?

will you remain in Christ and Christ in you, and your joy will be full.

But, Lord, you gave yourself up to death that I might live; how can I be happy about a freedom which is not wrought without your chains? How can I rejoice in my salvation, which 175 would not be without your sorrows? How can I enjoy a life which meant your death? Shall I rejoice with those who by their cruelty made you suffer? For unless they had done it you would not have suffered, and if you had not suffered these good things would not have been mine. But if I grieve because of their cruelty, how can 180 I also rejoice in the benefits that I only possess because of your sufferings? Their wickedness could have done nothing unless you freely permitted it, nor did you suffer except because in love you willed it. Thus I must condemn their cruelty, imitate your death and sufferings, and share them with you, giving thanks for 185 the goodness of your love. And thus may I safely rejoice in the good that thereby comes to me.

Now, little man, leave their cruelties to the justice of God, and think of what you owe your Saviour. Consider what he was to you, what he did for you, and think that for what he did for you 190 he is the more worthy to be loved. Look into your need and his goodness, and see what thanks you should render him, and how much love you owe him. You were in darkness, on uncertain ground, descending into the chaos of hell that is beyond redemption. A huge leaden weight hung round your neck, dragging you 195 downwards, an unbearable burden pressed upon you, invisible enemies were striking at you with all their might. You were without any help and you did not know it, for you were conceived and born in that state. What was happening to you, to what place were you rushing away? Remember and tremble; think and be 200 afraid.

Good Lord Jesus Christ, thus was I placed, neither asking nor conjecturing, when as the sun you gave me light, and showed me what a state I was in. You threw away the leaden weight which was dragging me down, you took off the burden that 205

235

pressed upon me, you drove off those who were attacking me, and opposed them on my behalf. You called me by a new name, which you gave me from your name. And I who was bent down, you made upright in your sight, saying, 'Be of good cheer. I have redeemed you. I have given my life for you. You shall leave 210 the evil you were in, and not fall into the pit to which you were going, if you cleave to me. I will lead you into my kingdom and make you an heir of God and co-heir with me.' From then on you accepted me into your care so that nothing could harm my soul against my will. And lo, even before I cleaved to you as you 215 counselled, you did not let me fall into hell, but looked forward to when I should cleave to you; even then you were keeping your promises.

Lord, it was so with me, and this is what you have done for me. I was in darkness, knowing nothing of myself, in a slippery place, 220 for I was weak and prone to fall into sin, I was descending into the chaos of hell, for in my first parents I had fallen from right-eousness into wickedness, which is the way to hell, and from blessedness to temporal misery for ever. The weight of original sin dragged me downwards, and the unbearable burden of the 225 judgement of God pressed upon me; my demon enemies thrust vehemently against me to make me do other damnable sins.

When I was destitute of all help, you illuminated me, and showed me what I was, for when I was still unable to see this, you taught others the truth on my behalf and you showed it to me 230 before I asked it. The load that dragged at me, the burden that weighed me down, the enemies that opposed me – you cast them all back when you removed the sin in which I was conceived and born and its condemnation. You forbade evil spirits to attack my soul. You made me a Christian, called by your own name, by 235 which I confessed you, and you acknowledged me to be among your redeemed. You have set me upright and raised me to the knowledge and love of yourself. You have made me sure of the salvation of my soul, for you have given your life for it, and you have promised me your glory if I follow you. And when I was not 240 following you, but was still committing many sins which you had forbidden, you waited for me to follow you till you could give me what you promised.

Consider, O my soul, and hear, all that is within me, how much my whole being owes to him! Lord, because you have made me, 245 I owe you the whole of my love; because you have redeemed me, I owe you the whole of myself; because you have promised so much, I owe you all my being. Moreover, I owe you as much more love than myself as you are greater than I, for whom you gave yourself and to whom you promised yourself. I pray you, 250 Lord, make me taste by love what I taste by knowledge; let me know by love what I know by understanding. I owe you more than my whole self, but I have no more, and by myself I cannot render the whole of it to you. Draw me to you, Lord, in the fullness of love. I am wholly yours by creation; make me all 255 yours, too, in love.

Lord, my heart is before you. I try, but by myself I can do nothing; do what I cannot. Admit me into the inner room of your love. I ask, I seek, I knock. You who made me seek, make me receive; you who gave the seeking, give the finding; you 260 who taught the knocking, open to my knock. To whom will you give, if you refuse my petition? Who finds, if this seeking is in vain? To whom is it opened, if to this knocking it is closed? What do you give to those who do not pray if you deny your love to those who do? By you I have desire; by you let me have 265 fulfilment. Cleave to him, my soul, and never leave off. Good Lord, do not reject me; I faint with hunger for your love; refresh me with it. Let me be filled with your love, rich in your affection, completely held in your care. Take me and possess me wholly, who with the Father and the Holy Spirit are alone 270 blessed to ages of ages. Amen.

Proslogion

Preface

At the pressing entreaties of some of my brethren I published a
short work as an example of meditation on the meaning of faith,
from the point of view of someone who, by silent reasoning in
his own mind, inquires into things about which he is ignorant.
When I reflected that this consisted in a connected chain of
many arguments, I began to ask myself if it would be possible to
find one single argument, needing no other proof than itself, to
prove that God really exists, that he is the highest good, needing
nothing, that it is he whom all things need for their being and
well-being, and to prove whatever else we believe about the
nature of God. I turned this over in my mind often and carefully; sometimes it seemed to me that what I was seeking was
almost within my grasp; sometimes it eluded the keenness of my
thought completely; so at last in desperation I was going to give
up looking for something that it was impossible to find. But when
I wanted to put the idea entirely out of my mind, lest it occupy
me in vain and so keep out other ideas in which I could make
some progress, then it began to force itself upon me with increasing urgency, however much I refused and resisted it. So
one day, when I was tired out with resisting its importunity,
that which I had despaired of finding came to me, in the conflict
of my thoughts, and I welcomed eagerly the very thought which
I had been so anxious to reject.

It seemed to me that this thing which had given me such joy
to discover would, if it were written down, give pleasure to any
who might read it. So I have written the following short work,
dealing with this matter and with several others, from the point
of view of someone trying to raise his mind to the contemplation
of God, and seeking to understand what he believes. It does not
seem to me that either this work or the one I mentioned before

deserves to be called a book or to bear the name of its author; but I do not think they should be distributed without some sort of title, which might make those into whose hands they come read them, so I have given them these titles: the first, 'An example of Meditation on the Meaning of Faith'; and the second, 'Faith in Search of Understanding'.

Under these titles they have both already been transcribed by several people, and many of them (above all the reverend archbishop of Lyons, Hugh, apostolic delegate in Gaul, who has commanded this by his apostolic authority) have urged me to put my name on them. For the sake of greater convenience I have called the first book Monologion, that is, a soliloquy; and the other Proslogion, that is, a colloquy.

Chapter 1

In which the mind is aroused to the contemplation of God

Come now, little man,
turn aside for a while from your daily employment,
escape for a moment from the tumult of your thoughts.
    Put aside your weighty cares,
    let your burdensome distractions wait,   5
    free yourself awhile for God
    and rest awhile in him. — *Rest*
Enter the inner chamber of your soul,
    shut out everything except God
    and that which can help you in seeking him,   10
    and when you have shut the door, seek him.
Now, my whole heart, say to God,
    'I seek your face,
Lord, it is your face I seek.'

             *

    O Lord my God,   15
teach my heart where and how to seek you,

where and how to find you.
Lord, if you are not here but absent,
　　where shall I seek you?
But you are everywhere, so you must be here,　　20
　　why then do I not seek you?
Surely you dwell in light inaccessible –
　　where is it? and how can I
　　have access to light which is inaccessible?
Who will lead me and take me into it　　25
　　so that I may see you there?
By what signs, under what forms, shall I seek you?
　　I have never seen you, O Lord my God,
　　I have never seen your face.
　　　Most High Lord,　　30
　　what shall an exile do
　　who is as far away from you as this?
　　What shall your servant do,
eager for your love, cast off far from your face?
He longs to see you,　　35
　　but your countenance is too far away.
He wants to have access to you,
　　but your dwelling is inaccessible.
He longs to find you,
　　but he does not know where you are.　　40
He loves to seek you,
　　but he does not know your face.
Lord, you are my Lord and my God,
　　and I have never seen you.
You have created and re-created me,　　45
　　all the good I have comes from you,
　　and still I do not know you.
　　I was created to see you,
and I have not yet accomplished that for which I was made.

*

240

How wretched is the fate of man   50
when he has lost that for which he was created.
 How hard and cruel was the Fall.
 What has man lost, and what has he found?
 What has he left, and what is left to him?
He has lost blessedness for which he was made   55
and he has found wretchedness for which he was not made.
He had left that without which there is no happiness,
and he has got that which is nothing but misery.
 Once man did eat angels' food,
 and now he hungers for it;   60
 now he eats the bread of sorrow,
 which then he knew nothing of.
 Ah, grief common to all men,
 lamentation of all the sons of Adam.
Adam was so full he belched, we are so hungry we sigh;   65
 he had abundance, and we go begging.
He held what he had in happiness and left it in misery;
we are unhappy in our wants and miserable in our desires,
 and ah, how empty we remain.
Why did he not keep for us that which he possessed so easily, 70
 and we lack despite such labour?
Why did he shut out our light
 and surround us with darkness?
Why did he take away our life and give us the hurt of death?
From whence have we wretched men been pushed down,   75
 to what place are we being pushed on?
From what position have we been cast down,
 where are we being buried?
From our homeland into exile,
 from the vision of God into our own blindness,   80
 from the deathless state in which we rejoiced
 into the bitterness of a death to be shuddered at.
Wretched exchange, so great a good for so much evil.

A grievous loss, a grievous sorrow,
   the whole thing is grievous. 85

*

Alas, I am indeed wretched,
one of those wretched sons of Eve,
   separated from God!
What have I begun, and what accomplished?
Where was I going and where have I got to? 90
To what did I reach out, for what do I long?
I sought after goodness, and lo, here is turmoil;
I was going towards God, and I was my own impediment.
   I sought for peace within myself,
and in the depths of my heart I found trouble and sorrow. 95
   I wanted to laugh for the joy of my heart,
   and the pain of my heart made me groan.
   It was gladness I was hoping for,
   but sighs came thick and fast.

*

   O Lord, how long? 100
How long, Lord, will you turn your face from us?
   When will you look upon us and hear us?
When will you enlighten our eyes and show us your face?
   When will you give yourself to us again?
   Look upon us, Lord, and hear us, 105
   enlighten us and show yourself to us.
Give yourself to us again that it may be well with us,
   for without you it is ill with us.
   Have mercy on us,
as we strive and labour to come to you, 110
   for without you we can do nothing well.
You have invited us to cry out, 'Help us':

I pray you, Lord, let me not sigh without hope,
    but hope and breathe again.
Let not my heart become bitter because of its desolation,   115
    but sweeten it with your consolation.
When I was hungry I began to seek you, Lord;
    do not let me go hungry away.
    I came to you famished;
    do not let me go from you unfed.   120
Poor, I have come to one who is rich,
    miserable, I have come to one who is merciful;
    do not let me return empty and despised.
    If before I eat I sigh,
    after my sighs give me to eat.   125
Lord, I am so bent I can only look downwards,
    raise me, that I may look upwards.
    My iniquities have gone over my head,
they cover me and weigh me down like a heavy burden.
    Take this weight, this covering, from me,   130
    lest the pit close its mouth over me.
    Let me discern your light,
    whether from afar or from the depths.
      Teach me to seek you,
    and as I seek you, show yourself to me,   135
    for I cannot seek you unless you show me how,
      and I will never find you
    unless you show yourself to me.
Let me seek you by desiring you,
    and desire you by seeking you;   140
    let me find you by loving you,
    and love you in finding you.

*

I confess, Lord, with thanksgiving,
    that you have made me in your image,
so that I can remember you, think of you, and love you.   145

But that image is so worn and blotted out by faults,
   so darkened by the smoke of sin,
    that it cannot do that for which it was made,
    unless you renew and refashion it.
Lord, I am not trying to make my way to your height,   **150**
for my understanding is in no way equal to that,
but I do desire to understand a little of your truth
   which my heart already believes and loves.
I do not seek to understand so that I may believe,
   but I believe so that I may understand;   **155**
    and what is more,
I believe that unless I do believe I shall not understand.

Chapter 2

That God really exists

Now, Lord, since it is you who gives understanding to faith,
grant me to understand as well as you think fit, that you exist as
we believe, and that you are what we believe you to be. We **160**
believe that you are that thing than which nothing greater can be
thought. Or is there nothing of that kind in existence, since 'the
fool has said in his heart, there is no God'? But when the fool
hears me use this phrase, 'something than which nothing greater
can be thought', he understands what he hears; and what he **165**
understands is in his understanding, even if he does not understand that it exists. For it is one thing to have something in the
understanding, but quite another to understand that it actually
exists. It is like a painter who, when he thinks out beforehand
what he is going to create, has it in his understanding, but he does **170**
not yet understand it as actually existing because he has not yet
painted it. But when he has painted it, he both has it in his
understanding and actually has it, because he has created it. So
the fool has to agree that the concept of something than which

nothing greater can be thought exists in his understanding, since 175
he understood what he heard and whatever is understood is in
the understanding. And certainly that than which nothing
greater can be thought cannot exist only in the understanding.
For if it exists only in the understanding, it is possible to think of
it existing also in reality, and that is greater. If that than which 180
nothing greater can be thought exists in the understanding
alone, then this thing than which nothing greater can be thought
is something than which a greater can be thought. And this is
clearly impossible. Therefore there can be no doubt at all that
something than which a greater cannot be thought exists both in 185
the understanding and in reality.

Chapter 3

That which it is not possible to think of as not existing

This *is* so truly, that it is not possible to think of it not existing.
For it is possible to think of something existing which it is not
possible to think of as not existing, and that is greater than something that can be thought not to exist. If that than which nothing 190
greater can be thought, can be thought of as not existing, then
that than which nothing greater can be thought is not the same
as that than which nothing greater can be thought. And that
simply will not do. Something than which nothing greater can be
thought so truly exists that it is not possible to think of it as not 195
existing.

This being is yourself, our Lord and God. Lord my God, you
so truly are, that it is not possible to think of you as not existing.
And rightly so. For if someone's mind could think of something
better than you, the creature would rise higher than its creator 200
and would judge its creator; which is clearly absurd. For whatever exists except you alone can be thought of as not existing.
Therefore you alone of all most truly are, and you exist most fully

of all things. For nothing else is as true as that, and therefore it has *less* existence. So why does the fool say in his heart, 'there is no God', when it is perfectly clear to the reasoning mind that you exist most fully of all? Why, except that he is indeed stupid and a fool? 205

Chapter 4

That what the fool said in his heart is something that it is not possible to think

Now how has he 'said in his heart' what it is not possible to think; for how could he avoid thinking that which he 'said in his heart', for to say in one's heart is to think. But if he really did, or rather because he really did, both think, because he said in his heart, and not say in his heart, because he was not able to think, then there is not only one way of saying in one's heart and thinking. For in a way one thinks a thing when one thinks the word that signifies the thing; but one thinks it in another way when the thing itself is understood. So in one way it is possible to entertain the concept that God does not exist, but not in the other way. For no one who truly understands that which God is, can think that God does not exist, though he may say those words in his heart, either without any, or with a special, meaning. For God is that than which nothing greater can be thought. Whoever truly understands this, understands that he is of such a kind of existence that he cannot be thought not to exist. So whoever understands this to be the nature of God, cannot think of him as not existing. 210 215 220 225

Thank you, good Lord, thank you, for it was by your gift that I first believed, and now by your illumination I understand; if I did not want to believe that you existed, still I should not be able not to understand it. 230

nothing greater can be thought

Chapter 5

God is whatever it is better to be than not to be; he exists in himself alone; and he creates everything else out of nothing

What are you, then, Lord God, you than whom nothing greater can be thought? What are you but that which exists alone over all things, and has made everything else out of nothing? For whatever is not that, is something less than can be thought; but this cannot be thought about you. Then what good can be lack- 235 ing to the highest good, through whom all other good exists? So you are just, true, blessed, and whatever it is better to be than not to be. For it is better to be just than unjust, blessed than not blessed.

Chapter 6

How he can be perceived, though he is not a body

Indeed it is better to be capable of perception, omnipotent, 240 merciful, and impassible, than not to be so; but how are you able to perceive if you are not a body, how are you omnipotent if you cannot do all things, and how can you be compassionate and beyond passion at the same time? For if only that which relates to the body can perceive things, since the senses are in the body 245 and concerned with it, how can he perceive, when he is not a body but the highest spirit, which is better than any body?

But if to perceive is nothing else but to know, or related to knowing, or if one perceives by knowing according to the appropriate sense, for instance, colours by seeing, tastes by 250 tasting – it is not inappropriate to say that whatever in some way is perceived, is also in some way known. Thus, Lord, although you do not have a body, you truly perceive in the highest way, for you know all things supremely, though not through the bodily senses like an animal.

255

Chapter 7

How he is omnipotent, though there are many things he cannot do

But how can you be omnipotent if you cannot do all things? How can you do all things, if you cannot be corrupted, or lie, or make false what is true – which would be to make what is into non-being – and so forth? If this is so, how can you do all things?

Or is it that these things proceed not from power but from powerlessness? For whoever can do these things, is able to do that which is harmful to him and which he should not do. And the more he can do these things, so much the more will adversity and perversity be in him, and he will be less opposed to them. Therefore he who can do these things, does them not by power but by powerlessness. It is not said that he can do them because he is able to, but because of his powerlessness another can do them in him; or it is meant in some other way, as many other words are used improperly. For instance we use 'to be' instead of 'not to be', and 'to do', when we mean 'not to do', or 'to do nothing'. So we often say when someone denies that something exists, 'that is as you say it is', when it would be more correct for us to say, 'it is not as you say it is not'. We also say, 'he is sitting', just as we say, 'he is doing something'; or 'he is resting', just as we say 'he is doing something'. But to sit is non-doing, and to rest is to do nothing. So when we say that someone has the power to do or suffer something which is not good for him or which he ought not to do, by 'power' we really mean 'powerlessness'. For the more someone has 'power' in that sense, the more power adversity and perversity have over him, and he is the more powerless against them. So, Lord God, you are in fact more truly omnipotent because you cannot do anything through powerlessness, and nothing has power over you.

powerlessness

5-26

Chapter 8

How he is both compassionate and beyond passion

But how can you be at the same time both compassionate and
beyond passion? If you are beyond passion, you cannot suffer 285
with anyone; if you cannot share suffering, your heart is not
made wretched by entering into the sufferings of the wretched,
which is what being compassionate is. But if you are not compassionate, where does so much consolation for those who are
wretched come from? 290

How then, Lord, can you be compassionate and yet not compassionate, unless you are compassionate from our point of view
and not from yours? According to our meaning, not according to
yours? When you look upon us in our wretchedness, we
experience the effect of your compassion, but you do not experi- 295
ence the emotion. So you are compassionate, when you save
wretches, and pardon those who sin against you; but you are not
compassionate because you do not experience the feeling of
compassion for wretchedness.

Chapter 9

How he who is entirely and supremely righteous spares the wicked; and that it is right for him to have compassion on the wicked

If you are entirely and supremely righteous, how can you spare 300
the wicked? How does the entirely and supremely righteous one
do something unrighteous? How can it be right to give eternal
life to one who deserves eternal death? God of goodness, good
to both good and wicked, how can you save the wicked, if it is
not right to do so, and you cannot do anything that is not right? 305
Because your goodness is beyond comprehension, is this

matter hidden in the inaccessible light wherein you dwell? Truly the source whence flows the stream of your compassion is hidden in the deepest and most secret place of your goodness. For in being entirely and supremely righteous, even in this you 310 are kind to the wicked, just because your goodness is entire and supreme. For you would be less good if you were kind to none of the wicked, for better is he who is good to both good and evil men, than he who is good only to good men. And better is he who is good to the wicked by both punishing and sparing them, 315 than he who only punishes them. So you are compassionate because you are entirely and supremely good. And although one can see why you should deal out good to the good and bad to the bad, what is indeed to be wondered at is why you who are entirely righteous and want for nothing should give good gifts to 320 your wicked and guilty sons. How deep is your goodness, O God. The source of your compassion is seen, but is not seen clearly; whence the stream flows is known, but it is not fully known whence it springs. It is the fullness of your goodness that makes you loving towards those who sin against you, but why this 325 should be so is hidden in the depths of your goodness. For even granted that it is out of your goodness that you deal out good to the good and bad to the bad, yet the consideration of justice would also seem to require this. But when you give good things to the wicked, we know it is because the highest good has willed 330 to do it, but we wonder why the highest justice was able to do it.

Ah, from what generous love and loving generosity
   compassion flows out to us!
Ah, what feelings of love should we sinners have
   towards the unbounded goodness of God! 335
   For you save the righteous
  who are commended by their righteousness,
  and you set free those
  who by their unrighteousness are condemned;
the one by the help of what they have deserved, 340

the other in spite of what they have deserved.
In those you look to find the good you gave them;
in these you overlook the evil which you hate.

    Ah, boundless goodness,
  far beyond all understanding,   345
  on me be your compassion
  which comes from such generosity!
Let that which flows from you, flow into me.
    Spare me out of mercy,
lest you take vengeance out of justice.   350
    It is hard to understand
how your compassion is no different
  from your righteousness,
  but it is essential to believe
that it is in no way opposed to righteousness,
for it flows from goodness,   355
which is nothing without righteousness
and even coincides with it.
For you are compassionate
because you are entirely good,
and you are not entirely good   360
unless you are entirely righteous.
So you are compassionate
because you are entirely righteous.
O righteous and compassionate God,
  whose light I seek,   365
help me to understand what I am saying!
Truly you are compassionate because you are entirely righteous.

Does not your compassion then proceed from your justice?
Do you not then spare the wicked out of justice? If this is so,
Lord, teach me how it can be so. Does justice lie in this, that you 370
are good in this way so that you cannot be conceived to be better,
and you act with such power, so that you cannot be thought to be
more powerful? What is more just than that? But that would not

be so, if you were good only in punishment and not in forgiveness, or if you made good men only out of the non-good, and not out of the wicked. So it is just that you should spare the wicked and make good out of bad. Finally, what is not done out of justice, ought not to be done, and what ought not to be done is unjustly done. If it is not right for you to have compassion on the wicked, you ought not to do it; and if you ought not to be compassionate, it is unjust for you to be so. If it is wrong to say that, then it is right to believe that you have compassion on the wicked with justice.

Chapter 10

How it is right for him to both punish and pardon the wicked

It is also right that you should punish the wicked. For what is more just than that the good should receive good and the bad bad? How then is it just for you to punish the wicked, and also just for you to pardon the wicked?

Is the solution that out of justice you in one way punish the wicked and in another way you spare them? When you punish the wicked, this is just, because it is what they deserve; but when you pardon them, this is just, not because of their deserts, but because it assorts well with your goodness. For in sparing the wicked you are just according to your own nature, not according to ours; in the same way as when we say you are compassionate it is not according to your nature but according to ours. When we say you are compassionate towards us we do not mean you experience the sentiment of compassion, but that we experience compassion as feeling; and when you save those whom with justice you might have deserted, you are just not because you give us our due, but because you act in accordance with your nature as being entirely good. So there is no inconsistency in saying that it is just both for you to punish and to pardon.

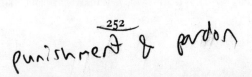
punishment & pardon

Chapter 11

*How 'all the ways of the Lord are mercy and truth',
and yet 'the Lord is righteous in all his ways'*

But does it not also belong to your very nature, Lord, to exercise justice in punishing the wicked? It is just for you to exercise such justice, for you cannot be thought to be more just. You would in no wise be so if you render good to the good and not bad to the bad. For more just is he who deals out what they deserve to both good and bad, than he who rewards only the good. So, just and merciful God, you act according to the justice inherent in your nature both when you punish and when you pardon. Truly, 'all the ways of the Lord are mercy and truth', and 'the Lord is righteous in all his ways'. And this is not inconsistent. For it would not be right for those to be saved whom you choose to punish; and it would not be right that those whom you choose to pardon should be condemned. For the only thing that is just, is what you will; and the only thing that is unjust, is what you do not will. So your compassion is derived from your righteousness, for it is right that you should be good in this way, that you might be good in forgiving. Perhaps that is why he who is entirely just can will good towards the wicked. But if in some way it is possible to grasp the reason why you can will to save the wicked, reason certainly cannot comprehend why through your supreme goodness you should save some, and through your supreme justice condemn others, when both are equally evil.

So in fact you can perceive and you are all powerful; you are compassionate and you cannot suffer; just as you are alive, wise, good, blessed, eternal, and whatever it is better to be than not to be.

Chapter 12

*That he is the very life which he lives and the same
is true of other attributes*

Clearly, whatever you are, you are in your self; you are not
derived from another. You are the very life by which you live, the 430
knowledge by which you know, the goodness by which you are
good, and so forth.

Chapter 13

*How he alone is without limits or time, yet other spirits
also are without limits and time*

Everything closed in by time or place in any way is less than that
which no law of place or time constrains. Since nothing is greater
than you, no place or time limits you, but you are always and 435
everywhere. Because I can say that only about you, you alone
know no bounds of place or time. How then can it be said that
other spirits are unlimited and eternal?

You alone of all things know no ending, just as you knew no
beginning, so you alone are eternal. But how are you alone with- 440
out limits? Is it that compared to you the created spirit is
limited, but compared to the body it is unlimited? Certainly that
which when it is entirely in one place cannot be at the same time
somewhere else, is in every way limited; and this is the case only
with bodies. That is truly unlimited which is everywhere at 445
once; and this is understood to be true of you alone. That which
when it is entirely in one place can also be entirely in another
place, but not in every place, is both limited and unlimited; and
that is the case with created spirits. For if the soul were not
wholly in each part of its body, it would not perceive wholly in 450
each of them. Thus, Lord, you are unlimited and eternal in a

Unlimited &
Eternal

Above all
things

special way, although other spirits are also unlimited and
eternal.

Chapter 14

How and why God is both seen and not seen by those who seek him

O my soul,
have you found what you were looking for?   455
I was seeking God,
and I have found that he is above all things,
and that than which nothing greater can be thought.
I have found him to be
life and light, wisdom and goodness,   460
eternal blessedness and the bliss of eternity,
existing everywhere and at all times.
If I have not found my God,
what is it that I have found and understood
so truly and certainly?   465
But if I have found him,
why do I not experience what I have found?
Lord God,
if my soul has found you,
why has it no experience of you?   470

*

If I have not found you,
what is this light and truth that I have found?
How did I understand all this,
except by the light and the truth?
How could I understand anything at all about you,   475
except by your light and your truth?
So if I see the light and the truth
I have seen you.

If I have not seen you
I have not seen the light and the truth.   480
Or is it that I both saw light and truth,
  and also did not see you,
because I only saw you in a certain degree,
  and not as you are?

*

  O Lord my God,   485
my Creator and my Re-creator,
my soul longs for you.
Tell me what you are, beyond what I have seen,
so that I may see clearly what I desire.
  I strive to see more,   490
  but I see nothing beyond what I have seen,
    except darkness.
  Or rather I do not see darkness
  which is no part of you,
  but I see that I cannot see further   495
  because of my own darkness.
    Why is this, Lord?
  Are my eyes darkened by my weakness,
  or dazzled by your glory?
The truth is, I am darkened by myself   500
  and also dazzled by you.
  I am clouded by my own smallness
  and overwhelmed by your immensity;
  I am restricted by my own narrowness
  and mastered by your wideness.   505
How great is that light from which shines out
  every truth that lightens the reasoning mind!
  How wide is that truth
  in which is everything that is true,
and outside which is nothingness and falsehood!   510
  How boundless is that which in its single gaze

256

sees all created things,
and by whom and through whom and how
they were created out of nothing!
What purity, what simplicity, 515
what certainty and splendour, are here!
It is indeed more than a creature can understand!

Chapter 15

That he is greater than it is possible to think

Lord, you are then not only that than which nothing greater can
be thought; you are something greater than it is possible to think
about. For since it is possible to think that this could exist, if you 520
are not that thing, then a greater than you can be thought; and
that will not do.

Chapter 16

That this is the 'light inaccessible in which he dwells'

In truth, Lord,
this is that light inaccessible in which you dwell.
Nothing can pierce through it to see you there. 525
I cannot look directly into it,
it is too great for me.
But whatever I see, I see through it,
like a weak eye
that sees what it does by the light of the sun, 530
though it cannot look at the sun itself.
My understanding cannot take it in,
it is too bright, I cannot receive it;
the eye of my soul
cannot bear to turn towards it for too long. 535
It is dazzled by its glory, mastered by its fullness,
crushed by its immensity, confounded by its extent.

light inaccessible

Light, entire and inaccessible!
Truth, whole and blessed!
How far you are from me who have come so close to you.   540
How remote you are from my sight,
while I am thus present in your sight.
Everywhere you are entirely present,
and I cannot see you.
In you I move and have my being,   545
and I cannot come to you.
You are within me and around me,
and I have no experience of you.

Chapter 17

*That in God, in his own unutterable way, are harmony,
smell, taste, softness, beauty*

Still, Lord, you hide from my soul in your light and beauty, and
therefore it still lives in darkness and in misery. I look all round,   550
but I do not see your beauty. I listen, but I do not hear your
harmony. I smell, but I do not gather your fragrance. I taste, but
do not know your savour. I touch, but do not feel your yielding.
For, Lord God, it is in your own unutterable manner that you
have these things; you have given them to what you have   555
created in a manner which can be felt, but the senses of my soul
have been hardened, dulled, and blocked by the ancient sickness
of sin.

Chapter 18

*That there are no parts in God or in his eternity, which is
himself*

I seek for joy and gladness, and once again there is confusion;
sorrow and grief stand in the way. My soul was hoping to be   560

filled, and once again it is overcome with need. I was striving to
be filled, and now I hunger all the more. I tried to rise up to the
light of God, and I have fallen back into the darkness of myself.
Or rather I have not only fallen into it, I feel myself surrounded
by it. 'Before my mother conceived me' I fell into it, I was con- 565
ceived in it, and when I was born it wrapped me round. In fact
we all fell once in him 'in whom we have all sinned'. There was
that which he held easily, and unhappily lost for us and for himself; in him we have all lost it, and when we want to seek it, we
are ignorant of it; when we look for it, we do not find it; when we 570
find it, it is not what we were looking for. Help me, 'according
to your goodness', Lord. 'I have sought your face; your face,
Lord, will I seek; hide not your face from me'. Raise me from
myself to you. Cleanse, heal, make keen, illuminate the eye of my
inner being, so that I may see you. Let my soul gather together 575
all its powers, and direct its whole understanding towards you,
Lord.

What are you, Lord, what are you,
What shall my heart understand you to be?
You are in very truth, life, wisdom and truth, 580
You are goodness, blessedness, eternity and all true good.
So many things you are; my narrow thought
Cannot behold them in a single glance
In order to delight in all at once.
So, Lord, how are you all these things? 585
Is each a part of you, or rather, is each wholly you?
For anything conjoined from several parts
Is not entirely one, but somehow plural and divided from
    itself,
It can be broken up, in fact or in the mind; such things 590
Are alien to the one than whom naught better can be
    thought.
No parts therefore are in you, Lord,
You are not many, you are so much one

And coextensive with yourself that nothing in you 595
   is dissimilar;
For you are unity that cannot be divided by the mind.
Life, wisdom and the rest, are then not parts of you
But all are one and wholly what you are, as all are
   in the others. 600
Therefore since parts are not in you or your eternity,
No part of you or your eternity
Is anywhere at any time,
But whole and everywhere at every time
Yourself and your eternity exist as one. 605

Chapter 19
That he is neither place nor time, but all is in him

'To have been' is not 'to be in the future'; 'to be' is not 'to have been' or 'to be in the future'; yet through eternity you have been, and are, and will be. How is it that your eternity is always a whole?

Is it that in your eternity nothing is past in the sense that it is 610 not now, or future, as though it were not already existing? So it is not that you existed yesterday, or will exist tomorrow, but that yesterday, today, and tomorrow, you simply are. Or rather, you exist neither yesterday, today, nor tomorrow, but you exist directly right outside time. For yesterday, today, and tomorrow 615 are nothing else but time; you however, though nothing can be without you, are not in place or time; but all are in you. Nothing holds you, but you hold all things.

beyond time

Chapter 20
That he is before and beyond all eternity

You then fill and enfold all things, you are before and beyond all things. You are before all things because before they were, you 620 already existed. In what way are you beyond all things? How are you beyond those things that have no ending?

Is it that without you they would not exist at all, while even if they return to nothing, your existence is in no way less? That is one way in which you are beyond them. Is it that they can be 625 thought to have an end, but that cannot in any way be thought of you? In that way they do indeed have an end and you do not. And clearly that which does not have an end is beyond that which has some kind of end. In that way you go beyond even eternal things, since your eternity and theirs is entirely present 630 to you; while they do not have their eternity that is still to come, nor do they now have what for them is past. Thus you are always beyond them, for that which they have not reached is where you always are, or rather it is always present to you.

Chapter 21
Whether this is 'the age of the age' or 'ages of ages'

Is this then 'the age of the age' or 'ages of ages'? Just as the age 635 of time contains all temporal things, so your eternity contains the ages of time. Because of its undivided unity this is an age; and because of its unlimited immensity, it is also ages. You are so great, Lord, that all things are filled by you and are in you; but you yourself have no dimension of space, so that there can be no 640 middle or half or other part in you.

Chapter 22
That he alone is what he is and who he is

Lord, you alone are what you are and who you are. For that thing is not entirely itself that is one thing as a whole, and another in its part, and in which there is that which can change. That thing does not strictly and absolutely exist that began to 645 exist out of nothing, that can be thought of as not existing, and that can return to not existing unless it subsists in something else, and that does not now have what it was before, and does not yet have what it will be in the future. You are what you are, truly, for whatever you are at any time and in any way, 650 that you are entirely and for ever.

You are that being who exists truly and simply, because you neither were nor will be but always already are, nor can you be thought not to be at any time. And you are life and light, wisdom and blessedness, eternity and many other such good 655 things, indeed you yourself are nothing other than the one and highest good, entirely sufficient to yourself, needing nothing, but he whom all things need for their being and well-being.

Chapter 23

That this good is equally Father, Son, and Holy Spirit; and that this is the one Being necessary, which is entirely and wholly and solely good

God the Father, you are this good; this good is your word, that is, your Son. For in the word which you yourself utter, there can 660 be nothing other than yourself, or anything greater or less than you. For your word is true just as you are true, and so it is the truth that is you yourself and no other. You are one, and from you nothing can be born except yourself. And this is the one love, between you and your Son – the Holy Spirit which pro- 665 ceeds from you both. This love is nothing less than you and your Son; for your love for him and he for you are as great as you are. That which is no different from you and him is not something other than you and him, for there cannot proceed from the height of your oneness anything that is not yourself. So Father, 670 Son, and Holy Spirit is wholly as Trinity what each is in himself; for each is none other than the highest single unity and the highest unity of persons, which can neither be multiplied nor made other.

'Moreover, one thing is necessary,' This is that one thing 675
necessary, which contains every good, or rather which is
wholly, uniquely, entirely, and solely, good.

Chapter 24
Surmises about the nature and extent of this good

Now arouse yourself, my soul, attend with all your mind, and
think as much as you can about the nature and extent of so great
a good. For if each good thing is delightful, think carefully how 680
delightful must be that good which holds within it the joy of
every good, and not such a good as we experience in created
things, but as different as Creator is from creature. For if life that
is created is good, how good must the life of the Creator be? If
salvation that is wrought is joyful, how joyful must that salvation 685
be that saves all things? If the wisdom that knows everything
that is made is lovable, how lovable must that wisdom be that
made all things out of nothing? Finally, since there is so much
and such deep delight in delightful things, how much better and
deeper is the delight which is in him who made these delights? 690

Chapter 25
Of the good that belongs to those who enjoy it, and
how great it is

He who would enjoy this good, what will be his and what will
not be his? He will have whatever he wants, and what he does
not want he will not have. There will be those goods of body and
soul, such as 'the eye has not seen, nor the ear heard, nor has the
heart of man' understood. So why do you wonder about so, little 695
man, seeking goods for your body and soul? Love that one good
in which are all goods, and it suffices. Desire that one good that

is every good, and that is enough. What does my flesh love, what does my soul desire? Whatever you love, whatever you desire, it is there, it is there indeed. 700

If beauty delights you, 'the just shall shine as the sun'. If you enjoy that speed, strength, and freedom of the body that nothing can withstand, 'they will be like the angels of God', for 'that which was sown a natural body, shall rise as a spiritual body', by a power beyond nature. If it is a long and healthy life 705 you desire, there is there a healthy eternity and an eternity of health, since 'the just will live for ever', and 'the salvation of the just is from the Lord'. If you want abundance, they shall be satisfied 'when the glory of God shall appear'. If it is drink you desire, 'they will drink of the fullness of the house of God'. If it 710 is melody, there the choirs of angels sing together unceasingly before God. If you delight in any pleasure that is not impure but pure, 'they shall drink from the torrent of the pleasures' of God. If it is wisdom you crave, the wisdom of God himself will show itself to them. If it is friendship that delights you, they will love 715 God more than themselves, and each other as themselves; God will love them more than they love themselves, because it is through him that they have love for him and themselves and one another; and it is through his own self that God loves both himself and them. If your joy is in unity, there will be one will for 720 them all, for they will have nothing except the one will of God. If it is power you want, their wills will be all powerful just like God's will. For as God can do what he wills in his own power, so through him they will be able to do what they will; for they will want nothing but his will, and therefore he will want whatever 725 they want; and what God wills needs must be. If it is honour and riches that you aim at, God will set his good and faithful servants over many things, even more, they will be called and will be 'gods' and 'sons of God'; and where his Son is they will be also, 'heirs of God and co-heirs with Christ'. If it is true security that 730 you long for, that security, or rather that good, will never in any way fail them, for they certainly will not lose it of their own free will, and the God who loves them will not take it away against their will from those who love him; and there is nothing more powerful than God, which could separate him and them against 735 their will.

Where there is such and so great a good, how rich and great must be the joy! If man abounded in all these things, how great would be the joy of his heart, that needy heart, well-versed in, indeed overwhelmed by, suffering. Question within yourself, 740 could you hold the joy of so great a bliss? But surely if another whom you loved in every way as yourself, had that same bliss, your joy would be double, for you would rejoice no less for him than for yourself. And if two or three or many more had this same blessedness, you would rejoice for each of them as much as 745 you do for yourself, if you loved each one as your self. So in that perfection of charity of countless blessed angels and men, where no one loves another any less than he loves himself, they will all rejoice for each other as they do for themselves. If the heart of man can scarcely hold the joy that comes to him from so great a 750 good, how will it hold so many and such great joys? In so far as each one loves another, so he will rejoice in the other's good; and as in that perfection of happiness, each one will love God incomparably more than he loves either himself or others, so he will rejoice more and without regard in the happiness of God than 755 in that of himself and of everyone else. But if they love God with their whole heart, mind, and soul, while as yet their whole heart, mind, and soul is not equal to the dignity of that love, truly they will rejoice with their whole heart, and mind, and soul, so that their whole heart, mind, and soul will not suffice for the fullness 760 of their joy.

Chapter 26

Whether this is the 'fullness of joy' promised by the Lord

My Lord and my God,
my joy and the hope of my heart,

tell my soul if this is that joy
which you spoke to us about through your Son, 765
'Ask and you will receive that your joy may be full.'
For I have found a fullness of joy
that is more than full.
It is a joy that fills the whole heart, mind, and soul,
indeed it fills the whole of a man, 770
and yet joy beyond measure still remains.
The whole of that joy cannot enter into those who rejoice,
but those who rejoice can enter wholly into that joy.
Speak, Lord, to your servant, in the depths of his heart,
tell him if this is that joy that your servants enter into 775
when they enter into 'the joy of their Lord'?
But, of course,
that joy in which your chosen ones will rejoice,
'neither has eye seen, nor ear heard,
nor has it entered into the heart of man'. 780
So as yet, Lord, I have not spoken about or understood
how greatly your blessed ones rejoice.
They will rejoice as much as they love,
and they will love as much as they know.
How much will they know you, Lord, 785
how much will they love you?
Truly in this life,
'neither has eye seen, nor ear heard,
nor has it entered into the heart of man',
how much they will know and love you in that life. 790

*

My God,
I pray that I may so know you and love you
that I may rejoice in you.
And if I may not do so fully in this life,
let me go steadily on 795
to the day when I come to that fullness.
Let the knowledge of you increase in me here,

and there let it come to its fullness.
Let your love grow in me here,
and there let it be fulfilled,   800
so that here my joy may be in a great hope,
and there in full reality.
 Lord,
you have commanded, or rather advised us,
 to ask by your Son,   805
and you have promised that we shall receive,
 'that our joy may be full'.
That which you counsel
 through our 'wonderful counsellor'
is what I am asking for, Lord.   810
 Let me receive
that which you promised through your truth,
 'that my joy may be full'.
 God of truth,
I ask that I may receive,   815
 so that my joy may be full.
 Meanwhile, let my mind meditate on it,
let my tongue speak of it,
let my heart love it,
let my mouth preach it,   820
let my soul hunger for it,
my flesh thirst for it,
and my whole being desire it,
until I enter into the joy of my Lord,
who is God one and triune, blessed forever. Amen.   825

Notes to the Prayers and Meditations

(References are to lines of the text)

(Prayer to God, p. 91)

2. Luke, 18, 13   28. Matthew 6, 10   30. Matthew 6, 13
12. Romans 8, 13

(Prayer to Christ, p. 93)

21. Psalm 38, 9   122. Matthew 28, 5   153. Psalm 73, 25
66. Anamnesis in   Mark 16, 6   155. Psalm 27, 8 and
    the Roman   128. John 20, 25   9
    Canon of the   132. Psalm 119, 8b   159. Psalm 10, 14
    Mass   133. Psalm 39, 12   167. Psalm 80, 3
74. Baruch 3, 38   139. Acts 1, 9   172. Psalm 63, 1
80. Luke 2, 35   Luke 24, 50   174. Psalm 42, 2
82. John 19, 34   142. Acts 1, 11   178. Psalm 17, 15
87. Matthew 27, 34   146. Canticle 2, 5   180. Psalm 36, 8
90. cf. John 19, 25   147. Lamentations 5,   182. Psalm 42, 3
104-5. John 19, 27   15   184. Matthew 25, 6
109. Matthew 27, 57   148. Psalm 73, 26   191. Hebrews 10, 37
116. Luke 24, 23   152. Psalm 77, 2   192. Romans 11, 36

(Prayer Before Receiving the Body and Blood of Christ, p. 100)

11. 1 John 1, 7   29. Romans 6, 5   34-5. Ephesians 4,
13. Luke 7, 6   30. Romans 6, 6   15, 16
16. John 10, 15 and   31. Romans 6, 4   35. John 15, 4
    17   33. Colossians 1, 24   37. Philippians 3, 21
23-5. Roman
    Canon of the
    Mass

(Prayer to the Holy Cross, p. 102)

12. Introit for the   34. Romans 4, 17   68. Galatians 6, 14
    Mass of the   59. Philippians 2, 8   72. Matthew 26, 24
    Holy Cross   and 9   95. Psalm 51, 5
15. Galatians 6, 14   62. Psalm 9, 4   101. Romans 1, 25
32. Acts 3, 15

Notes to the Prayers and Meditations

(Prayer to St Mary (1), p. 107)

5. Luke 1, 32
40. Luke 1, 42
89. Luke 1, 42

90. The Nicene
. Creed

91. Daniel 3, 53
(Septuagint)

(Prayer to St Mary (2), p. 110)

21. Romans 11, 15
23. Romans 3, 25
and 1 John 4, 10
36-7. Luke 19, 10

47. Luke 5, 32
125. cf. Matthew 14,
31

139. Daniel 3, 53;
cf. end of prayer
5

(Prayer to St Mary (3), p. 115)

25. Psalm 27, 1
32. Psalm 18, 28
65. Luke 1, 42
67. Titus 3, 5
76. Isaiah 30, 1
159. Luke 1, 28.
174. Lamentations 3,
25

181. Philippians 2, 6
195. The Nicene
Creed
199. Luke 1, 28
263. Matthew 12, 49
282. cf. Galatians 4, 5
and Ephesians 1,
5

289. Romans 8, 29
297. Canticles 2, 5
298. Psalm 73, 26
333. Genesis 18, 27
357. Philippians 2, 8
361. Luke 11, 27
374. Psalm 89, 52

(Prayer to St John the Baptist, p. 127)

3. cf. Luke 1, 15
8. cf. Luke 1, 41-45
13. Matthew 11, 11
19. cf. John 3, 29
44. Psalm 51, 5
45. 1 Corinthians 6,
11

59. 1 Corinthians
15, 53
63. Ephesians 2, 3
67. cf. Genesis 1, 26,
1 Corinthians 11,
7 and Colossians
3, 10

117. Psalm 38, 8
187. John 1, 29
220. Jeremiah 17, 14
223. Luke 1, 15
226. Psalm 136, 1

(Prayer to St Peter, p. 135)

2. cf. Antiphon on
Magnificat, 1st
Vespers SS
Peter and Paul
3. ibid.
5. Matthew 16, 19

72-3. 1 Peter 5, 8
78. cf. Matthew 26,
75
79. Revelation 9, 4
85. John 21, 15-18
95. Luke 15, 5

97. 1 Corinthians 6,
20 and 1 Peter 1,
19
122. Romans 5, 21
125. Matthew 16, 19
186. Psalm 84, 4 .

(Prayer to St Paul, p. 141)

3. 1 Corinthians 15, 8
4. 1 Corinthians 15, 10
7. 2 Corinthians 12, 2 and 4
9. 1 Thessalonians 2, 7
11. Galatians 4, 19
13. 1 Corinthians 9, 22
160. Matthew 9, 13 and 1 Timothy 1, 15
175. Matthew 7, 7
195. James 2, 20, James 2, 26
207. Romans 1, 17
211. Matthew 3, 10
230. Matthew 26, 24
258. Luke 16, 22

273. cf. 1 Kings 17, 21 and 2 Kings 4, 34
278. 1 Corinthians 9, 22
281-2. 1 Kings 17, 21 and 2 Kings 4, 34
291. 2 Corinthians 12, 9
292. 1 Corinthians 9, 22
300. 2 Corinthians 12, 9
334. Luke 5, 32
335. 1 Corinthians 15, 10
336. Isaiah 53, 4 and John 1, 18
337. 2 Corinthians 11, 29
340. cf. Hebrews 2, 9

343. 1 Corinthians 9, 22
359. 1 Thessalonians 2, 7
360-61. Galatians 4, 19
371. 1 Corinthians 15, 10
375. Psalm 42, 4
380. 1 Thessalonians 2, 7
397-8. Matthew 23, 37
410. Hebrews 2, 9
419. cf. John 3, 3-5
442. cf. 1 Corinthians 7, 40
466. cf. Matthew 23, 37
467. Psalm 91, 4
471. Matthew 23, 37
486. Romans 1, 25

(Prayer to St John the Evangelist (1), p. 157)

8. John 13, 25
10. John 19, 26
64. 2 Corinthians 4, 10

99. John 13, 23
108. John 13, 25
135. Job 10, 3

166. Wisdom of Solomon 11, 24

(Prayer to St John the Evangelist (2), p. 163)

10. Psalm 37, 14, Psalm 72, 12 and Psalm 74, 19
37. Psalms 70, 5 and 109, 22
41. Psalm 34, 8

42. Psalm 77, 2
50. James 1, 17
175. ff. cf. 1 John 3, 17
186. Hebrews 10, 34
229. Psalm 42, 2
240. Luke 10, 36

245 and 251. Luke 10, 37
246. 2 Corinthians 8, 6 Philippians 1, 6
266. Psalm 84, 2
267. Psalm 103, 1

Notes to the Prayers and Meditations

(Prayer to St Stephen, p. 174)

9. Acts 6, 15
11. Acts 7, 56
13. Acts 7, 60
63. Acts 7, 59–60
67. Stephen: Greek for crowned
69. Psalm 102, 13
88. Psalm 31, 2 and Psalm 70, 1
94. Psalm 69, 15

123. Acts 7, 60
131. Romans 1, 25
135. Acts 7, 60
155. Acts 7, 58
157. Acts 7, 57
174. Acts 7, 51
174. Acts 7, 54
179. Acts 7, 60
195. Psalm 34, 8

214. Psalm 63, 5
219. Psalm 107, 9
224. Acts 7, 60
228. Psalm 17, 15
233. Psalm 42, 2
235. Psalm 36, 8
259. Revelation 7, 17
276. Romans 7, 24
285. Psalm 4, 8

(Prayer to St Nicholas, p. 184)

2. Ephesians 4, 30
11. Psalm 143, 8
18. Psalm 42, 4
34. Psalm 13, 1
36. Psalm 111, 4
42. Joel 2, 13
65–6. Luke 11, 11
97. Psalm 58, 7

126. Psalm 51, 17
127. Genesis 43, 30
129. Canticle 5, 6
204. Matthew 15, 14
227. John 8, 34
230. Psalm 78, 39
241. Psalm 42, 7
253. Psalm 36, 6

256. Romans 11, 33
283. Daniel 3, 55 (Septuagint)
285. Psalm 139, 7
308. 2 Corinthians 8, 6
346. Psalm 78, 7
360. Romans 1, 25

(Prayer to St Benedict, p. 196)

8. Rule of St Benedict, Prologue
21. ibid., chapter 58
25. chapter 1
35. Prologue, and chapter 1
36. Prologue and chapter 2

38. chapter 58
40. cf. Ezekiel 11, 19 and 36, 26
66. Rule, Prologue
68. ibid., Prologue
71. chapters 1 and 5
80. chapters 1 and 58
82. Daniel 13, 22 (Septuagint)

84. Rule, Prologue
92. Psalm 25, 18
94. Psalm 27, 9
95. Psalm 143, 10
98. Psalm 5, 2
102. Rule, Prologue
123. ibid., Prologue
124. Psalm 35, 1

(Prayer to St Mary Magdalene, p. 201)

2. Luke 7, 38 and 44
9. Luke 7, 37 and 39

13. Luke 7, 47
56. cf. Luke 7, 39–40
57. Luke 10, 40

58. John 12, 45
61. John 20, 11 ff.
78. John 20, 15
81. Luke 24, 1

92. cf. John 19, 25
109. John 20, 15
112. cf. 1 Corinthians 3, 6–8

140. cf. John 20, 16
152. John 20, 16
153. John 20, 15
154. John 20, 13

157. cf. John 20, 18
169. Psalm 51, 17
171. Psalm 80, 5

(Prayer by a Bishop or an Abbot to the Patron Saint of his Church, p. 207)

33. Job 25, 6
60. Psalm 104, 24
82. 1 Corinthians 6, 19

93. Acts 20, 28 and 1 Timothy 3, 5

128. Job 7, 20
149. Psalm 89, 52

(Prayer for Friends, p. 212)

2. John 15, 13
6. 1 John 3, 16
7. Luke 23, 34
9. Romans 5, 10 and 2 Corinthians 5, 18
11. John 15, 12 and 17

15. Psalm 116, 12
21. Psalm 16, 2
23. Psalm 50, 12
24. Psalm 40, 17
25. Job 25, 6 and 30, 19
28. John 15, 12 and 17

36. Psalm 40, 17
68. 1 Peter 4, 8
84–5. Matthew 22, 37
90. Ephesians 2, 4

(Prayer for Enemies, p. 216)

5. Psalm 7, 9
11. Matthew 13, 25
21. Luke 19, 21
24. Psalm 100, 3

27. Psalm 130, 3
37. John 1, 9
38–9. John 14, 6
41. 1 John 3, 14

43. Matthew 22, 37 and 39
49. 1 Peter 2, 8
76. Matthew 6, 12

(Meditation 1, p. 221)

10–11. Matthew 3, 10
18. Psalm 22, 6
19–20. Job 10, 1
28–32. Zephaniah 1, 14–16
33. Revelation 3, 16

36. Matthew 3, 10
46. Luke 23, 31
59. Psalm 102, 13
73. Jeremiah 14, 17
95. 1 Peter 4, 18
102. Isaiah 9, 6
103. Luke 2, 11

104. Matthew 1, 21
108. Psalm 109, 21
119. Psalm 102, 13
120–21. Psalm 30, 9
122. Psalm 115, 17
127. Psalm 5, 11

Notes to the Prayers and Meditations

(Meditation 2, p. 225)

8. 2 Corinthians 11, 22
24. Deuteronomy 24, 1
36. Isaiah 14, 15
86. Luke 18, 13

94. Job 10, 21
100. Matthew 8, 12
101. Revelation 14, 10
103. Mark 9, 43–48

110. Matthew 25, 41
123–4. Ezekiel 33, 11
144. Psalm 30, 8
150. Psalm 118, 1
151. Romans 1, 25

(Meditation on Human Redemption, p. 230)

2. Galatians 5, 1
2. Ephesians 1, 7
15. Luke 10, 33 ff.
18. 2 Corinthians 12, 9
18. Habakkuk 3, 4
22. 2 Corinthians 12, 9
29. Mark 15, 27
30. John 12, 32
45. John 5, 36
54. John 8, 44
74. Philippians 2, 8
90. Mark 12, 25

148. Philippians 2, 8
149. John 14, 31
150. John 18, 11
160. Hebrews 7, 25
165. Galatians 4, 31
169. Luke 11, 3
171. John 6, 57
171. John 16, 24 and 1 John 1, 4; cf. Proslogion 26
196. Ephesians 6, 12
207. Revelations 2, 17

209. Matthew 9, 2 and 22
210. Isaiah 43, 1
210. John 10, 15
213. Romans 8, 17
240. John 17, 24
258. Canticle 3, 4; cf. Proslogion 1
259. Matthew 7, 7 ff.
267. Canticle 2, 5
268. Lamentations 1, 2
271. Romans 1, 25

(Proslogion, p. 238)

8. Matthew 6, 6
13. Psalm 27, 8
22. 1 Timothy 6, 16
41. Psalm 51, 11
59. Psalm 78, 25
61. Psalm 127, 2
92. Psalm 122, 9
92. Jeremiah 14, 19
95. Psalm 116, 3
97. Psalm 38, 8
100. Psalm 13, 1
103. Psalm 13, 3

106. Psalm 80, 3
112. Psalm 79, 9
124. Job 3, 24
128. Psalm 38, 4
131. Psalm 69, 15
144. Genesis 1, 27
157. Isaiah 7, 9
205–21. Psalm 14, 1
307. 1 Timothy 6, 16
411. Psalm 25, 10
412. Psalm 145, 17
471. Psalm 43, 3

484. 1 John 3, 2
491. 1 John 1, 5
524. 1 Timothy 6, 16
545. Acts 17, 28
559. Jeremiah 14, 19
565. Psalm 51, 5
567. Romans 5, 12
571. Psalm 25, 6
572. Psalm 27, 8
574. Psalm 13, 3
619. Psalm 90, 2

Prayers and Meditations

Appendix: The Development of the Prayers
I. The Circulation and Influence of the Prayers

When Anselm wrote the *Prayers and Meditations* between 1070 and 1080 he wrote out of a tradition, objective and liturgical in form, which had changed little in the two previous centuries. They were the answer to a new demand for personal and more intimate forms of prayer, and expressed the fervent devotion to the humanity of Christ and his mother in a way which influenced piety to the end of the Middle Ages and beyond. They had in Anselm a firm theological basis in the doctrines of the undivided Church, but it was the tone of personal commitment and affection, the reference to real personal experience – '*affectus*', '*cor*', '*experientia*', those key words to this school of prayer – that took the imagination and answered the need of the next centuries.

The prayers had a circulation among monks and educated laity alike during Anselm's life-time. In 1081 he sent six prayers and one meditation to Adelaide, the younger daughter of William the Conqueror, who lived not far from Bec as the ward of Roger de Beaumont; she seems to have lived a secluded life without in fact being a nun. The Princess had asked Anselm to send her a selection of psalms for her private use, a common practice, and this he did, adding some prayers addressed to the saints. This was also a usual procedure and the saints addressed are familiar in such a context – St Mary Magdalene, St Stephen, probably St Peter and St Paul, St John the Baptist, and St John the Evangelist. These prayers, however, are no brief collects but long meditations for use in the inner chamber; it is significant that they have survived while the *florilegium* from the psalms has not. The prayers were accompanied by a letter containing directions about their employment.

In the next year Anselm sent three more prayers to a friend, this time to Gundolf, a monk of Bec, who had followed Lanfranc to Caen in 1063. The *Vita Gundolfi* describes him as 'a man whose obedience was perfect, his fasting rigorous, his prayer constant, and his compunction so remarkable that if you had seen the tears pouring from his eyes you would have thought them to be the sources of two streams'.[1] He is described as the intimate friend of Anselm though they could only have shared the monastic life at Bec together for three years, and Gundolf was ten years Anselm's senior. The *Vita* also mentions Gundolf as devoted especially to St Mary, 'who became as it were his friend and initiated him into all her mysteries'.[2] It has this to say about the three prayers Anselm sent to Gundolf: 'Knowing that Gundolf was assiduous in prayer, the same divine instrument, namely Father Anselm, sent him three prayers, or rather meditations, on blessed Mary, which he had framed under the inspiration of the Holy Spirit; and indicated the method he should use in meditating on them.'[3] The letter accompanying these prayers explains that another monk had asked Anselm to write a prayer to St Mary; he had felt no enthusiasm about this at first, but he was stirred to composition, he says, when he thought of his friend. He wrote a short prayer first (Prayer 5), was dissatisfied with it, and tried again (Prayer 6); finally he wrote the third prayer (Prayer 7), and sent all three to Gundolf. It seems that Anselm worked over this final version with great care, and Dom Wilmart has examined two extant versions which were first drafts of it.[4] It also seems to have satisfied him to the end of his life, for it was included in the collection sent to Countess Mathilda in 1104. These prayers and those sent to Adelaide were written at the request of others; and this is what Eadmer says too about the composition of the *Prayers and Meditations*: 'His prayers which at the desire and request of his friends he wrote and published.' This in no way detracts from the integrity of the prayers, but indicates rather the reputation of Anselm even as a young monk as a man of prayer, from whom others were eager to learn, both inside the cloister and farther afield. It was through these prayers, and therefore as a spiritual guide, that Anselm first became known as a writer.

Two of the meditations, numbers 1 and 2, seem to have circulated outside Normandy at this time, for the Abbot Durandus of Casa-Dei in Auvergne wrote to Anselm when two of his monks visited Bec, praising these meditations and mentioning especially the tears of compunction they had evoked.

Another prayer, to St Nicholas, is mentioned in a letter from Anselm to the community at Bec in 1090, when it seems to have been a recent composition. The final meditation, the *Meditation on Human Redemption*, was certainly composed in 1099 and added to the collection as a prayed version of the *Cur Deus Homo*.

Anselm sent the completed collection of the *Prayers and Meditations* to Mathilda of Tuscany in 1104; this is the first mention of the shorter prayers, the Prayer to God, to Christ, to the Holy Cross, and Before Receiving the Body and Blood of the Lord, but they may well have been written earlier and added to the collection to complete it at this time. By 1104 the prayers had ceased to be an addition to a selection from the psalms; it is the psalms that have disappeared, leaving the prayers to circulate as a book in their own right.

Within a few years this collection had received additions. They were sufficiently of the same genre to be accepted as the work of Anselm at this very early date, but they do in fact differ from them both in quality and in content. Some of these were older Carolingian prayers, such as the *Singularis Merita*; writers of others included John of Fécamp, Elmer of Canterbury, Ekbert of Schonau, Aelred of Rievaulx, and others. These spurious prayers influenced the tradition of medieval devotion equally with the genuine prayers of Anselm, and it is useful to see some of the contrasts between the prayers that are by Anselm and the rest. The additions made within fifty years of Anselm's death, by Ralph and Elmer, are very close to the kind of prayer he wrote, but present already some significant differences.

II. Early Additions to the Collection

Ralph of Battle

In his work of separating the genuine prayers of Anselm from the rest Dom Wilmart[1] distinguished a group of prayers and meditations which had been added to the collection early in the twelfth century and which seemed to be the work of one person. He tentatively suggested John of Fécamp as their author, and later put forward the name of Anselm the Younger, the archbishop's nephew. More recently Professor Southern has examined what is substantially the same group of prayers and meditations in the Bodleian MS. Laud Miscellany 363, a twelfth-century MS. from St Albans Abbey.[2] He has shown that they are the work of Rodolphus, a monk, whom he at first identified with Ralph D'Escures, Bishop of Rochester, and later Archbishop of Canterbury, who was a pupil of Anselm. He has since suggested the name of Ralph of Battle and this, though not conclusive, seems highly probable.[3]

This Ralph was a monk of Caen who came to England with Lanfranc and was made Prior of Rochester under Bishop Gundolf. He later became third abbot of the royal foundation at Battle, where he died in 1124. The Chronicle of Battle Abbey describes him as '*vir venerabilis*', and says that under him Battle was 'judged second to none in England for goodness, kindness, charity and good deeds'.[4] Ralph left a reputation for sound administration and for learning and sanctity; he was '*vir agricola … et spiritualis agricolae*', caring for both the temporal and spiritual needs of his monastery. He extended the library, and among his devotions it was noted that he read the whole psalter daily. '*Quies et pace*', '*mansuetudine*', '*venerabilis*', are the kind of words the Chronicle uses about Ralph; it is a picture of a scholarly and devoted monk, a preacher and teacher, concerned with his own monastery, able rather than brilliant, and this picture is confirmed by his writings. Ralph's most important works were a series of discussions between Reason and Ignorance in the Anselmian manner, but he was also known as a writer of prayers and meditations, some of which are put after the treatises in the Laud MS. By their connection with the name of Anselm they reached a wider public than any of Ralph's other writings, and thereby had a greater influence than in a sense they deserved.

Ralph's long and complex meditations belong to the kind of writing that Anselm popularized; they are for use in private, in solitude, and are meant to stir up the soul from its torpor to look inwards and understand its own need as a way to come to the knowledge of God. The most immediate difference between Ralph and Anselm is in their style of writing. The introduction to Ralph's meditation, 'To stir up the soul to amend its sins' (Meditation IV), provides an example of this at once: like Anselm in Meditation 2, Ralph addresses himself, *'Anima mea, anima misera et foeda, diligenter recollige ad te intrinsecus omnes sensus corporis tui, diligentiusque intuere, et videre quam graviter intus vulnerata atque prostrata sis.'*[5]* The contrast with Anselm writing in the same vein is obvious, *'Anima mea, anima aerumnosa, anima inquam, misera miseri homunculi, execute torporem tuum, et discute peccatum tuum, et concute mentem tuam ...'*[6] Ralph's style is quieter, flatter; he makes no use of rhyme; he has simply *'intuere'* and *'videre'* where Anselm has the brilliant *'execute ... discute ... concute'* climax. The contrast is perhaps not only that of an artist in words and a less gifted writer, a vigorous personality and a less colourful one, but also between a monk still under forty and the 'old man' that Ralph calls himself.[7] However, Anselm's style proved inimitable; it was Ralph's that provided a model for others.

Anselm uses the literary device of addressing himself as 'my soul', and Ralph attempts to use it in most of his meditations;

* My soul, my wretched, filthy soul, carefully gather within yourself all the senses of your body, and understand more carefully and see how gravely hurt and cast down you are.

but what Anselm uses with complete control is for Ralph a half-understood technique which he cannot sustain. In Meditation IV he begins by addressing himself as '*anima mea*', but he soon slips into the second person, and by the middle of the meditation he is definitely exhorting someone else; the end of the meditation has more the style of a sermon, with an awkward return to '*anima mea*' in the last paragraph. This moral and dialectical concern is something almost entirely absent from Anselm's meditations and prayers, perhaps with the exception of parts of the *Meditation on Human Redemption*; but it occurs again and again in Ralph. Meditation V is full of exhortations directed towards other people: 'In all your works keep careful watch'; in Meditation VI he has, 'Let us amend our sins'; Prayer VI is for the sins of others rather than about his own; in Prayer III he is talking about God, not to God; in Prayer XV, he discusses rather than confesses sins.

There is an important difference here between Anselm and Ralph. Ralph writes as a preacher, a pastor of souls, whereas Anselm is simply praying out of his own need. This contrast can be seen clearly when in Meditation VI Ralph describes the fall of Adam; he sees the fall at a remove, 'I have heard', 'they say', and he describes the history of redemption as a series of events he has heard about; the direct prayer which applies this to his own condition comes later. In the Prayer to St John the Baptist Anselm makes the whole human tragedy immediate and personal to himself; he himself is 'worse than the devil' in his rejection of God; it is not a story known about but an experience undergone.

There is one sphere, however, where the quieter approach of Ralph makes a wider appeal than the heights and depths of Anselm; this is in self-abasement. In Anselm there is an intense, overwhelming horror of sin as such; it springs from his awareness of the holiness of God and the infinite offence of any sin against him: 'Where then is the sinner who dares to call any sin small?'[8] Few have this degree of impassioned understanding of theological truth, and without it such self-abasement can seem over-done. Ralph works from a more familiar starting-point: his repentance comes from a steady and honest examination of himself and his actual sins and weaknesses; and he expresses his self-knowledge with simplicity and discernment: 'If it happens, and it sometimes does, that I, unhappy man, do something that seems in the judgement of men to be good, not a little do I pride myself upon it. If anyone does not mention it, or fails to praise me for it, I despise him as a fool and ignoramus; or if I flee from the praise of men, as if I did not care about it, I glory not a little in doing so, in my heart of hearts, where only God sees me; and thus when I avoid praise, in a strange way I seek praise and vainglory all the more.' [9] Such self-revelation is less universally applicable than that of Anselm since it is connected with particular sins; but it has for most men a more sincere ring, a more human note. It was this practical moral concern for the individual that shaped the manuals and sermons of preachers and confessors in the next centuries.

In his dialogues Ralph shows himself to be the pupil of Anselm, but in his meditations this is not nearly so obvious. In some ways the prayers of Ralph are closer to the older tradition of devotion that formed the Carolingian prayers. Prayer XV, for instance, has more in common with a prayer in section IV of the *Libellus Turonensis* than with anything in Anselm. It is a meditation in litany form on the life of Christ from the Annunciation to the Second Coming, leading to a detached kind of confession of sin and a petition for mercy. In this prayer it is significant that Ralph uses the old understanding of the rights of the devil as if Anselm's view of the Atonement was unknown or unacceptable to him.

It is the pedestrian tone of Ralph's meditations which appears most when they are set beside those of Anselm. In Ralph's prayers there is less variety in every way; there is no third person of a saint to add interest to the dialogue; there is none of the vivid understanding of the Bible of Anselm. There is the same ardent devotion to the person of Christ, but in Ralph this too finds less varied expression. '*Dulcissimus, benignissimus, et mitissimus*' are his favourite and often repeated adjectives in addressing Christ – nor is it always quite clear whom in fact he is addressing. By '*dulcissime Pater*' in Prayer XXVIII he seems to mean Christ, but elsewhere he uses expressions normally associated with Christ for the Father. Anselm too spoke of Christ as the Father of the redeemed creation and also as him 'by whom all things were made', but he holds this firmly in the theological framework of God's creative action through Christ. Ralph seems to confuse the functions appropriate to the Persons of the Trinity, and speaks of creation *by* Christ instead of *through* Christ. Perhaps for this reason Anselm could go further than Ralph and speak also of the Motherhood of Christ.

The last group of prayers by Ralph is a collection of private devotions for a priest before saying Mass. They are addressed to Jesus, and are acknowledgements of the unworthiness of the minister, and prayers for purity. One of them found its way into the Roman missal under the name of St Ambrose for this purpose.[10] Anselm's Prayer before Receiving the Body and Blood of Christ is the obvious point of comparison here. Ralph's prayers are longer, more diffuse, and their theme is moral, a desire for cleansing from sin, whereas Anselm's prayer has a more theological and biblical content.

The difference in kind and in quality between Ralph and Anselm is clear, but these prayers went under the name of Anselm until this century and exercised a deep influence on piety. Indeed they may have been popular just because they were less demanding, perhaps more sentimental, than the genuine prayers. Plain teaching and moral effort mingled with sentiment may be dull in some ways, but they seem to have a more general appeal than mystical and intellectual fervour. Ralph was concerned for 'the salvation of souls', and he writes first and foremost as a pastor. The tone of his prayers is in line with this passage describing his life: 'He was vigilant in his care for all exterior things, and let it not be thought burdensome if I relate how zealously he set forward the salvation of souls; he was always adapting himself to the characters of those under him; never did he give orders as a master. He bore with the infirmities of others and led them on to great things. He himself practised what he preached; he lived what he taught ... a Daniel in his sparing diet, a Job in his sufferings, a Bartholomew in his prayers.'[11]

Elmer of Canterbury

The tradition of prayer in Anselm's meditations was continued by another of his immediate circle – Elmer, who was a monk at Christ Church, Canterbury, and prior until his death in 1137. He wrote a great deal, and two at least of his meditations have survived, one of them under the name of Anselm.

Ralph shared and continued Anselm's theological interests, but in some ways it is Elmer who is more truly the successor of Anselm in meditative writing. He was pre-eminently a monk, a man of the cloister, and his preference was for a life of prayer and meditation. He wrote to William of the '*paradisi claustralis*', saying, 'I have such joy in study, in meditation and writing that I count a day wasted in which I have not engaged in these employments.'[1] Like Anselm he took pleasure in friendship and wrote to his friends at length about spiritual matters. It is in these letters that he shows himself to be a doctor of *suspira*, of desire, like St Gregory, Anselm, and John of Fécamp. His was a single eye, a single concern: 'What else ought we to meditate,' he wrote to William, 'unless how our devotion to Christ can be more and more increased?'[2] And in his letter to Nicholas of Gloucester he claims eagerly his descent from St Gregory: 'I perceive', he wrote, 'that you have a great love for the writings of St Gregory, my sweetest master, and I greatly rejoice at it.'[3] Like Anselm Elmer prayed the prayers he wrote personally:

'You see in these meditations in what misery I am involved . . .
lament with me and of your mercy pray for me, lest the number
of my sins cut me off from the mercy of God.'⁴

Elmer sent the two meditations that are certainly his to the
same Nicholas, whom he had found to be a fellow disciple of St
Gregory. Meditation XX is concerned with man's alienation
from God and his desire to return to him. It recalls the *Proslogion*, and it is significant that the meditation that follows it in
Migne is in fact an abridgement of the more meditative parts of
the *Proslogion*. Both the *Proslogion* and Elmer's prayer are concerned to 'stir up the soul to seek after God', and both begin
with the awareness of the soul of its distance from God, and its
weariness in the land of unlikeness. This awareness of sin, which
is the first compunction, leads to the second compunction of
desire for God, and in Elmer's prayer this is done in a passage
strongly reminiscent of St Gregory: 'My whole heart, delight in
sighs, that by their practice your beauty may be illuminated and
your inner eye raised to contemplate the brightness of heavenly
light. My whole soul, leave aside your wanderings, and gaze only
upon the splendour of God; desire him, shed copious showers of
tears, that they may wash away your foul and numberless sins;
then will the natural beauty which the good Creator gave you be
restored by his mercy.'⁵ Equally familiar in St Gregory and
Anselm are these ideas of the 'inner eye of the soul', the
'heavenly light', and the 'tears' that wash away defilement and
restore the image of God in man.

The end of this meditation echoes Anselm's *Meditation on
Human Redemption* with its use of 'I ask, I seek and I knock',
and the last passage in it is similar to the end of the *Proslogion*:
'Let my soul long always for the glory of thy countenance, let
my mind love it, my thought reach out to it, the entire love
of my heart sigh for it, all my being be gathered up in love
for it . . .'⁶

A very notable difference between Anselm and Elmer is in
their use of the Bible. Elmer constantly uses an allegorical inter-

pretation of the scriptures which is entirely absent from Anselm. In Meditation XX, for instance, Elmer introduces the parable of the Prodigal Son, and uses each detail in a symbolic manner – the prodigal son is the repentant soul returning to God; the ring he receives is faith, the robe righteousness, the arms of the father are God's mercy, and the servants of the household are angels; the calf is seen as the Son of God, presumably seen as a sacrifice. The difference between this approach and that of Anselm is still more clearly illustrated in the other of Elmer's meditations, where he refers to the forgiveness accorded to David, St Peter, and St Mary Magdalene.[7] When Anselm prays to St Peter he talks to him as a friend, asks for his help, is encouraged by his life, and is even on such familiar terms with him as a person that he can reproach him for his denial of the Lord. But Elmer is not concerned with Peter as a person at all; for him there is a truth behind the surface meaning of scripture, a spiritual meaning. So he makes St Peter's confession of Christ into a revelation of the doctrine of the Trinity to the Church: 'He knew the Father's revelation of the Son, he understood the Son by knowing the Father, by the inspiration of the Holy Spirit he merited to know the full truth of the Father co-equal with the Son; so he deserved to be called Peter because he knew him to be truly Father, Son, and Spirit, one God . . .'[8] This kind of exegesis belongs to the Patristic writings and continued down into the late Middle Ages, but it is a stream of biblical understanding as alien to Anselm as to the present day.

Elmer's prayers are of the same type as the meditations of Anselm and in its most important aspect, that of compunction, he echoes the thought of his master. But he was not a writer of the stature of Anselm, and while a phrase here and there catches Anselm's ardour it is not sustained and there are long and tedious passages. His style is rhetorical, he makes great use of antithesis, but much of this is artificial and superficial. There is in the meditations, however, a quality of sheer goodness, of single-minded dedication, which redeems them. They are in the Anselmian tradition, but the work of a different man, of whom Gervase of Canterbury wrote, 'Prior Elmer, a man of great simplicity and of outstanding religion'.[9]

Notes

The Circulation and Influence of the Prayers

1. *Vita Gundolfi*, PL 159, part II, 816D.
2. ibid., col. 816D.
3. ibid., col. 819C.
4. Wilmart, A., 'Les propres corrections de S. Anselme dans sa grande prière à la Vierge Marie', in *Recherches de Théologie Ancienne et Médiévale*, vol II, 1930, pp. 189–204.

Early Additions to the Collection (Ralph)

1. Wilmart, A. *Auteurs spirituels et textes dévots du moyen âge latin*, Paris 1932, pp. 158–98.
2. Southern, R. W., *Anselm and His Biographer*, Cambridge University Press, 1963, pp. 206–9.
3. Southern, R. W. 'St Anselm and His English Pupils', in *Medieval and Renaissance Studies*, ed. Hunt and Klibansky, Warburg Institute, appendix, 'The Monk Rodolphus', pp. 24–29.
4. *Chronicon Monasterii de Bello*, London 1846, p. 51.
5. Ralph, Meditation IV, PL 158, 729D–733B.
6. Anselm, Meditation 1.
7. Ralph, Oratio IV, PL 158, 870C.
8. Anselm, Meditation 1.
9. Ralph, Oratio IV, PL 158, 869C.
10. Ralph, Oratio XXIX, PL 158, 921.
11. *Chronicon Monasterii de Bello*, op. cit., p. 59.

(Elmer)

1. Elmer of Canterbury printed by Leclercq, J., in *Analecta Monastica* (2nd series), 31, '*Écrits Spirituels d'Elmer de Cantorbéry*', Rome, 1953, p. 63.

2. ibid., p. 63.

3. ibid., p. 87.

4. ibid., p. 87.

5. Meditation XX, PL 158, 812B.

6. ibid., 814C.

7. '*Écrits Spirituels d'Elmer de Cantorbéry*', pp. 110–114.

8. ibid., p. 114.

9. *Historical Works of Gervase of Canterbury*, ed. Stubbs, Longman, 1878, pp. 98, 100.